Cooperative
Vocational
Education

Cooperative
Vocational
Education

Principles, Methods, and Problems

E. F. Mitchell

Professor Emeritus · Mississippi State University

Allyn and Bacon, Inc.
Boston • London • Sydney

Library of Congress Cataloging in Publication Data

Mitchell, E. F.
    Cooperative education.

    Includes index.
    1. Education, Cooperative. I Title.
LB1029.C6M54   373.2'7   76-58830
ISBN 0-205-05768-3

To my wife Evelyn and our three daughters: Barbra, Lynda, and Evelyn Ann

Contents

Contents

Contents

Foreword

Cooperative vocational education provides an excellent vehicle for students to develop desired vocational capabilities through a program which balances the acquisition of skills learned on the job with related skills and information learned in the classroom. Over the past years there has been an increasing awareness among educators of the value of cooperative programs in the comprehensive school curriculum. Such programs have been recognized as an extremely effective means of providing practical vocational education designed to accomplish desired occupational outcomes.

Since this program is so vitally important to the total aspects of vocational education, a more complete understanding of the concepts of coordination and learning in a cooperative education program must be achieved. For those persons who are currently involved in cooperative programs, this book can very well be utilized as an in-service guide. For those who are entering this field and are preparing themselves as teacher–coordinators, its value is immeasurable.

Having been acquainted with the author of this book for many years, first as an undergraduate student in his classes and later on a professional basis in our vocational programs, I know that with his knowledge and dedication, and with his reputation as an outstanding educator, this book will serve as a valuable tool, not only for teacher–coordinators in cooperative programs, but for school administrators, teacher educators, and others involved in the educational process.

Donald E. Milner, State Supervisor
Cooperative Vocational Education
Mississippi Department of Education

Preface

An important purpose of this book is to characterize cooperative education as an integral part of well-rounded educational programs. In this role it may range from a single course designed to meet the entire need for vocational education in small schools to more complex forms that provide occupational breadth in comprehensive educational programs in large school districts. Although cooperative education may embrace occupationally specialized fields such as trade, industrial, distributive, office, health, agricultural, and home economics in a single class, separate courses in these areas should be offered where they are justified by student and community needs.

Another aim is to deal specifically with the principles, methods, and techniques common to all types of cooperative education on the secondary level, with emphasis on *how* to perform successfully as a teacher–coordinator.

The author envisions several uses for this material, the most important being its application in basic teacher–coordinator preparatory and in-service professional improvement programs on the undergraduate and graduate levels.

The fact that school administrators control the destiny of cooperative education suggests that this book may be appropriately extended into school administration preparatory and in-service programs. The vital role of guidance in the student referral process lends equal prestige to the use of this material as required reading in preparatory and professional improvement courses for guidance counselors.

Teachers from other areas of vocational education who have had little or no contact with cooperative education may enter the program as teacher–coordinators. Such qualified vocational educators in other fields could gain a creditable concept of cooperative education through study of this material.

The fact that emphasis is placed on principles, methods, and problems suggest that in-service teacher–coordinators should find this book of value as a day-by-day reference, especially for inexperienced individuals who find themselves faced with difficult situations.

The content results from forty-three years of professional experience—including the developmental period of reimbursable cooperative education. The author has served as a local teacher–coordinator, local director of vocational education, district supervisor, state supervisor, state teacher educator, and as head of a university department of industrial and occupational education. In the office of state supervisor and state teacher educator he has visited hundreds of teachers and administrators in local programs.

A vital part of these educational experiences is the twenty-two years devoted to teaching undergraduate and graduate courses in a teacher–coordinator preparatory and professional improvement program. The students who sat in these classes and the contacts with local programs, as well as extensive professional relationships on state, regional, and national bases, contribute to the book's philosophical foundation.

Attention is called to the chapter design in Parts II, III, IV, and V, with special reference to the "Typical Problems" section that follows the rationale in every chapter but Chapters One and Twelve. This format is logical in that it tends to compensate for the inevitable divergence between philosophy and practice. The problems were selected to identify the points at which difficulty might be expected. Being able to anticipate typical difficulties should constitute an escape from many troublesome situations. The author has found the use of typical problems as points of departure to be more conducive to student participation in teacher education courses than the traditional questions which often serve as chapter endings.

The accomplishment of a judicial selection of the suggested activities at the end of each chapter will prepare the new teacher–coordinator for initial responsibilities that may otherwise be overlooked in the preparatory program. Being prepared for such responsibilities in the beginning will often be the difference between success and failure.

For inexperienced teacher–coordinators will be able to measure up to the idealistic standards of accomplishment described in this book. The author envisions complete mastery of all principles and methods as an ultimate goal rather than an immediate accomplishment. The embryonic teacher–coordinator should prepare for initial employment by identifying and developing those methods and techniques which are most compatible with immediate capabilities. Aspiration to perfection, in service, should forge a persistent personal improvement program. The nearer the teacher–coordinator approaches the ideal in the perfection of technique, the higher the quality of the program.

In service the teacher–coordinator should develop an action pattern involving methods and techniques that feature personal strengths and compensate for deficiencies. Successful teacher–coordinators are individualists, each applying their own repertoire of skills and techniques in pursuit of the same goals.

Cooperative education offers opportunity to men and women as teacher–coordinators. The nature of the occupations involved in any given program, however, may be the basis of preference on the part of either sex. The suggestion is that men may function more effectively in some occupational areas while women will be more comfortable in others.

Appreciation is expressed to Dr. Richard J. Vasek, professor and head of Industrial and Occupational Education at Mississippi State University, and the entire staff of the department for their interest and encouragement.

Appreciation is also expressed to Dr. James E. Wall, associate dean for Research and Development, College of Education at Mississippi State University; Dr. James F. Shill, director of the Research and Curriculum Unit and professor of Industrial and Occupational Education at Mississippi State University; and Charlene Callaway, Carol Schuster, Karen Moreland, and other members of the staff, for their assistance during the development of this publication.

The interest shown and helpful suggestions made by members of the supervisory staff of the State Department of Vocational Education for Mississippi (many of whom were recipients of the content of this book as students at MSU) have been a source of encouragement and are greatly appreciated.

The help Mr. Harry L. Cole, retired professor of English, gave in editing the manuscript was indispensable and is gratefully acknowledged.

Special recognition is given to the hundreds of students, teacher–coordinators, and school administrators who have contributed to the development of a firm philosophy for cooperative education. Their success and loyalty to the program have contributed greatly to the content of this book and to the author's personal satisfaction in having had the opportunity of working with them.

E. F. Mitchell

Part I

Introduction

chapter one
Introducing Cooperative Education

chapter one

Introducing
Cooperative Education

One of the most important needs of youth is to have the opportunity to attend a school dedicated to preparing them for the next step after high school. This purpose should not reduce emphasis on basic general education or on college preparatory work. Basic general education should be strongly maintained to assure the development of communication, computation, and other basic skills essential to successful living and working in modern society. It necessarily follows that career emphasis in the high school should not curtail the availability of college preparatory courses for those students whose educational plans require college attendance.

The Emerging Philosophy of Public Education

A point of view prevalent in the emerging philosophy of public education is that all education that equips the individual with the skill and knowledge needed to enter and make progress in the world of work at any level, skilled or professional, is vocational education. College preparatory courses, therefore, may be considered vocational when they precede college preparation for employment.

This philosophy departs drastically from that found in many schools where courses designed to prepare for employment not requiring a college degree are known as "vocational" and courses preceding college entrance are called "college preparatory." This practice feeds the illusion that courses designed to prepare individuals for work on

3

nonprofessional levels are for economically poor youths, while college preparatory courses are for the more affluent.

The Career-Centered High School Curriculum

If the high school is to be consistent in meeting the needs of all students, it must provide educational experiences in sufficient scope and depth to satisfy the occupational goals that normally exist in high school student populations. This consideration requires that college preparatory courses be available as well as appropriate occupational education.

Another important student group that finds little interest in either of the above programs is made up of those unable or unwilling to establish career interests because of immaturity or other reasons. Coping with the needs of this group presents an entirely different and more difficult problem than that of meeting the needs of the first two groups—those who have decided to go to college and those requiring occupational education as a prerequisite to entering the world of work.

Public education has failed to serve effectively the youth group without career interest as well as those destined to step from high school into the world of work. These two groups, a vast majority of contemporary high school populations, are destined to play an important role in the pattern of educational change, a change that is inevitable if the public school is to survive in its present form.

Meeting Diverse Occupational Needs

The number of occupational interests in the noncollege student group will exceed the number of vocational courses that feasibly can be established within the physical plant of the school. Alert and enlightened school administrators will seek additional methods of meeting this diversified need for preparation, since the need exceeds the diversification feasible in conventional institutionally contained vocational courses. The solution adopted must be workable economically and must also be flexible enough to adapt to student needs, which vary from year to year.

Failure to provide vocational education in all areas of need would be failure to activate completely the career-centered educational plan because many students would be denied the opportunity to develop occupational interests which may have been established in earlier phases of the curriculum.

4

An obvious and practical approach to a solution of the above problem would be to call on the community to enter into partnership with the school to make business and industrial establishments available as laboratories with appropriate personnel to serve as occupationally competent on-the-job instructors. This plan makes it possible for the school to enrich its curriculum by providing specific preparation in all acceptable occupations represented in the community, including those for which no instruction and no facilities have been provided in the school itself. Such a program may take the form of *cooperative education* (CE).

Introducing CE to School and Community

CE may provide the occupational breadth essential to well-rounded career-centered educational programs on secondary school levels without discounting its value and applicability to occupationally specialized programs in all areas of vocational education, such as distributive education. Programs enrolling students without occupational restrictions may be referred to as *diversified occupations, diversified cooperative education*, or any other title that characterizes its occupationally diversified nature.

It should be emphasized, however, that the basic principles and methodology described in this text are applicable to all CE whether or not it is occupationally specialized or diversified in nature. The primary differences are in the methods of presenting directly related subject matter.

Definition of CE

The nature of CE requires that its responsibilities be divided between the school and the community. Local employers selected by the school become responsible for on-the-job instruction and work experience for students selected and recommended by the school.

The responsibility of the school includes the selection and recommendation of students in accordance with their individual career interests, the provision of related instruction, and effective coordination and supervision of the total program. Selected students are placed with the selected employers to work on the job for a period each week, and this time should equal or exceed the time in school. The program is carried out in accordance with a schedule of work experiences and related instruction prepared jointly by the teacher–coordinator and the employer before the student goes to work.

Two regular high school credits are normally awarded for each year of successful participation in the program, and concurrent enrollment in two additional high school courses will enable the student to earn the four traditional credits per year to fulfill graduation requirements in the usual four-year period. This book deals primarily with the form of CE that provides work and school attendance on alternate half-days for regularly enrolled students who receive instruction in both vocational and general education each school day.

Other program forms may require work and school attendance on alternate days, weeks, terms, semesters, or other suitable time periods. In all cases the time at work must equal or exceed the time in school. CE in appropriate form will fit into school systems ranging from small institutions with insufficient numbers of students to justify any type of specialized occupational class, to schools with large student bodies.

Within this range, many schools will be found that cannot justify occupationally specialized programs of any kind. Such schools may find CE in diversified occupations to be the best answer to their need for specific occupational education. A program of this kind may be successfully operated in any school that has sufficient student interest and is located in a community large enough to provide the required number of acceptable training stations.

Preparing the School and the Community

Those publics that contribute most to the environment in which CE will function should be carefully informed as to the basic purposes and values of the program. Misunderstandings at the outset may make acceptable program operation extremely difficult. In the beginning it should be understood, in the school and in the community, that CE is an educational program and that it must be considered as such by everyone concerned, but especially by the employers and the students. This consideration may be emphasized by pointing out that students entering the program as juniors invest one-fourth of their high school time and credits.

This investment is far too great a part of the total educational opportunity to jeopardize by allowing students to engage in activities deficient in educational value. The school must assume the responsibility of assuring the quality and the educational worth of CE. The first step, therefore, should be the development of understanding and acceptance of the foregoing program definition and the following statement of purpose by the school administration and faculty.

The purpose of CE is to provide the opportunity for high school juniors and seniors to pursue their career goals through work experience in selected jobs in the community and through related instruction in the school, to the end that they will be qualified for beginning employment in their chosen occupations, after graduating from high school.

Other publics—including employers, students, and parents—must come to understand and accept the authentic purposes and values of CE if the environment in which the program functions is to be conducive to successful operation. The employer, for example, who understands and accepts the program definition and statement of purpose above will assume the responsibility of on-the-job instructor, teaching the student how to do the job, as opposed to considering the program to be a means of securing inexpensive labor.

The student who understands and accepts the legitimate advantages of the program will see it as an opportunity to prepare for entrance into the world of work after graduation from high school rather than as an opportunity to earn spending money without regard for career interest. Parents who are properly informed will accept the program as an educational experience rather than as an opportunity to supplement the family income.

All these considerations place a high priority on the development of appropriate awareness as an initial phase of CE, and on continued relationship development as an integral part of operational procedure. Such relationships should always be based on the valid purposes and expected outcomes of the program. This insistence is necessary because purposes arising from within the various publics will be based on values compatible with their own experiences rather than on educational criteria.

It would be natural for potential employers and students to assume inappropriate attitudes such as those suggested above. It would also be natural for members of the faculty to assume the program to be an arrangement for students to work part-time because they need financial assistance.

Uninformed school administrators and guidance personnel could easily get the idea that CE provides a haven for students who are unsuccessful in other phases of the school program. Individual members of all publics will see in the program what they want to see when left to form their own opinions. Their own educational experiences do not include precedents through which they can relate to the program.

Attitudes such as those described above would result in a part-time work program. Such a program would randomly place students in the most readily available jobs, disregarding the quality of the experience and the career interests of the student.

In these circumstances the school could be expected to channel its problem students as well as those needing financial assistance into the program for placement with employers primarily concerned with production. Such an arrangement would have little educational value.

The only safeguard against such negative attitudes is a deliberately planned educational program designed to acquaint those publics that make vital contributions with the true advantages of well-founded CE. Such a program should be initiated by school administrators as the first step in program establishment. After the teacher–coordinator is employed, it should become his or her responsibility to continue the development of these relationships.

Teacher–Coordinator Qualifications

The most important single factor in the successful operation of CE is the teacher–coordinator, and accordingly the selection of a qualified person for the position is of great significance. As a general rule, state certification requirements for teacher–coordinators in reimbursable programs will include the following:

1. A Bachelor of Science degree, preferably from a teacher-education program with a major in coordination of CE.
2. Occupational competence, requiring not less than one year of successful work experience outside the teaching profession.
3. At least two years of successful teaching experience in the absence of a teacher-education major in CE, and in addition a fixed number of teacher-education courses, with a given number of them required before employment.

Additional qualifications should be judged in terms of the responsibilities of the teacher–coordinator as they are graphically depicted in Figure 1. According to this chart analysis, the teacher–coordinator must be able to function effectively in four major areas.

The first of these areas has to do with coordination, which is defined as the development and maintenance of cooperative relationships among all school and community elements involved in the success-

8

Figure 1 Analysis of Cooperative Education

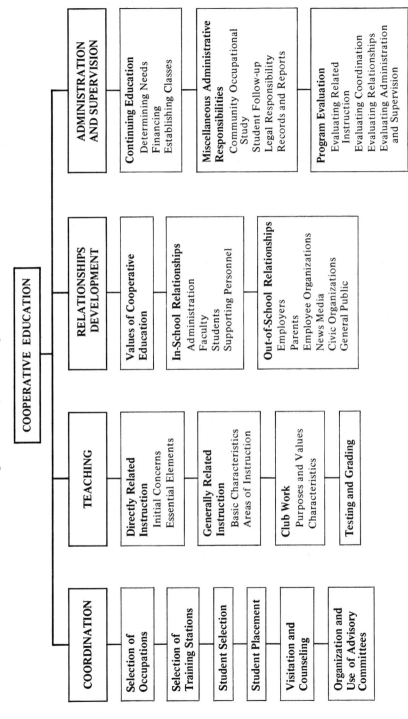

9

ful operation of CE. Discharging the responsibilities of coordination moves the teacher–coordinator into activities that are not expected of regular teachers.

Another major area of responsibility is teaching. The teacher–coordinator should be a master teacher able to apply a broad variety of methods and techniques to the teaching process. This requirement places a premium on individuals who are teacher-education graduates with majors in CE. Recruits from other majors should be required to take a sufficient number of methods courses to initiate the development of a background in principles, philosophy, and methodology before going to work.

A third major area of responsibility has to do with relationships development. To succeed in this area the teacher–coordinator must apply many of the skills of the public relations director in large business or industrial organizations, skills not required of regular teachers.

In addition to being a coordinator, a master teacher, and a director of public relations, the teacher–coordinator is also required to assume many supervisory and administrative responsibilities. Here again, his responsibilities differ from those of other teachers.

Selecting the Teacher–Coordinator

Since the successful teacher–coordinator, as indicated above, should be qualified to function in multiple areas, the school administrators may fear that such individuals will not be available at a price the school can afford to pay. On the contrary, it is suggested that the extraordinary functional area affords an unexcelled and attractive opportunity for personal and professional growth. An ambitious young person will realize that a successful teacher–coordinator presents strong credentials for many top-notch positions in business and industry as well as higher-level positions in vocational administration and supervision. These potential opportunities do not discount the wisdom of a career in cooperative education. As a matter of fact, the opportunity for service and the rewards accruing therefrom are unexcelled in the teaching field.

Teacher-education graduates with majors in CE coordination and promising young teachers who will take qualifying courses are the types of individuals the administrator should screen in his search for a teacher–coordinator. Within these groups the following personality traits should be looked for.

Initiative

The teacher–coordinator must be a self-starter, one who is able to determine what should be done at a given time and to do it without administrative direction. For the most part the high school principal and other administrative officers will not be fully aware of the teacher–coordinator's responsibilities during unscheduled time. In some cases the coordinator may be scheduled for only one or two periods, and have most of the school day free from scheduled class activities. Indeed, the results of the teacher–coordinator's efforts during unscheduled time should be so dynamic that feedback from the community will dispel any suggestion of time that is not well spent.

Such desirable results come only from good judgment in determining what should be done and how it should be done to serve the best interests of the program. The business and the industrial community will respond to this kind of service in a manner favorable to the entire educational program. It stands to reason that an individual without initiative would fail to function effectively as a teacher–coordinator in unscheduled time.

Procrastination is a pitfall and probably one of the greatest hazards confronting the teacher–coordinator. Most duties are not scheduled or signaled by the ringing of a bell and are not required by administrative mandate. Consequently, many duties can be postponed to another time. The teacher–coordinator who becomes a victim of procrastination will eventually be hopelessly lost in a maze of program responsibilities.

Occasionally, however, circumstances may require more time than available. On such occasions, good judgment must be exercised in determining what should be postponed. Responsible postponement under justifying circumstances should not be confused with procrastination.

A teacher–coordinator's failure to cope successfully with responsibilities may not be noticed immediately by school administrators. In fact, such failure may not be recognized until a program breaks down completely.

Versatility

The teacher–coordinator must be versatile enough to function effectively in a variety of circumstances. The following description of a typical day is intended to illustrate the importance of versatility.

The day probably will begin in the classroom with the teacher–

coordinator teaching a generally related unit such as one on employer–employee relationships. *Generally related information* is defined as subject matter of general interest to all students regardless of their occupational areas. The teaching of generally related information requires the use of a variety of conventional teaching methods. Much of the strength of the program lies in the teaching ability of the teacher–coordinator and in willingness to devote the necessary effort to preparing each lesson. (See Chapter Nine.)

The second period could find the teacher–coordinator conducting a class involving information directly related to work experience, through the supervised and directed study method. This kind of teaching is designed to provide technical information directly related to and correlated with the work experience of each student. Inasmuch as the daily work experience of each student can be expected to differ from that of others, the directly related information each day must be provided on an individual basis. The supervised and directed study method makes this individual adaptation possible. (See Chapter Eight.)

There are circumstances under which the teacher–coordinator would be justified in "farming out" a student to an occupational class for technically related instruction that is difficult to provide. It must be understood, however, that resorting to this method will introduce a number of problems, the most important of them being correlation with work experience.

Although the teaching of one, two, or possibly three periods may complete the regular classroom schedule for the day, the teacher–coordinator is far from through. The next task could be to address the local Rotary Club at its regular weekly luncheon meeting. The rest of the afternoon may then be devoted to visiting students on the job as well as their employers.

During the course of the afternoon the teacher–coordinator may visit training agencies representing the skilled trades, a variety of professional areas, retail establishments, and industrial organizations. The point here is that the teacher–coordinator must be appropriately presentable in the diversified occupational areas involved in daily contacts. Those contacted may range from the skilled tradesman to a lawyer or a doctor.

Following the afternoon visitation, the teacher–coordinator may look forward to one or more of the following activities: an organizational meeting of an adult evening class, a presentation on local radio or television, a meeting with an industrial development committee of the local chamber of commerce, or a host of other activities.

12

This description of a typical day casts the teacher–coordinator in the role of teacher, public speaker, supervisor, and public relations envoy. The next day may be repetitive to some extent, but will undoubtedly provide a variety of new experiences during the unscheduled part of the day.

The teacher–coordinator who functions well in this variety of tasks will reflect great credit on the school and on CE. Increasing involvement with local business and industrial leaders will eventually forge a connecting link between the school and the community.

Grooming

Teacher–coordinators must be groomed appropriately at all times. It is not suggested that they resort to special costumes for each activity, but rather that they present the appearance of professionals. Consistency in attire so as to be presentable at all times in diverse environmental circumstances is an essential personal characteristic of successful coordinators. Attire must be rated a factor in the professional image that the individual seeks to develop as a representative of the school.

The possibility of being considered overdressed for visits in some occupational areas should be overcome by the ability to converse intelligently with these encountered. Teacher–coordinators necessarily become students of occupations in order to communicate acceptably with those they meet in any of the community's occupational areas. Although the selection and care of clothing is important, it is only one of the essential factors in good grooming; for example, consistency in hygenic practices is obviously desirable.

Sincerity

Ideal teacher–coordinators show a sincere and abiding desire to be of service to their students, the school, and the community. Such an inclination will bring to bear every reasonable effort to provide meaningful educational experiences for each student in the program, together with help in successfully adjusting to problems of living and working in modern society.

With these services in mind, teacher–coordinators deal with students as individuals. Their sincere personal interest in all students and constant concern with providing a challenging educational program will not go unnoticed. As a matter of fact, students are not likely to respond fully until they are convinced that the teacher–coordinator has their best interests at heart.

Other publics will respond in ways consistent with their own nature. The collective response, however, should be general community acceptance of the teacher–coordinators and CE as integral and valuable parts of the community's total educational program.

Loyalty

Successful teacher–coordinators can be counted on for a sincere loyalty to the school in all its functions. Every day may present circumstances requiring evidence of their loyalty in some form, for example:

1. Defending school policies to which various elements of the community may take exception.
2. Reacting positively to irate patrons of the school concerning discipline or other school–student relations.
3. Representing the school in a professional manner wherever appropriate.

Not all circumstances that test the loyalty of teacher–coordinators can be anticipated. Nevertheless, school officials are not likely to accept them fully as agents of the school until their loyalty is proved. Those who find themselves unable to be loyal to the school should sever their relations and seek employment elsewhere.

The Teacher–Coordinator Begins Work

As a general rule teacher–coordinators will be contracted on a twelve-month basis, covering the fiscal period July 1 to June 30. Accordingly, new teacher–coordinators would report to work July 1 with approximately two months to get the program under way by the time school opens. The possibility of being successful in this endeavor will depend largely on how well the program has been introduced to the school and the community and on how favorable an initial climate the school provides.

The first and most pressing responsibility will be to make contacts with eligible students and with potential employers. Making student contacts will require the help of guidance personnel and probably of a representative from the principal's office. Initial contacts with potential employers will be greatly facilitated if information concerning the program and its purposes and values has been projected effectively into the community. Administrative actions similar to those suggested below should assure teacher–coordinator success in the discharge of initial responsibilities.

A news article should be released from the office of the superintendent announcing that the teacher–coordinator is on the job and is in the process of setting up the program. The article should include information concerning program purposes and values in sufficient scope to enable concerned publics to associate this new item with previous news releases on the subject.

Diplomatic reference should be made to initial teacher–coordinator contacts with students and employers. Appropriate personal information such as a photo of the teacher–coordinator, office hours, and telephone number may encourage potential students and employers to make contact. The office of the superintendent should request that the article be given a prominent place in the local newspaper.

Arrangements should be made for the superintendent or another appropriate administrative officer to introduce the teacher–coordinator on local television and radio. The educational nature of the program should be emphasized, and statements should be made directly to employers concerning visits to their places of business to discuss the possibility of their cooperation with the school.

If possible and feasible, an opportunity to speak briefly to one or more local civic clubs should be helpful. Diplomatic contact with the chairman of an appropriate committee of each club may result in an invitation to address the club.

A representative of the guidance system should be made available to help identify students who are eligible for enrollment. The administration should suggest to guidance personnel that full cooperation will be needed in the initiation and development of CE. Student personnel files should be made available by the principal of the high school.

The principal should advise the teacher–coordinator of all the prior efforts to alert students to the opportunity of enrolling in the program. Since one method of contacting prospective students will be through the mail, secretarial service should be made available.

Special administrative effort should be made to advise the faculty of the part it will be expected to play in the new CE program. The teacher–coordinator may be permitted to speak briefly to the faculty during preschool workshops or on other occasions. Such talks offer unexcelled opportunity to explain program purposes and values, and to ask for faculty help and cooperation.

Suggested Activities

1. After reviewing appropriate sources of information, outline a career-centered educational plan for the elementary school, junior high school, and senior high school. Define each phase clearly.
2. Prepare a statement explaining fully how CE provides occupational breadth in vocational education in the secondary school.
3. Prepare a brochure defining CE in terms that will be understood by school administrators, faculty, and students who are not familiar with the program.
4. Prepare a news article to be released from the office of the superintendent announcing that the teacher–coordinator is on the job and is in the process of setting up the program.
5. Prepare a 20- to 25-minute talk suitable for presentation to a civic club or on television, introducing CE and briefly outlining program purposes and values together with the contribution it is designed to make to the local educational program.
6. Compose a minimum of five objectives for CE. Justify each objective by listing its contribution to one or more of the seven cardinal principles of education.

Part II

Coordination of Cooperative Education

chapter two
Selection of Occupations

chapter three
Selection of Training Stations

chapter four
Selection of Students

chapter five
Placement of Students on Jobs
for Training Purposes

chapter six
Visitation and Counseling

chapter seven
Organization and Effective Utilization of Representative Advisory Committees

Introduction to Part II

Chapter Two marks the beginning of specific treatment of the basic parts of CE that are vital to its successful operation as one integral part of the educational system. The order in which the various items are treated has no significance because a chronological arrangement of program elements according to importance is not feasible.

The fact that "Selection of Occupations" is the first element to be treated, therefore, does not imply that it is more important or that it should be known about before other aspects of the program are introduced. In practice it may be difficult to determine which of the program elements is being emphasized by an experienced teacher–coordinator at any given time because all of them may require equal attention at the moment.

For this reason teacher–coordinators are not likely to commit their time to one part of the program to the total exclusion of all others. Rather they will be involved in many activities dividing the time among several program functions. Successful performance of multiple activities requires good management and judicial budgeting of time, and those who fail in these respects may find themselves in difficulty.

Coordination has been defined as bringing into harmonious relationship the parts of the school and the community essential to CE. In its broadest sense coordination includes all teacher–coordinator activities that involve a joint and functioning relationship between elements of the school and the community—activities such as selecting occupations and training stations, selecting and placing students, and visiting and counseling students.

As the study of this book proceeds, the reader should remember that the principles and the methods recommended are basic and applicable to CE relating to specialized occupational areas as well as to "across the board" or "diversified occupations" programs. The basic difference in these course types is the manner in which the directly related instruction is presented.

chapter two

Selection of Occupations

One of the most important aspects of CE is the nature and character of the occupations in which students are placed to gain their work experience. An examination of the following occupational characteristics should be helpful in the evaluative process that precedes selection.

Occupational Qualifications

Learning Time

The placement of students in occupations that do not require learning periods worthy of the school time and credit involved is a common program malfunction. In order to ensure program integrity in this respect, the teacher–coordinator must exercise every possible effort to restrict student placement to occupations requiring learning periods of at least two thousand hours. The learning-time estimate is based on the time needed for related study and on-the-job work experience. In addition to being able to produce at beginning employment level, the program graduate should also have the technical background and ability to become highly skilled with practice.

An apprenticeable occupation normally requires more than two thousand hours learning time. Such an occupation, therefore, should always satisfy the learning-time requirement. However, placing students in apprenticeable occupations does not mean that the complete training requirements can be met within the CE program.

On the contrary, it simply means that the student who enters the program as a junior can complete approximately two thousand hours training in an apprenticeable occupation before graduating from high school. By the same token, the senior entering the program could complete approximately one thousand hours of training. Both students, after graduating, would need additional learning time to satisfy requirements.

The acceptability of CE-sponsored work experience as a part of the apprenticeship will depend upon agreements between the school and local "joint apprenticeship committees." Some committees have developed plans for the time spent by the CE student to be applicable to local apprenticeship programs.

Arrangements of this kind are mutually beneficial because local labor organizations are thus assured of a dependable supply of high-caliber apprentices, and the local high school would gain additional opportunities to offer satisfying career openings to the students. Representative advisory committees should be helpful in working out arrangements with local joint apprenticeship committees.

Since the placement of students is not restricted to apprenticeable occupations, it may become difficult at times to determine whether a given occupation actually requires enough learning time to justify its inclusion in the program. At such times authentic sources of information are needed to establish the learning time required to reach proficiency levels.

Business and industrial firms may be consulted to determine if there are established training programs requiring two thousand or more hours for completion. If it is found that such programs do exist, the occupation in question should be acceptable from the standpoint of learning time.

Other sources of information may be vocational schools in other communities or state educational agencies having to do with vocational education. And in some cases employee organizations having jurisdiction over occupations in question may supply the needed information.

An occupation may also be acceptable if a craft or occupational committee of at least three members, each of whom has expertise at acceptable levels in the occupation in question, is able to develop a "job analysis" with training-time assignments totaling at least two thousand hours.

Post-Training Opportunity for Employment

After it has been determined that sufficient learning time is required for a given occupation, the opportunity it presents for post-training employment should be examined. Vocational education that is not premised on suitable employment opportunity for program graduates is futile and fails to meet the first requirement to justify its establishment.

It should be understood, however, that vocational education in an occupation that cannot be justified in one community may be completely justifiable in another that provides employment opportunity for program graduates. In other words, programs may vary from community to community depending upon the availability of acceptable post-training opportunities for employment.

The second phase of the occupational selection process, therefore, should consist of an examination of projected employment opportunity to be expected at the time current students would be seeking employment.

Educational Feasibility

The third prerequisite to the acceptability of an occupation is its adaptability to CE. Occupational characteristics should be examined from the following standpoints:

1. Availability of directly related reference materials.
2. Accessibility and stability of training stations.
3. Seasonal nature of employment.

Inexperienced teacher–coordinators may fail to realize the importance of deficiencies in these areas until they have witnessed the frustration of students victimized by such circumstances. If students are placed in occupations for which directly related reference materials are not available, these students would be unable to satisfy the requirements of directly related instruction through normal procedures.

Occupations may present training stations that are improperly located or are too far from the school to be reasonably accessible to students and school officials. Training-station instability in any form may create circumstances incompatible with the educational plan of the school.

Another important consideration is whether the employment is

23

seasonal. Occupations of this type may provide employment for only a few months during the school year, thus failing to lend themselves well to the educational plan of local schools.

Hazardous Occupations

A fourth consideration has to do with whether the occupation is hazardous, and this question can be answered by referring to the standard listing established by the Fair Labor Standards Act. Students under eighteen are prohibited from working in occupations thus classified as hazardous.

For a complete and up-to-date listing of hazardous occupations the teacher–coordinator should contact the nearest office of the Wage and Hour Division of the U.S. Department of Labor. Such an office is normally located with other federal offices in state capital cities. Summaries of those parts of the Fair Labor Standards Act and Amendments pertaining to CE are available upon request.

The Occupational Evaluation Process

The evaluative instrument shown in Figure 2 may be used as it is, or it may be helpful to the innovative teacher–coordinator in developing an original evaluative plan. In either event, the instrument used should be as practical and objective as possible. After deriving the best possible answers to the three major questions concerning each occupation under consideration, the findings should be presented to the local advisory committee for judgment. Action may be delayed when the committee feels that additional information or study is necessary. In such an event, student placements may be delayed until final judgment is made.

As each occupation is approved by the advisory committee, it should be added to the approved list, which in its entirety will constitute the occupational breadth of the vocational opportunity in any given school district. Once the list is completed, it can be kept current from year to year by simply adding and deleting occupations as advised by the advisory committee in accordance with business and industrial development. Hazardous occupations may be included on the list for placement of students eighteen or older.

The teacher–coordinator and the advisory committee should develop occupational sensitivity and alertness to occupational changes and the resulting implications for CE. This awareness should be of great

Figure 2 Occupational Evaluative Instrument for Cooperative Education

An affirmative answer to the three major questions which follow should indicate that the occupation is acceptable. A negative response to any one of the major questions should render its acceptability subject to conditions that may be imposed by the advisory committee. A negative answer to all three major questions should eliminate the occupation from consideration. In responding to the minor questions, the yes and no answers indicate definite presence or absence of the condition under consideration. An indef. (indefinite) response indicates doubt that the condition exists or can be accomplished, or indicates that additional investigation is necessary.

Occupation: _____

A. Does this occupation require a learning period of sufficient length to justify the student's devoting school time and credit to the program?

Yes ___ No ___

(A positive response to any one of the following minor questions should substantiate an affirmative answer to this major question.)

1. Does the learning period involve 2,000 hours or more for completion?

Yes ___ Indef. ___ No ___

2. Is it an apprenticeable occupation?

Yes ___ Indef. ___ No ___

3. Are there training programs in business or industry requiring 2,000 hours or more for completion?

Yes ___ Indef. ___ No ___

4. Are there public or private school programs requiring 2,000 or more hours for completion?

Yes ___ Indef. ___ No ___

5. Does a representative craft or occupational committee agree that 2,000 hours are required or that a sufficient learning period, judged on other bases, is required?

Yes ___ Indef. ___ No ___

B. Does this occupation offer acceptable post-training employment opportunity?

Yes ___ No ___

(Negative responses to the following minor questions will bolster an affirmative answer to this major question.)

1. Is the occupation becoming obsolete?

Yes ___ Indef. ___ No ___

2. Is it crowded or becoming automated?

Yes ___ Indef. ___ No ___

3. Is employment restricted to a small geographical area?

Yes ___ Indef. ___ No ___

4. Are employment and career progress dependent on qualifications other than training, experience, and ability?

Yes ___ Indef. ___ No ___

(continued)

Figure 2 *(continued)*

5. Is the work involved socially unacceptable as judged by local standards?

Yes ___ Indef. ___ No ___

C. Is in-school and on-the-job training feasible and justifiable through
cooperative education?

Yes ___ No ___

1. Are ample and appropriate instructional materials available?

Yes ___ Indef. ___ No ___

2. Is the work involved full-time as contrasted with seasonal employment?

Yes ___ Indef. ___ No ___

3. Are training stations normally accessible and stably located?

Yes ___ Indef. ___ No ___

Date of Initial Evaluation _____

Signed _____ Teacher–Coordinator

Approved _____ Disapproved _____ , by the Gen-

eral Advisory Committee in Executive Session on _____ .

Date

Signed _____

Chairman of Advisory Committee

value in counseling students relative to their career interests, and in the
perpetual reevaluating of occupations to determine whether they continue to merit a place on the approved list.

Typical Problems in Selecting Occupations

The following problems are typical because most teacher–coordinators will be confronted with them throughout their careers, but
especially during their first months in the program. These problems,
with their attending commentaries, should serve to crystallize understanding of the nature of the difficulties that may be encountered in
maintaining the quality and reputation of the occupations in which
students are placed for their work experiences. Consideration of these
problems, and of others that may arise during the formative period of
philosophical development, should help the teacher–coordinator to deal
intelligently with them when they occur.

Problem 1 *Dealing effectively with students who seek enrollment with the request that they be permitted to continue current employment in an occupation that does not meet established occupational requirements*

Students who already have jobs will often seek enrollment in CE in order to get additional compensation in the form of "school time for work" and "school credit" for work experience in an occupation, even though it does not offer career potential. For purposes of illustration, let it be assumed that a high school student has a lucrative paper route. CE seems to offer several benefits, including getting out of school early, delivery of papers before dark, and two credits.

It is not difficult to visualize the disappointment of this student when told that paper delivery does not qualify as a CE job. Often the student does not understand or appreciate the difference between the type of work experience provided by jobs such as paper delivery as compared with that of qualified occupational areas being pursued by bona fide CE students.

This student's misunderstanding and disappointment may be shared by parents and friends, and they may protest to educational officials of the community. The reaction of school officials to such a protest reveals how well they understand and appreciate the aims of CE, and the extent of their support. Although teacher–coordinators have no alternative but to accept administrative mandates, they should find legitimate ways to preserve occupational standards.

The above example does not imply that the publishing business does not include occupations that justify the placement of CE students; it simply means that delivering newspapers fails to meet occupational requirements, as may be verified by applying the criteria given in the occupational evaluative instrument (Figure 2). But if the student could develop career interest in "newspaper circulation" or other reputable occupational areas within the publishing field, it is quite likely that excellent training opportunities could be developed.

Problem 2 *Effectively withstanding insistence that the enrollment in CE produce a student-hour teaching load that compares favorably with that of other teachers*

Pressure of this kind tends to force a lowering of occupational standards in order to reach enrollment goals. Pressure may be generated by faculty misunderstanding of the nature and the extent of the teacher–coordinator's duties and responsibilities.

Negative attitudes will inevitably result from the following faculty observations of the teacher–coordinator at work:

1. Curious teachers will notice that the teacher–coordinator may have only thirty students with two scheduled periods per day as compared with their own daily load of five classes of thirty students each.
2. They will also notice that the teacher–coordinator leaves the campus early in the day and seldom returns, thus raising questions as to where he goes and what he does.
3. They will be prone to accept a consistent rumor that the teacher–coordinator's salary exceeds that of experienced master teachers.

Resulting attitudes will tend to generate hostility if positive administrative action is not taken without delay, but all too often faculty indignation is fed by similar administrative attitudes. The administration may seek to appease the faculty by insisting that CE enrollment be increased or that extra responsibilities be assigned to the teacher–coordinator during the unscheduled portions of the school day.

Although the teacher–coordinator must follow administrative orders, he or she should explain to appropriate individuals that a student load of thirty compares favorably with the 150 students hours normally carried by regular academic teachers. Each CE student will be enrolled in the related subjects class for a minimum of one period per day.

Although this one class may account for only thirty student-hours, it is significant that the teaching time may be spread over two or more periods, with 60 percent of it being devoted to individual instruction. All CE students leave the school to work on their respective jobs for at least three hours of the school day; but if they were to remain in school, they would require the time of one teacher three hours of the school day.

Since the absence of CE students relieves the regular faculty of ninety student-hours per day, it seems logical that the load of the teacher–coordinator should be credited with proportionate teaching time, because he or she works with the students on the job, thus carrying a total daily load of 120 student hours. Hence the teaching load compares favorably with that of regular teachers, and it should be emphasized that the teacher–coordinator has many responsibilities over and above those required of the regular teacher. (See Figure 1, page 9.)

Criticism and resentment of the teaching load should not develop when CE is properly introduced in the first place. Administrative officers and faculty members who understand and accept the purposes, values, and operational procedures of the program will approve its operation and champion its cause rather than raise a barrier of doubt.

Problem 3 *Working with local employers who see CE as an oppor-tunity to secure labor at less than normal cost in occupations that require little or no learning time*

Employers such as these may not wait for the local teacher–coordinator to call on them to examine the possibility of placing students in their places of business, but rather they will be aggressive in claiming student labor. If the occupations involved are not on the approved list, they should be subjected to the standard evaluative process and presented to the advisory committee for judgment.

If the occupations are not approved, the requesting employers should be told of the decision and they should be given a full explana-tion of the reasons for rejection. It would be wise to inform all concerned individuals, and to give appropriate administrative officials a written explanation of the rejection.

For illustration, let it be assumed that a local employer draws the conclusion that CE presents an opportunity to secure student help in jobs requiring little or no learning time. It may seem to be a solution to a pressing labor problem in that high school students could be made available to work approximately half of each school day and all day Saturday, as a part of their school work. The employer reasons further that two students working during the morning hours and two working in the afternoon would be the equivalent of two full-time employees at a fraction of the normal cost.

Full production could be expected in a short time, because very little learning time is required in the types of jobs being considered. Such reasoning could be the basis of enthusiastic and aggressive contact with school officials to request that four students be recommended for placement.

It is not difficult to envision the employer's disappointment when the proposal is not accepted, for students may not be used to replace regular employees or those needed in the basic operation of the busi-ness. The intensity of the disappointment may prompt a protest to school officials, and here again the staunchness of the school adminis-trators will be tested.

If occupational standards fail to withstand the pressure, the ability of the program to serve the purposes for which it is designed will have been weakened. The approved list of occupations in which students may be placed, a functioning advisory committee, and staunch adminis-trative support are the best safeguards against those who try to lower occupational standards to levels that could result in exploitation of students.

Problem 4 *Resistance from local employee organizations relative to* *placement of students in occupations over which they have jurisdiction*

Labor organizations are normally strong supporters of vocational education in the public schools, and all the federal legislation that supports vocational education has been passed with the full backing of organized labor. This national labor union endorsement provides an excellent basis for beginning good relations with local employee organizations.

Under normal circumstances, however, it will be necessary for the teacher–coordinator to take the lead in making it known that the school desires to be cooperative. The local labor leaders should be given a full explanation of the purposes and values of CE. Such an explanation should leave no doubt about what the program is designed to do, and should describe it as an excellent medium through which the public school can support the apprenticeship program.

It should be explained, for example, that CE graduates are advanced learners and excellent candidates for the apprenticeship program. The best possible result of a good relationship with organized labor would be the development of a cooperative plan that would accord advance apprenticeship rank to graduates from CE.

Failure to cultivate a constructive relationship with a union may result in misunderstanding of the purposes of the program and it might appear, for example, that the local school was competing with organized labor in producing skilled workers for the occupational areas over which the union has jurisdiction. This fear could cause opposition and might result in a problem about placing students in the occupations involved.

Proper representation of employee organizations on the local advisory committee should prove an effective safeguard against the development of problems such as that described above. In fact, a representative advisory committee should eliminate the possibility of the development of such a problem.

Problem 5 *Overcoming a previously established program image that discounts the occupational stature essential to CE*

A teacher–coordinator who enters a school that has a low regard for CE will face severe problems in establishing recommended standards for occupations to be included in the program. Such problems may stem from any one or all of the publics that make contributions to the environment in which the program functions.

Coping with resistance of this nature in initial tenure, the inexperienced teacher–coordinator may be unable to find an immediate solution and consequently may be forced to accept some undesirable

30

conditions and make the best of the situation, at least temporarily. Under no circumstances, however, should the coordinator succumb to pressures to the extent of permanently qualifying or reducing occupational standards. On the contrary, an immediate educational program should be designed to develop understanding and appreciation of the purposes and values of CE and the occupational stature necessary to make the program successful.

It would be a wise precaution on the part of a teacher–coordinator who is considering a move into a school in which CE has previously operated to carefully assess the attitudes of all concerned publics to determine the intensity and nature of the program image in the community. The findings of such a study should be used as a basis of the conditions under which employment would be acceptable. Agreements made with the administration as conditions of employment should smooth the way to necessary changes in operational standards and policies after employment. Without administrative support, however, these changes probably could not be accomplished, and CE would have to continue to serve ends different from those intended.

In the event that initial administrative rapport can be developed and the environment seems favorable for improvements in operational standards and policies, the teacher–coordinator is cautioned to be patient in regard to the time required to accomplish such changes. It may be necessary to cope with adverse attitudes on the part of some publics for an extended period before harmony can be achieved.

Persistence is the key word here, for definite and deliberate relationship development programs should be designed, and relentlessly pursued, in order to replace adverse attitudes with those conducive to proper program operation. The teacher–coordinator should not expect complete and immediate change but should be willing to accept continuous and positive progress. A strong, representative advisory committee is of great value in reconciling out-of-school publics.

Suggested Activities

1. After study of the occupational evaluative instrument (Figure 2), develop an alternative instrument involving personal innovations in content and form.
2. Develop a step-by-step procedure for the selection of occupations to be included in CE.

3. Prepare a statement portraying the hazards involved in including occupations of insufficient stature in CE.
4. Prepare a plan for the effective use of a general advisory committee in the occupational selection process.
5. Prepare a statement for presentation to school officials comparing a CE enrollment of thirty students with conventional teaching loads.
6. Develop a policy statement relating to the selection of occupations to be included in CE, for presentation to school officials for consideration and approval prior to the opening of school.

chapter three

Selection
of Training Stations

The terms *training station* and *occupation* are frequently used interchangeably by those not well versed in CE terminology. It becomes necessary, therefore, that the prospective teacher–coordinator be acquainted with the significance of these two terms and the difference in their meaning.

Occupation may be defined as a specific division or an entity in the world of work—an entity that requires the application of specific manipulative skills or technical knowledge in the performance of a job—skills not necessarily required in other jobs. *Training station* refers to the place where the student receives on-the-job educational experiences.

It may be that an acceptable occupation will fail to provide acceptable training stations in a given community. Salesmanship, for example, is an acceptable occupational area well represented in all communities. It may be found, however, that some places of business representing this occupation do not provide suitable training conditions for high school students.

Training-Station Characteristics

A responsibility of the school, through the teacher–coordinator and the local advisory committee, is to establish training-station standards to guarantee acceptable on-the-job educational experiences for all CE students. Accordingly, the teacher–coordinator should develop criteria for use in the tentative selection of training stations before presenting the matter to the advisory committee. The following listing and discussion of training-station characteristics may be helpful in judging them.

Employer Attitudes

The attitude of the employer is an important factor in the desirability of a training station, for even though all other desirable characteristics exist, educational values could disappear if the employer does not understand or accept the true purposes of CE.

For example, the employer may get the idea that the principal purpose of the program is to provide opportunity for high school students to earn money to help defray the cost of their education. Naturally, the employer would approve such a purpose, and he would not overlook an opportunity to obtain low-cost student labor. Other publics—students, parents, administrators, and teachers—may share the employer's misconceptions.

The fact that federal legislation requires that students be paid a monetary wage establishes the "earning of money" as an essential feature of CE. However, the wage must not be permitted to become the paramount consideration. When the money paid to the student becomes the most important concern of the employer, educational values tend to be replaced by concern for weekly production in return for weekly pay. It is imperative that the teacher—coordinator develop the concept that wages must be relegated to a place of minor importance in comparison with the major importance of educational values.

Perhaps the first indication of the right employer attitude would be insistence, during the training-station selection period, that the student assigned possess aptitudes and vocational interests compatible with success. Another indication of an appropriate attitude on the part of the employer could be interest in securing a student with the personal characteristics desired in potentially permanent employees.

In public and private statements about the program, the employer should show understanding and acceptance of the purposes and values of CE. Reaction to the memorandum of training, when it is explained as part of the placement process, should reveal the employer's real intent in the program.

For example, what is the reaction to the statement that the "student while in training will have the status of noncompetitive worker, neither displacing a regular worker now employed nor substituting for a worker needed by the training agency"?

34

Positive reaction to the above statement should reliably indicate an acceptable attitude on the part of the employer, but a negative response would indicate an attitude that could make cooperation with the school difficult.

Another test of attitude could be to examine the employer's interpretation of program values. If immediate returns in production are expected as opposed to the potential values the program is designed to produce, the employer can be expected to regulate on-the-job training accordingly. (See Program Values to Employers, page 252.) In the final analysis, what the employer understands and believes will determine the character of the on-the-job experiences of the student.

Range and Scope of On-the-Job Experiences

The teacher—coordinator should carefully examine the probability that the student can be employed for the entire school year. Some employers are reluctant to promise employment for so long a period, particularly in the field of distribution during periods of low business activity. However, the employer must be advised that laying the student off during the school year presents a problem to which neither the student nor the school has a ready solution.

During the process of training-agency selection, if the employer believes that it may be necessary to lay the student off for one or more periods during the school year, this place of business should be eliminated from the list. Such action will avert embarrassing circumstances later in the year. An employer attitude of this kind may be an honest reflection of the business, or it may indicate a personal disregard of the educational values of the program.

In any event, it should be made clear that training agencies are expected to provide on-the-job experiences for the entire school year. A rigid policy in this respect must not discount circumstances that may inadvertently develop and require that student employment be discontinued. In such a case, the school should promptly remove the student and make the best possible adjustment.

Another important point to be carefully considered during the selection of the training station is the range of experience available to the student. Although final determination of the total range may require further study, it should be immediately discernible whether sufficient experience potential is available to merit further consideration.

For example, there may be doubt about an adequate range of

experience being offered to a student working in an automotive repair shop restricted to minor repair with limited equipment; whereas there would be no doubt of an adequate range of experience available in a well-equipped shop with capacity to completely service the modern automobile.

Another example would be a retail store that depends on display selling, thus eliminating the need for sales ability, as contrasted with a specialty store dealing in "ladies' ready-to-wear" merchandise, which requires an appropriate learning time to acquire the necessary technical knowledge and sales ability. The suggestion is that the two places of business that obviously do not provide acceptable ranges of experience should not be listed. Nevertheless, potential training agencies should not be rejected before being accorded the total training-station evaluation process.

Equipment and Facilities

The physical capacity of the training agency to provide the training desired for the cooperative student will depend upon a sufficiency of appropriate equipment of proper vintage. There may be instances where enough equipment is available, but it is so antiquated or obsolete that it cannot be applied effectively to the solution of modern problems.

Another important consideration is the attention given to the maintenance of equipment necessary for dependable service and minimum safety hazards. The employer should be reminded of his responsibility for any injury sustained by the student on the job. In this respect the student has the same legal status as any other employee, and hazards could justify rejection of an agency.

The general condition and appearance of facilities such as the inside and the outside of the building that houses the training agency contribute to the environment where the student will work. If the building is in good repair and provides adequate heating, ventilation, and cooling, it will tend to lift the morale of all employees; but a poorly equipped and maintained building can be expected to lower the morale of employees. The resulting environment may not be good for the placement of students.

Employee Morale

The general morale of the employees of a potential training agency affects the environment in which the student gets on-the-job experience. If employees are generally dissatisfied with the conditions under which they work, they will not provide wholesome and desirable working conditions for students. Furthermore, insecure workers who fear that management is plotting to replace them may view CE students as potential replacements. Consequently, the worker may withhold essential information or refuse to teach the student how to do the job. An employee who is hostile to management or to his coworkers can be expected to resent the student and to make circumstances as difficult as possible.

In the final analysis, employee morale should be considered an important factor in training-station selection. Before a student is placed, it should be determined that the on-the-job environment would be receptive to the training of high school students.

On-the-Job Instruction

The availability of a qualified on-the-job instructor should be a matter of important consideration in selecting training agencies. This individual frequently will not be the employer, but an employee appointed to assume this responsibility. The teacher–coordinator should be satisfied that the potential on-the-job instructor, whether the employer or an appointee, understands the responsibility and that the student will get the attention needed. On-the-job instructors should be informed of their responsibilities for student educational opportunities on the job, and of their function as members of the high school faculty.

If the employer does not desire to serve as the on-the-job instructor and if there is not an employee qualified to discharge the responsibility, the place of business should be eliminated as a training station, because a satisfactory learning situation cannot be developed without a qualified on-the-job instructor. Under such circumstances the student's work experience could only be a series of job assignments of doubtful educational value.

Location of the Training Station

An important consideration during the training-station selection process is the location of the training agency. The distance from the school should not be greater than can be feasibly accomplished by the student under all weather conditions. It should also be readily accessible to the school for coordination and supervisory purposes.

The location of the training station should be stable; that is, the student would be expected to report for work at the same time and place each day. An example of a violation of this principle would be placing a student with a building contractor, with carpentry as the vocational objective. In this case the location of the training station could vary from day to day according to periodic assignments to buildings in various stages of construction. The result might prove unsatisfactory because the school and the employer would find it difficult to coordinate and supervise the on-the-job experience of the student. A too-frequent change in location might also become confusing to the student.

The above statements are not intended to imply that carpentry is not a suitable occupation for the placement of students, for it is highly acceptable when placement conditions are satisfactory. The point is that the teacher–coordinator should carefully examine potential training stations in order to be sure that the location enables the student to report for work daily at a time and place commensurate and compatible with the school program.

The training agency should be completely outside the school to guarantee that the student's on-the-job experience will be a genuine sample of the world of work. Accordingly, students should not be placed in school jobs such as part-time secretaries and library assistants, because the working environment would be dominated by student–teacher relationships as opposed to real job circumstances.

Training stations restricted to placing a son or a daughter of the employer are seldom acceptable. For example, a son working for his father will be the victim of an on-the-job environment dominated by the father–son relationship, and being enrolled in CE will make little or no difference in the student's attitude toward the parent. Indeed, the son can be expected to continue to employ the same methods he has found to be successful in getting his way with his parents. Although there may be exceptions, students working for their parents will seldom experience on-the-job training up to the standards of CE.

The Training-Station Selection Process

Figure 3 is an evaluative instrument that may be helpful in its present form. It is suggested, however, that its greatest value would be in serving as a guide to the teacher–coordinator in the development of an instrument in accord with personal innovative ideas and local circumstances. In its final form the instrument should be as objective as

Figure 3   Training-Station Evaluation Instrument for Cooperative Education

An affirmative answer to all the following major questions would strongly indicate that the training station is acceptable. A negative response to one or more of the major questions should either eliminate the station from further consideration or render its acceptability subject to the judgment of the advisory committee. In responding to the minor questions, the yes and no answers indicate definite presence or absence of the condition under consideration. An indef. (indefinite) response indicates doubt that the condition exists or can be accomplished, or indicates that additional investigation is necessary.

Potential Training Agency _____

Address _____   Phone _____

Occupational Area Represented _____

A. Is the employer's attitude conducive to effective cooperation with the school in the operation of cooperative education?

   Yes ___ No ___

   (A positive response to three or more of the following minor questions, including No. 1, will substantiate an affirmative answer to this major question.)

   1. Does the employer understand and accept the purposes and values of CE?

   Yes ___ Indef. ___ No ___

   2. Can the employer be expected to honor educational purposes in dealing with the student and the school?

   Yes ___ Indef. ___ No ___

   3. Does the employer recognize that the principal values are potential, not immediate?

   Yes ___ Indef. ___ No ___

   4. Is the employer concerned about the student's basic aptitudes and vocational interests as they relate to occupational requirements?

   Yes ___ Indef. ___ No ___

   5. Is the employer concerned about the student's personal characteristics as they compare with those of desirable permanent employees?

   Yes ___ Indef. ___ No ___

B. Does the training station provide a satisfactory range and scope of on-the-job experience?

   Yes ___ No ___

   (A positive response to three or more of the following minor questions, including No. 1, will substantiate an affirmative answer to this major question.)

   1. Does the employer agree that employment of the student will continue for the entire school year?

   Yes ___ Indef. ___ No ___

(continued)

Figure 3 *(continued)*

2. Does the training-station experience potential range from initial uncomplicated activities to the more difficult and complex operations involved in the total expanse of the occupation?

Yes ___ Indef. ___ No ___

3. Does the employer agree that the student is not to remain in any one operation or phase of the occupation beyond the time required to reach the point of job proficiency?

Yes ___ Indef. ___ No ___

4. Does the employer agree to work with the teacher–coordinator in the development of a schedule of work experiences based on an analysis of the occupation represented by the training agency?

Yes ___ Indef. ___ No ___

C. Are the equipment and facilities satisfactory?

Yes ___ No ___

(A positive response to three or more of the following minor questions, including No. 1, will substantiate an affirmative answer to this major question.)

1. Are tools and machines present in sufficient amounts and quality to provide experience in the total expanse of the occupation?

Yes ___ Indef. ___ No ___

2. Are tools and equipment of reasonably modern design?

Yes ___ Indef. ___ No ___

3. Are tools and equipment well enough maintained and equipped with safety devices to ensure safe working conditions?

Yes ___ Indef. ___ No ___

4. Does the general condition of the building and facilities contribute to an attractive environment?

Yes ___ Indef. ___ No ___

5. Do the facilities provide adequate heating, ventilation, and cooling?

Yes ___ Indef. ___ No ___

D. Is employee morale conducive to satisfactory on-the-job relationships for the student?

Yes ___ No ___

(A negative answer to three or more of the following minor questions, including No. 1, will bolster a positive response to this major question.)

1. Are employees generally dissatisfied with working conditions?

Yes ___ Indef. ___ No ___

2. Is the absence of one or more of the basic morale factors obvious?

Yes ___ Indef. ___ No ___

3. Are feelings of insecurity or hostility toward management reflected in conversations with employees?

Yes ___ Indef. ___ No ___

4. Is absenteeism a problem?

Yes ___ Indef. ___ No ___

5. Is the "lost-time accident" record above normal for comparable types of businesses?

Yes ___ Indef. ___ No ___

E. Is the instructional potential of the training agency satisfactory?

Yes ___ No ___

40

Figure 3 *(continued)*

(A positive response to three or more of the following minor questions, including No. 1, will substantiate an affirmative answer to this question.)

1. Does the employer agree to designate a qualified individual for on-the-job instruction?

     Yes ___ Indef. ___ No ___

2. Does the on-the-job instructor understand and accept his responsibility to the student and the school?

     Yes ___ Indef. ___ No ___

3. Will association with the on-the-job instructor be a desirable experience for the student?

     Yes ___ Indef. ___ No ___

4. Does the instructor understand and accept the educational significance of the on-the-job experiences as opposed to emphasis on production?

     Yes ___ Indef. ___ No ___

F. Is the training station satisfactorily located?

     Yes ___ No ___

(A positive response to all the following minor questions will substantiate an affirmative answer to this major question.)

1. Is the training station within reasonable commuting distance of the school?

     Yes ___ Indef. ___ No ___

2. Is the training station readily accessible to the teacher–coordinator and other school officials for coordination and supervision?

     Yes ___ Indef. ___ No ___

3. Is the location of the training station stable enough for the student to report for work at the same time and place each day?

     Yes ___ Indef. ___ No ___

4. Are the time elements of the on-the-job experience compatible with school scheduling?

     Yes ___ Indef. ___ No ___

5. Does the training station involve normal work circumstances as opposed to a part-time job in the school or in a family business?

     Yes ___ Indef. ___ No ___

Date of Initial Evaluation _____

Signed _____ Teacher–Coordinator

Approved _____ Disapproved _____ , by the General Advisory Committee in Executive Session on _____ .
                                                                                        Date

Signed _____
                        Chairman of Advisory Committee

---

possible, so that undesirable training stations can be rejected "objectively." Subjective justification for rejecting a training station frequently becomes painfully unsuccessful.

Tentative List of Training Stations

As the teacher–coordinator approaches the problem of training-station selection, he or she will recognize that the first need is for a tentative listing of training stations potentially available. There are sources from which such a list might be developed, the most obvious being the local telephone directory, with particular reference to the Yellow Pages. All places of business representing approved occupational areas should be listed for further study.

It may be found that the local chamber of commerce can be helpful by making business or industrial studies available. Such studies may have been made in conjunction with industrial development projects.

A study of all available sources of information should produce a tentative listing of training stations that appear to qualify for student-placement purposes. Such a listing will serve as an excellent point of departure in the training-station evaluation process. The process might continue by purging the list of those firms that obviously offer inadequate possibilities.

The advisory committee may be helpful by identifying places of business with the best potential, thus compensating for the new coordinator's unfamiliarity with the community. The new teacher–coordinator may find it advisable to further restrict the list to those potential training stations that are representative of the occupational interests of tentatively selected students.

Preliminary Survey

In choosing training stations, there is no substitute for the teacher–coordinator's personal contact. The training-station roster developed during the preliminary study will list the potential training agencies that the teacher–coordinator must visit as the second step in the evaluative process. Under no circumstances should a phone call be substituted for the first visit to a potential training agency.

Attention is called to an earlier suggestion that the best understanding, on the part of the reader, will result from the assumption that he or she is a new teacher–coordinator in a school system in which CE has not previously been a part of the educational program. Thus it is obvious that the preliminary survey will bring the teacher–coordinator into contact with potential employers for the first time.

This first meeting will provide opportunity to tell the CE story to its most important public. The importance of this first contact cannot be overestimated because from it the potential employer will get a concept of the program. Effective presentation will tend to overcome self-assigned values or those stemming from rumor or other unreliable sources.

In addition, the teacher–coordinator will make that inevitable "first impression." If this first meeting demonstrates appropriate poise and stature, the response of the employer should be positive, regardless of any previously developed attitudes. Consequently, it is imperative that the teacher–coordinator carefully and thoroughly prepare for initial presentation to potential employers.

It is important that the teacher–coordinator make contact with the "head man" of the firm. Time and energy used in talking with lesser officers or employees below the decision-making level may be wasted. It would not be wise to have the one who will eventually make the decision concerning cooperation with the school get information secondhand from a subordinate. Therefore, it is suggested that the teacher–coordinator ask for the top executive, and if this individual is not available, request an appointment at a later time.

During the course of the interview, the teacher–coordinator should carefully observe the employer's reaction. If the response is favorable, it may be advisable to suggest a short tour of the area of the potential training opportunity. The teacher–coordinator should assess the range and scope of training, the quality and quantity of equipment and facilities, and employee morale indicators. A relatively complete observation during the first visit will make the initial evaluation more reliable.

It would be poor taste to take notes or check an evaluation sheet during the interview or the tour of facilities, but this checking should be done as soon as possible after leaving the place of business. Subsequent visits may be necessary to get additional information needed in the evaluative process.

The question of the employer's cooperation need not be raised during the first interview; in fact, it may be better to delay the decision until the evaluative process has been completed. Subsequent visits or phone calls may be necessary to obtain additional information.

Many employers will respond warmly, and during the first interview they will ask to cooperate. Still, it would be wise to refrain from a definite commitment until the evaluative process is completed.

Application of Evaluative Criteria

After the initial visit to potential training agencies, the evaluative instrument given earlier in this chapter should be applied to each agency. This application should be as complete as possible and should involve additional contacts with the agencies whenever needed. Training agencies that score negatively should be removed from the list for the time being, but they can be reinstated if later information should justify it. Even affirmative ratings should be subject to final approval by the advisory committee.

Advisory Committee Action

After the teacher–coordinator has applied the evaluative criteria to all potential training agencies, a meeting of the advisory committee should be called to confirm the tentatively selected training stations.

It is quite possible that information coming from the advisory committee will be of sufficient weight and authenticity to justify a change in the initial classification of some training agencies. Here again the wisdom of the advisory committee can be expected to exceed that of the teacher–coordinator, because its members are substantial citizens. Teacher–coordinator wisdom would be shown by acceptance of the committee's recommendation.

After the committee has made its recommendation, the teacher–coordinator should compile the tentatively approved list of training agencies for submission to administrative officers for approval before placements are made. Information used in the evaluation, including the completed evaluation forms, should become a part of a permanent training-agency file.

Typical Problems in Selecting Training Stations

The problems listed and discussed below are typical, and they present some critical difficulties encountered by new teacher–coordinators in introducing themselves and CE to uninformed schools and communities. Such problems also serve to temper the preceding, some-

44

what idealistic, rationale with typical job circumstances that tend to bridge the gap between theory and practice.

Problem 1 *Making appropriate and effective initial presentation to potential employers*

The degree to which this problem can be effectively solved will depend on how deeply and thoroughly the teacher–coordinator has absorbed the principles upon which CE is based. A full and complete grasp of the program in all its ramifications, coupled with abiding confidence in its ability to provide educational opportunities not otherwise available, will generate enthusiasm that should prove to be contagious in dealing with potential employers.

Problem 2 *Getting sufficient insight into potential training-station characteristics to support intelligent application of evaluative criteria*

On the surface it appears that there is not enough time to accomplish the essential functions of the teacher–coordinator, and the delinquent individual may offer this excuse for failure. Rather than to accept such an excuse at face value, however, administrative superiors should regard it as a danger signal. Teacher–coordinators must organize their work and budget their time so that efforts may be devoted in appropriate measure to functions currently most essential.

Organizational ability coupled with sufficient sensitivity should enable the coordinator to select properly the training stations needed for the initial placement of students. Admittedly, the process is complicated by the fact that the selection of students is going on during the same period.

Furthermore, public relations responsibilities will also be demanding and difficult to postpone, and there will be other demands. In these circumstances the weak-hearted may accept training agencies without subjecting them to the suggested evaluative process. Consequently, the program may become employer-centered rather than student-centered.

Problem 3 *Temptation to allow educational values to be submerged in favor of mercenary values*

The publics having the most intimate relationships with the CE environment may accept its tangible mercenary values more readily than they realize its somewhat remote and less tangible educational values. Without being prompted, the employer will recognize the possibility of profit from the work of students, and the fact that the student works a given amount of time for a mutually satisfactory wage may seem to be sufficient justification.

The employer may not realize that the school would not be justified in allowing students to miss half of the school day unless by this arrangement they could gain as much or more educational value as they would by remaining in the full school day. An employer who denies the student the educational value which should result from CE work experience in effect causes the student to pay an educational penalty in order to add to the employer's profit.

The students' need for money may influence them to apply for enrollment. To them the wages seem to justify their sacrifice of school time, and thus it becomes the responsibility of the school to protect them from this mistake.

Parents often favor the opportunity for their sons or daughters to work because of their low income, and they may not realize the price their progeny would pay in lost educational opportunity. The school also may attach too much importance to the money earned by the students.

This mercenary emphasis would be demonstrated if, for example, the local newspaper should carry a feature story headlined: "Vocational Students Earn $100,000." An article with such a headline would probably win favorable attention from several segments of the community, and many readers would think that it correctly indicated the principal value of CE in the minds of the school officials. The best insurance against this misconception is a qualified teacher–coordinator with a dependable philosophy and an intense faith in the purpose and values of the program.

Problem 4 *Resisting the use of substandard training stations in the face of the personal desires of employers, students, school officials, or parents*

The teacher–coordinator may find it difficult to resist an insistent request from influential employers to place students in their places of business. Such requests may arise from such circumstances as the following:

1. Parents who wish to employ their son or daughter.
2. An employer who wants to cut operating costs through the use of student labor.
3. An employer who wishes to employ the son or daughter of a friend.
4. An employer who wishes to employ students to satisfy short-term or seasonal needs.
5. An employer who wishes to employ students for dead-end jobs requiring little or no learning time.

Requests such as those suggested above will be especially difficult to resist if they are transmitted through a member of the school board, an important city official, or the superintendent of schools. Students may insist that they be permitted to continue to hold jobs they already have, or that they be placed with specific employers for reasons other than to pursue their vocational education.` Such students may enlist employers, parents, and school officials to intercede for them.

School officials may insist that students be placed in school jobs in order to cut labor costs, and indeed the teacher–coordinator who requests secretarial help may be required by the administration to employ a CE student. The most effective defense lies in adhering to a definite set of training-station standards previously approved by the administration.

Problem 5 *Effective organization and utilization of the advisory committee in the training-station evaluative process*

The pressure of deadlines such as the beginning of school and the last day for changing schedules sometimes places new teacher–coordinators in difficult positions. The time element may become so acute that they no longer have time to apply the evaluative criteria to potential training stations, and to wait for the advisory committee to meet and pass judgment on tentative selections. The situation may be further complicated by such circumstances as the following:

1. The pressure from students and employers waiting for assignments.
2. Delay because of inability to make contact with appropriate training agency officials.
3. Delay in getting the advisory committee selected and organized.
4. Inability of the teacher–coordinator to organize and direct the collective efforts of the advisory committee to the problems at hand.

Although the new teacher–coordinator is vulnerable to circumstances such as the above, prior recognition and consideration of these possibilities in various combinations should help avert serious complications. After the first year, however, only gross negligence could result in comparable circumstances.

Suggested Activities

1. After a review of the training-station evaluation instrument (Figure 3), develop an alternative instrument involving personal innovations in content and form.

2. Describe in detail how the instrument above might be used in the training-station selection process.

3. Compose a statement designed for presentation to potential employers during the first visit in the training-station selection process. Keep in mind that this presentation will probably be the basis of the employer's "first impression" of CE as well as that of the teacher–coordinator.

4. Describe in detail how the wisdom of the advisory committee can serve most effectively in the training-station selection process.

5. Prepare a statement detailing the "preliminary survey" the new teacher–coordinator should conduct in the initial quest for training stations.

6. Design a policy statement relating to the selection of training stations for consideration and approval by school officials. Specify regulations regarding jobs in the school and in family-owned business and industrial firms.

chapter four

Selection
of Students

No other aspect of CE is more vital than a selection plan to ensure that students enrolled are qualified. The teacher–coordinator should have the authority and the responsibility of finally determining who may be enrolled. To accomplish the purpose of the program, it is necessary to have students who want, need, and are capable of profiting from the instruction.

The teacher–coordinator is cautioned to remember that the term "selection of students" may be misunderstood by school administrators and teachers. They may resent and resist this essential feature of CE because they assume that it will result in their loss of good students. The typical reaction of a school principal who has not recognized the valid requirements of the program would be to refuse the teacher–coordinator a part in selecting students on the grounds that other teachers accept the students who are assigned to them.

Perhaps it would be better to use the term *determining enrollment* instead of *student selection.* Teacher–coordinators do not actually select students, but they should have the responsibility of deciding whether each applicant is qualified for enrollment. Administrative assignment of this responsibility to the teacher–coordinator should be coupled with the mandate that students who finally fail to meet requirements, for whatever reason, be returned to the regular program on or before the last day for schedule changes. Such an arrangement is essential if enrollment is to be limited to qualified students.

Distinguishing Characteristics of Qualified Students

The importance of having the right students enrolled in CE suggests that a listing of ideal student characteristics would be helpful. Such a listing follows with brief commentaries.

Clearly Defined Vocational Purpose

The student's declaration of vocational purpose is a legal enrollment requirement, but there is a tendency for such declarations to be made as a matter of course rather than as an honest statement of career interest. This danger prompts the suggestion that the process of selecting students include the validation of their stated vocational purposes through accepted guidance procedures. These procedures should help students designate their vocational purposes on the basis of personal aptitudes, vocational interests, and knowledge of the occupational areas that offer the best possibilities of success.

Academic Ability

Job skills and technical knowledge are essential to success in the world of work, but of equal importance are knowledge and skills in communication and computation, as well as ethics and good citizenship. Becoming a vocational student, therefore, should not be allowed to enhance the idea that conventional high school courses in language arts and mathematics cease to be important. On the contrary, the vocational student should attach great importance to competence in these areas, for his or her occupational progress may depend heavily upon them.

Communicative skills, including ability to read and write, are essential to successful participation in directly related instruction when the "supervised and directed study" method of teaching is used. This method requires that the students find, read, and understand technical information related to their on-the-job experience.

Within reasonable limits and in accord with good judgment, grade averages should not be the most important consideration in deciding on the qualifications of students applying for CE. Although A and B students may be ideal, their chances of success may not be so great as the chances of those with less academic ability, but with more desirable character traits and ambition. Students with C and D averages often present chances for success, and even individuals with failing averages

50

should not be eliminated without a full investigation of the causes of failure.

Character Traits

Both vocational purpose and academic ability are essential to success in the pursuit of excellence in vocational education, but little of lasting value will result if the basic character of individuals does not enable them to secure and hold a job after graduating from high school. By virtue of early training, or perhaps the lack of it in the home and the school, the character patterns of students are largely fixed before they enroll in CE.

Of paramount importance are character traits such as integrity, courtesy, cheerfulness, cooperativeness, dependability, sincerity, self-reliance, and willingness to take correction. Although some improvement can be expected to result from insistent attention to these elements of character, much more progress is likely if students are properly oriented in these respects before they are enrolled. The teacher–coordinator should be aware of the futility of preparing individuals for jobs they could not be expected to hold because of character deficiencies.

Ambition To Acquire Related Knowledge

Students of good character would still be deficient if they did not have enough ambition to prepare themselves for occupational success. Clearly defined vocational purpose, academic ability, and desirable character traits will not compensate for a lack of interest in acquiring the knowledge and skills essential to current job performance and to future progress and promotion.

On the other hand, students who are sincerely interested in a broad preparation will accept the challenge to find the information they need, and to apply it to the solution of job problems. Teaching such students in related subjects becomes a matter of simply giving the help and guidance they need in the pursuit of excellence.

Making Contact with Potential Students

During the initial development of CE, teacher–coordinators should make special efforts to contact potential students before the beginning of school. They will also find it necessary to continue the practice after the program becomes established in order to inform potential students of this opportunity at an opportune time. The fact that CE is a relatively new feature of the high school curriculum requires that it be given promotional treatment for the foreseeable future.

Promotional efforts should be organized and effective prior to spring registration or any similar event designed to give high school students an opportunity to identify courses they are interested in taking the following semester. There follows a list of suggested activities, with attending descriptions, intended to inform students about enrollment requirements.

Assembly Program

In the schools that still hold them, general assemblies offer an effective medium of student contact. Assembly programs should be focused on sophomores and juniors who will be eligible for enrollment at the beginning of the next fall term. Novel ways of presenting program values should be designed to catch the attention of eligible students.

An approach that is effective, although not innovative, would be for the teacher–coordinator to introduce three or four students, and to have each one present a prepared statement on the values of CE to them. The teacher–coordinator should work with the students in preparing their statements, to be sure that they will emphasize the true values of the program. The general suggestion is that qualified students should be encouraged to take the lead in school activities whenever feasible, and to take advantage of opportunities to inform other students of the educational value of the program.

Newly employed teacher–coordinators, although not scheduled to report for work until fall, might seek opportunities to introduce themselves to student bodies at general assemblies during the preceding spring semester.

These assembly appearances could also be used to relate program information in the best way available. For example, a film that tells the story of CE might be shown. All such programs should inform students how they can make their interest known and to whom they should go to get additional information. When teacher–coordinators report for work at their respective schools, office hours should be announced together with invitations to prospective students at their convenience.

Visit Homerooms or Activity Periods

Teacher–coordinators should seek administrative approval to visit homerooms or other comparable student assemblies. They should work out a definite schedule and procedure, and inform both the administration and the homeroom teacher about them. The message may be the same as in assembly programs, but with smaller groups the approach can be less formal and more conducive to questions from the students. In either event, the students should be told how and when they can obtain more information.

This advice about homeroom appearances also applies to club meetings and activity periods, where discussion of this nature would be appropriate. It is desirable to make such appearances before the mass meeting of all interested students, which will be discussed later as a phase of the student selection plan.

News Releases

The school paper is a most effective medium in relaying information to eligible students. However, the fact that the paper is a student publication subject to faculty supervision sometimes makes it difficult to obtain the desired publicity. Stories written by students are preferred to stories written by the teacher–coordinator. Therefore, the following suggestions are offered:

1. Contact the sponsor of the paper early in the school year.
2. After a suitable explanation of CE, request that a student reporter be assigned to write a feature story on the program.
3. Suggest that a student photographer be assigned to work with the student reporter.
4. When and if these young journalists report, give them undivided time and attention. Provide the information they want, and be sure that they see all facets of the program, including qualified students on the job and engaging in related study.

Gratifying results should be forthcoming because sponsors of student publications will recognize the project as an excellent opportunity for desirable student experiences. Such results may range from pictures of students at work with captions briefly explaining the program from the student's point of view, to full-page feature stories with pictures and commentary designed to inform students about the program.

The local newspaper may not be so well read by the students as the school paper, but it is an excellent medium for transmitting program information to prospective students through their parents and friends.

A paid advertisement in the local newspaper is not always deemed appropriate, but it does offer a possibility of reminding eligible students that the time is at hand for them to enroll in the program. A similar purpose could be served by free announcements the editor may be willing to publish.

Radio and Television Appearances

Local radio and television stations normally will be receptive to spot announcements if they judge that enough listeners will be interested. Usually, they will welcome personal appearances by the teacher–coordinator and CE students, and the response should be good if the quality of the performance is high. The station managers normally would not expect to be paid for broadcasting a program such as suggested here, for they would regard it as a public service.

Bulletin-Board Announcements

An attractively designed bulletin board located in a convenient place offers a good medium for transmitting information to the students. A sample bulletin-board layout is shown in Figure 4.

Innovative thinking on the part of the teacher–coordinator should produce suitable messages to attract the desired attention. As part of the student recruitment, such messages could be in the form of want ads for student–workers in occupational areas where good training stations are available. Featuring the demand for a worker in a less common occupation, such as a lens grinder, for example, as opposed to an accountant should enhance student interest. Here again, the time and place the students can make their interest known should be clearly indicated.

Bulletin-board announcements and displays should be changed periodically, perhaps daily, in order to maintain student interest. Clever ideas will attract the attention of all students, and will help to generate curiosity and interest.

Figure 4 Sample Bulletin-Board Layout

COOPERATIVE EDUCATION

WANTED

(Insert want ads such as that pictured on page 71.)

4

If interested, do not delay.

See _____ 5 _____ at once.
        Teacher–Coordinator

1

2

3

6

7

8

CODE

1,2,3: classroom scenes
4: want ad
5: contact
6,7,8: students at work (pictures)

Letters to Potential Students and Parents

Often the best approach to potential students is through letters to those supposedly qualified for enrollment. A list of such students may include all juniors and seniors remaining after the roster has been purged by counselors and appropriate administrative officials. If feasible, the teacher–coordinator should diplomatically resist this purging, since it cannot be assumed that the criteria likely to be used in the purge would be based upon real insight into the character of students who are capable of profiting from CE. However, the teacher–coordinator should not pass up the opportunity to discuss the matter with the counselors and administrative officials, since a constructive relationship with them is vital to the success of the program.

Inasmuch as the parents of potential students will be involved in the student selection process, it is suggested that a letter be addressed to them as an initial step in student recruitment. This letter should ensure parental knowledge of the basic purposes of CE and of its values to the student, and it should point out to the parents the school time and credit the student must invest. Unless a joint letter to parents and potential students is deemed advisable, the letter to the parents should precede the letter to potential students.

The sample shown in Figure 5 should be helpful to the teacher–coordinator in designing letters to be used in initial efforts to interest qualified students.

The methods of contacting potential students that have been described above are the most obvious. The alert teacher–coordinator will find other ways to disseminate appropriate information concerning the time, place, and means of enrollment. Appropriate administrative officials should be kept informed of all plans employed to interest qualified students. Plans that involve any school organization for which other teachers are responsible should be prepared in writing and submitted for administrative approval before any action is taken.

Student Selection Plan

The most logical first step in the student selection plan is to make sure that qualified students know about CE and how they may secure enrollment information. Any one or all of the previously suggested avenues of student contact may be employed together with other methods that may stem from local circumstances or the ingenuity of

Figure 5   Sample Letter to Parents and/or Students

The _____ High School is offering cooperative ed-
ucation for the first time, beginning in September of the 19____–19____
school year.   The program is designed to provide vocational education
through real work experience on real jobs in the community, and related
technical instruction at school.   Through this program the entire community becomes a laboratory in which future citizens can be prepared for
jobs vital to its economic development.

Students interested are requested to apply for enrollment without delay
so that their credentials may be fully judged before the spring registration.

The purpose of this letter is to alert you to the characteristics of cooperative education. The following information should be helpful:

1. To be eligible for enrollment, the student must be a junior or a senior,
   at least 16, and have vocational intent, acceptable moral and physical
   characteristics, and suitable scholastic background.
2. If accepted for enrollment, the students are required to divide their
   time between school and work. The time on the job shall be equal to
   or in excess of the time in school and should not involve less than 15
   hours of school time per week.
3. A monetary wage is paid to the student comparable to that paid other
   beginning workers in the same occupation.
4. Students receive two high school credits per year for satisfactory participation in the program. They are required to schedule two additional high school courses to enable them to satisfy graduation requirements at the end of the usual four-year high school period.
5. Cooperative education is an integral part of the regular high school
   program and should not be confused with any form of youth, adult,
   or relief educational programs fostered by agencies outside the school.
6. Cooperative education features educational values to the student such
   as the following:
   a. Opportunity to acquire occupational competence as a part of the
      regular high school program.
   b. Meeting and solving problems of adjustment to the world of work
      while teachers and other elements of the school are available to
      help.
   c. Motivation that should carry over into other subjects.
   d. Opportunity for personal development leading to desirable level of
      maturity.
7. A student enrolling as a junior is required to invest one-fourth of the
   total high school schedule in the program. This investment is justified
   only by sincere career interest in the occupational area in which work
   experience is to be gained.
8. Students can arrange course work so as to be prepared for college
   entrance to pursue career interests on technical or professional levels.
   If they prefer not to attend college, sufficient preparation is available
   through cooperative education for desirable and permanent employment upon graduation from high school.
9. It is not feasible for the school to guarantee that every student who

(continued)

Figure 5 *(continued)*

desires to enroll will be accepted in the cooperative education program. But all qualified students who apply will be considered for enrollment to the extent that acceptable training stations are available, and the class quota will permit.

After carefully considering this letter, you are invited to present any questions you may have by calling me at _____ during office hours. If your questions cannot be resolved properly by a phone call, an appointment will be made for a conference at a mutually convenient time and place.

Let us work together to serve the best interests of our youth.

Very sincerely yours,

Signed _____
Teacher–Coordinator

the teacher–coordinator. Timing is important and should be considered carefully in relation to the school calendar. The student contact program should culminate prior to spring registration for the obvious reason that students who are accepted for enrollment should be able to design their class schedule accordingly.

Mass Meeting

After all students have been alerted to the time, place, and means of enrollment, the teacher–coordinator may call a mass meeting of interested students for the purpose of explaining the basic elements of CE and the responsibilities of its enrollees. The date for this meeting should be well in advance of spring registration, and should be approved by the administration.

Examine Applications and Personal Data Sheets

A study of applications and personal data sheets should indicate those students who are best qualified for enrollment in CE, and by the same token the weaker applicants should be fairly obvious. (See sample student application form in Figure 6, pages 60–61.) The applicants may well be divided into two groups, the first composed of apparently qualified students, the second of doubtfully qualified. Errors in this initial classification will naturally be corrected later when and if additional and more favorable information surfaces. The better group should proceed to the succeeding steps in the enrollment process.

Study School Records

The cumulative records for each student under consideration should be examined carefully. The fact that this record is a résumé of important facts in the entire school life of the individual makes it an illuminating document. It should make clear the strong and the weak subject-matter areas, and it should authenticate or discredit the student's statement of vocational intent. For example, if a student should indicate a vocational interest in an occupational area that requires competence in science and mathematics, school records should show reasonable achievement in these areas. If a discrepancy should appear, the student may need help in identifying the occupational areas that are compatible with personal qualities.

Insight into character traits may be gained from the student's attendance record. Excessive absences or tardinesses may be indicative of personal characteristics about which the teacher–coordinator should be concerned.

Another possibility is that the student may have found little interest in the school program, with the result that there was no incentive or ambition to achieve a good school record. Such students may be most receptive to the opportunity offered by CE. They have much to gain, and they can be expected to respond promptly in newly acquired respect for themselves with desire to develop the personal characteristics and abilities that they find prerequisite to success in the world of work.

If it is found that student applicants have been disciplinary problems, they should not necessarily be rejected, but a thorough effort should be made to identify the underlying reasons for failure to abide by school regulations. Although there are many causes of undesirable conduct, lack of interest and challenge in the school program are prominent reasons.

Here, again, the whole attitude toward life might be changed by proper placement in an occupation that presents success requirements that basically coincide with the individual's aptitudes, vocational interest, and personal characteristics. It may be that the absentee and the problem student are both rejecting the same set of circumstances in different ways, and that CE offers a solution for both of them.

Although the teacher–coordinator should not allow rehabilitation cases to dominate the CE enrollment, great satisfaction will stem from the successful launching of such individuals into the world of work. In many instances CE could be the last chance for these students because of their failure to profit from the conventional educational program.

Figure 6   Sample Student Application for Enrollment in Cooperative Education

Date _____

Name _____   Grade _____

Address _____   Telephone _____

Sex _____   Age _____   Date of birth _____   Weight _____   Height _____

Parents' names _____

Do you live with both parents at the above address? _____

Church preference _____

What do you plan to do after graduation from high school? _____

_____

_____

_____

Do you plan to go to college? _____   If so, where? _____

What course do you plan to major in at this college? _____

Briefly state your principal reasons for seeking admission to cooperative

education. _____

_____

_____

_____

Give your first and second choices of occupations in which you desire to

receive training.

(1) _____

(2) _____

Upon what do you base your occupational choices? (Explain.) _____

_____

Previous work experiences:

Employed by	Types of work	Dates worked
_____	_____	_____
_____	_____	_____
_____	_____	_____

Figure 6 *(continued)*

Can you type? _____ Words per minute? _____ Can you take dictation? _____ Words per minute? _____ Have you had bookkeeping? _____ Industrial arts? _____ Home economics? _____ Vocational agriculture? _____ Other vocational courses? _____

_____

Is your father living? _____ Place of employment? _____

Occupation? _____

Is your mother living? _____ Place of employment? _____

Occupation? _____

Subjects and grades earned:

	9th grade	10th grade	11th grade
1. English			
2. Mathematics			
3. Social studies			
4.			
5.			
6.			
7.			
8.			

If this application is accepted and I am placed in a training agency, I pledge myself to be alert at all times, both on the job and in the classroom, to opportunities which will enhance the development of my skill and knowledge. I will also abide by all regulations which the school sees fit to impose on program participants.

Signed _____
Applicant

Signed _____
Parent or Guardian

If anecdotes are a part of the cumulative record, they may reveal character traits useful in judging desirability for enrollment. Anecdotes may reveal the presence or absence of characteristics such as sociability, integrity, cooperativeness, dependability, and courtesy.

Teacher References

Although the teacher–coordinator should make every effort to enlist the help of the other teachers in recruiting students, it should be understood that they will recommend students according to their own understanding or misunderstanding of the purposes and values of CE. Suppose, for example, that a teacher conceives of the program as primarily an opportunity for the student to earn money, or as a class for those who will not or cannot do acceptable work in other parts of the educational program. This teacher will recommend only those students who need financial assistance, or those who have failed to do satisfactory work for whatever reason. The new teacher–coordinator is in trouble if such attitudes prevail among the faculty, and therefore it is clear that the first step in beginning a program should be to give the faculty a clear-cut understanding of its real purposes and values.

The teacher–coordinator should design a questionnaire to submit to teachers under whom students have had at least two courses in high school. There should be no difficulty in identifying these teachers when the cumulative record is examined, and the questionnaire should simply request a recommendation relative to the student's readiness for the responsibilities to be assumed if enrolled in CE.

Examine and Validate Vocational Purpose

One of the legal requirements for enrollment in all vocational programs is that the vocational intent of students be a matter of record. As suggested earlier, student statements of this nature are frequently recorded without serious consideration. It becomes necessary, therefore, that the teacher–coordinator make every effort to check basic aptitudes, vocational interests, and personal characteristics.

A general intelligence test and a vocational interest inventory would provide minimal information. An ideal arrangement would be full cooperation of the school counselor in selecting, administering, scoring, and interpreting a battery of standardized tests, including multifactor scholastic aptitude test, general development or achievement test, interest inventory, and one or more general aptitude tests.

62

The results of testing and other efforts to examine the basic psychological characteristics of students should strongly support the authenticity of the stated vocational purposes of applicants, or reveal the lack of authenticity.

List Qualified Applicants

Each step in the student selection plan will serve to eliminate some students and to bolster the application of others until a final list of those qualified for tentative enrollment is evolved. Full enrollment cannot be accomplished until job placement has been arranged.

Personal Interviews

When the list of qualified applicants is completed, each one should be scheduled for an interview even though the teacher–coordinator may have talked with them several times.

One or both parents should be present at this interview, and they should be encouraged to raise questions to help them to understand their responsibilities in the program. It should be made clear that the program is a cooperative arrangement between the school and local employers, and that all complaints should be made to, and adjusted by, the teacher–coordinator as an agent of the school. The effect of being in the program as it relates to qualifying for college entrance should be explained.

Parents and students should be made aware of the fact that entering the program as a junior will require one-fourth of the high school educational opportunity. Only a sincere vocational purpose on the part of the student will justify a decision to make this sacrifice, and a misstep here could make enrollment in CE an expensive educational interlude with damaging effect on the student's future.

Typical Problems in Determining Enrollment

Problem 1 Overcoming pressure to accept students for enrollment without due process

"Due process" is defined as being a course of procedure carried out regularly in accordance with established rules and principles. The course of procedure should be the student selection plan described in this chapter.

The application of this plan to a large number of applicants would present many problems, including a great deal of time at a critical period of the school year. Pressure may come from students, faculty, and administrators faced with unalterable deadlines established in the school calendar. In fact, to an inexperienced teacher–coordinator, it may seem, under the circumstances, to be impossible to hold to the student selection plan.

The coordinator may find it much easier simply to accept the students who apply and attempt to find jobs for them or allow them to find their own jobs. To hold to the student selection plan requires dedication and strength of purpose.

To complicate the situation further, other and perhaps more glamorous phases of the program will be competing for the teacher–coordinator's time. These demands will test strength of purpose and measure ability to organize and apply time in the manner necessary to honor essential priorities in all phases of the program.

Problem 2 *Keeping the selection process "student-centered"*

Keeping the student selection process "student-centered" is a paramount responsibility of the teacher–coordinator. Difficulty in this matter may stem from a number of sources. The most potent of these may be the student applicants, for they cannot always be depended on to arrange the wisest course for themselves. Their tendency may be to allow obvious and immediate values to take precedence over less tangible and somewhat remote educational values.

Suppose, for example, that a student wants a motor bike to ride with friends during leisure time. Since the parents cannot afford to buy the bike, ways of earning the money are sought. CE seems to be an ideal way to get a job without undue interference with the high school education program. Unwary parents may agree to this plan without considering the cost in terms of educational opportunity. Under such circumstances, the student is likely to scorn serious consideration of vocational purpose.

Some students place a high value on "getting out of school" for half the school day; others may think of CE as a way to relieve fear of failure; and still others may regard it as an opportunity "to be with a friend." The tendency of students to value these and other fringe benefits to the exclusion of educational values frequently renders them incapable of making judgments to their own best interests. It becomes necessary, therefore, for the teacher–coordinator to make every effort to limit enrollment to those students who are motivated by genuine vocational purposes.

Keeping the student selection plan student-centered, therefore, simply means that the best interests of the student must be the ruling factor. Here again the teacher–coordinator may stand alone in the face of misunderstanding on the part of publics vital to the program. If this stand is based firmly on the best interests of the students, the administration will scarcely take a stand against the teacher, for all education should be based on this concern.

Applying the student selection plan should cease to be a problem as CE becomes established in the school. Ill-advised precedents in the beginning, however, are extremely difficult to overcome. Firmness of purpose as an initial characteristic, therefore, is necessary.

Problem 3 *Getting enough qualified students to meet administratively established quotas*

In some states an enrollment of thirty students per teacher–coordinator has been determined to be optimal. Meeting the needs of a student group of this size, coupled with other responsibilities, will tax the ability of capable individuals. If the student load increases beyond this number, the efficiency of the teaching can be expected to decrease proportionately.

Since an enrollment of thirty students is a teaching load comparable with that of regular teachers, the teacher–coordinator should be prepared to present this justification in support of what may appear to be scant enrollment.

Difficulty in enrolling a sufficient number of qualified students may stem from a number of causes. One of these may be a lack of student interest resulting from failure to get information concerning the program to eligible students prior to enrollment time. Student indifference may also result from rumors that the program is designed for a specific group.

Another contributing factor could be the tendency of referring students for enrollment on the basis of criteria that do not coincide with the actual enrollment requirements.

A possibility that might reduce the number of students who could be accepted could be a lack of balance in the occupational interests of those applying for enrollment. If too many students are interested in too few occupations, a sufficient number of training agencies may not be available in the community.

Any one or a combination of these possibilities together with others of local significance may bring the teacher–coordinator face to face with the enrollment deadline before the quota is reached. The teacher–coordinator then has the alternative of inducing students to enroll without serious regard for proper standards, or entering the school year with a low enrollment subject to criticism by the faculty and the administration.

Problem 4 *Preventing CE from becoming earmarked for a special student group*

The supposition that CE is for a special group may be forestalled if the teacher–coordinator can inform the publics concerned before misconceptions begin to arise. Suppose, for example, that the coordinator had failed to communicate with these publics before they heard rumors that CE is intended for students coming from poor families that need financial assistance.

Naturally, if this rumor gains credence, only students who are from impoverished families would apply for enrollment. Furthermore, teachers and advisers would not recommend that students from prosperous families should apply.

Or the program might gain the undeserved reputation of being a haven for failures, or for those who are at cross-purposes with the regular program of the school. Such misconceptions would obviously restrict enrollment.

These dangers highlight the vulnerability of CE and the necessity that it be nurtured carefully throughout the developmental period in any school system. Once the program reaches maturity, however, it should have developed enough momentum, dignity, and strength of character to command respect.

Problem 5 *Dealing with superficial vocational purpose on the part of students applying for enrollment*

The fact that most students possess general aptitudes that qualify them to function satisfactorily in a rather broad occupational spectrum complicates judgment on the authenticity of stated vocational purpose. Misrepresentation of vocational interest may result from ignorance rather than from deliberate intent to deceive. On the other hand, desire to gain an opportunity to earn money, or to get away from school for half of the school day, may tempt the student to invent a false vocational purpose to satisfy the enrollment requirements.

Since it is the teacher–coordinator's responsibility to limit enrollment to students whose best interests will be served thereby, procedures must be established that will ensure the rejection of superficial purposes as justification for enrollment.

Problem 6 *Rejecting the enrollment of students with conflicts in interest*

Participants in major sports will often see in CE an opportunity for relief from the academic pressure of the school. The requirement that certain academic standards be maintained coupled with misunderstanding or disrespect for the standards and purposes of the program frequently provides ample motivation for seeking enrollment. Furthermore, keeping star athletes eligible may be a concern of all the publics involved with CE. Hence it follows that the teacher–coordinator may again stand alone in opposition to those who control the environment in which the program must function.

Suppose, for example, that one or more members of the football squad apply for enrollment. Special accommodations are requested at once: the football player would prefer not to begin on-the-job experience until the season is over, then make up for lost time. Or, to be free for the afternoon practice during the season, it is suggested that work time be arranged in the morning, say from 7 to 10 A.M. Aid in placing such students may be offered as an extra incentive.

Avid sport fans as employers may welcome the opportunity to subsidize star athletes through providing part-time jobs without too much concern for the time actually spent on the job. Similar circumstances may apply to other major student activities.

Here again the teacher–coordinator's strength of purpose and administrative support will be the determining factor in dealing with these problems. The fact that proposed enrollments of this kind are based on false premises should be sufficient justification for their rejection. It should be explained to students and to other concerned individuals, however, that rejection is necessary because major activities such as football require almost all the student's interest and capability.

CE is also a major interest demanding much interest and time. Furthermore, participation in football or any other major sport is in conflict with CE because work time and practice time both usually require afternoon hours, and past attempts to remove this conflict by scheduling the work time in the forenoon have not proved satisfactory. The arrangement is particularly unsatisfactory if placements are made with employers who are primarily interested in football as opposed to vocational education.

Consequently, student applicants who have another major interest should be required to make a choice: They should choose CE *or* a major activity or sport: They should not have both.

The establishment of appropriate administrative policy in the initial phases of program development would facilitate the solution of many problems such as those suggested above. Such a policy would back up the teacher–coordinator in placing proper restrictions on enrollment with ample provision for dealing with exceptions to the rules.

Most teacher–coordinators have to experience the futility of the circumstances that normally develop as a result of accepting enrollees with conflicts of interest such as those described above before they are willing to exercise the necessary precautions and rejection techniques. It is not suggested that athletes are not qualified for enrollment in CE, but rather that the two programs are completely incompatible. As a general rule, enrollment in both programs will not serve the best interests of the student, and will detract from the integrity of CE.

Suggested Activities

1. Compose a CE enrollment policy designed to admit only those students who want, need, and are qualified to profit from the instruction; for presentation to school officials for approval as an initial step in the establishment of a CE program.
2. Prepare a talk suitable for a high school assembly, depicting the values of CE to qualified students.
3. Prepare a series of spot announcements for radio and/or television, describing appropriate aspects of the enrollment process.
4. Using the sample bulletin-board layout on page 55 as a point of departure, design a layout incorporating personal ideas and characteristics stemming from anticipated local circumstances.
5. Prepare an agenda suitable for an initial mass meeting of all students interested in enrolling in CE. (See page 58.)
6. Devise a plan for validating the vocational intent of students applying for enrollment in CE. (See page 62.)

chapter five

Placement of Students on Jobs for Training Purposes

The following commentary on Placement of Students on Jobs for Educational Purposes presupposes that training stations and students have been tentatively selected according to the processes described in Chapters Three and Four. If the recommended procedures have been followed, the placement process becomes a matter of matching the aptitudes and vocational interests of individual students with occupational characteristics and requirements represented by available and qualified training stations. Students should not have been even tentatively enrolled in occupational areas not represented by qualified training stations in the geographical service area of the school.

The process of placing students on jobs is the final and perhaps the most vital step in the student-enrollment process. It is futile to attempt to accomplish program purposes if students are not placed in job situations which present characteristics and requirements compatible with their basic aptitudes, vocational interests, and personal qualities.

In effect, the teacher–coordinator serves as a community personnel director with the responsibility of identifying qualified students, matching their aptitudes, vocational interests, and personal qualities with the requirements of jobs that are vital to the community's economic stability and development.

The student-selection process consists of the identification of juniors and seniors who want, need, and are qualified to profit from the instruction and work experiences provided through CE. The placement process involves the matching of aptitudes, vocational interests, and personal qualities of students with job success requirements.

Failure to place students in appropriate jobs will defeat the entire program even though all other vital requirements may have been satisfied. Very little vocational value will accrue to the students if the work experience is in occupational areas in which there is no vocational interest. This situation would negate the value of directly related instruction and create a set of invalid circumstances, since the students would lack motivation. Thus educational opportunity would be traded off for work experience of little or no educational value.

Students who reach agreements with employers to work in jobs that meet their vocational needs in accordance with the teacher–coordinator's judgment are fully enrolled. Those who cannot be suitably placed should be returned promptly to the regular program.

The Placement Procedure

Matching Aptitudes and Vocational Interests with Job Requirements

It is vastly important that the teacher–coordinator be familiar with requirements of the occupational areas represented by available training stations. Such familiarity should be of sufficient caliber and extent to make it possible to determine the degree of compatibility between the occupational characteristics and requirements of the job, on the one hand, and the student's aptitudes, vocational interests, and personal characteristics, on the other.

When the teacher–coordinator is not sufficiently familiar with the characteristics and requirements of given occupations, employers should be requested to provide job descriptions according to a standard format. In the final analysis, a determination should be made that available training stations either do or do not meet the requirements of students being considered for enrollment. When this decision is reached, the actual placement process can get under way.

Examining the Community for Specific Training Opportunities

The teacher–coordinator can expect to find students with vocational interests not represented on the list of approved training stations. When this occurs the community should be reexamined to determine whether training opportunity is available in the occupational areas in question. If suitable training agencies are not available, students should not be accepted for enrollment in these occupations, for their best interests will be served by remaining in the regular academic program. Under no circumstances should students be encouraged to change their vocational objectives simply because training opportunity is not available. On the contrary, they should be encouraged to cultivate their interests until opportunity for training does develop, even though it may have to be delayed until the post-high school period.

In the process of reassessing the community in search of occupational opportunities to satisfy special student interests, the teacher–coodinator should be alert to new opportunities for training in occupational areas not previously requested.

If an occupation discovered in this manner can satisfy the criteria included in the occupational evaluative instrument in Chapter Two (Figure 2), it should be presented to the advisory committee for approval. Such occupations, if represented by acceptable training stations, may become the subject of special student recruiting efforts in the form of "want ads" in bulletin-board displays and other available media, such as the school paper, the local newspaper, and the radio and television stations.

Suppose, for example, that a local teacher–coordinator finds that opportunity for training is available in less common occupational areas such as lens grinder, dental laboratory technician, X-ray technician, and so on. There are students who would be interested in these occupations if they knew about them. It therefore becomes a responsibility of the teacher–coordinator to reach the student body with information concerning opportunities in such occupational areas. An ad similar to the following sample could appear on a bulletin board located near the office of the teacher–coordinator or in any other appropriate location:

Wanted: A beginning lens grinder. Good pay while
learning. This is an occupational area that
offers excellent CAREER OPPORTUNITY
for the right person. If interested, do not
delay: see _____ at once.
                    Teacher-Coordinator

With some variation this ad could be put in a local newspaper; however, it should be fully identified with the school and the CE program.

It is not recommended that the teacher–coordinator devote a great deal of time to recruiting efforts of this kind. It may be found, however, that such efforts will frequently result in bringing together qualified and deserving students and career opportunities which would not otherwise occur. Such students respond to the new horizons encountered through contact with legitimate phases of the world of work. They are pleased to find an occupational environment responsive and receptive to their aptitudes, vocational interests, and personal qualities.

All CE students should be inspired and motivated by the discovery that they possess what it takes to be successful in occupations that present desirable career opportunities. Discoveries of this kind serve to relieve youth of unexpressed anxiety often resulting from uncertainty about ability to enter successfully and to make progress in the world of work. Being relieved of such anxieties will often remove the roadblocks that have been a problem to students and will promote rapid strides in the maturing process. Replacing doubt with assurance tends to make the student confident, ambitious, mature, and motivated. Having the opportunity of working with students of this kind constitutes the greatest satisfaction and reward for the teacher.

Preparation of Students for the Job Interview

Actually meeting an employer and applying for a job will be an important experience for students. In preparation for this phase of the job placement process, the teacher–coordinator should assume that it is a new experience and that students are not well versed in acceptable protocol and procedures. This assumption justifies a carefully planned program to prepare students for their first job interview.

Although it may be necessary to talk individually to some students concerning personal problems, as a general rule good results can be expected from group activities. It may be advisable, however, to meet with boys and girls separately in order to provide opportunity to deal more forcefully with those facets of the problem that refer specifically to one sex and not to the other. A male teacher–coordinator may find it desirable to call on a female member of the faculty for help in dealing with the problems peculiar to the girls. By the same token, a female teacher–coordinator may call on a male member of the faculty to help her deal with certain problems of the boys. In either event, the teacher–coordinator should prescribe the information to be presented and the points to be emphasized.

72

The agenda for preinterview conferences should include the following points for emphasis:

1. Cleanliness of clothes and body.
2. Good grooming.
3. Apparel in good taste for work environment.
4. Shoes clean, polished, and in good repair.
5. The hair of both boys and girls clean and neatly groomed in accordance with current and acceptable styles appropriate for *work* environments.

Regardless of how teacher–coordinators elect to counsel students concerning these matters, they should establish a checkpoint in the placement process to be sure that students have followed instructions. The most obvious checkpoint would be to have the students come by the office on the way to their job interviews. Students found to be improperly dressed or groomed should be instructed to correct the deficiencies before proceeding to the interview.

The employer should be advised of the delay and asked to set a new time for the appointment. Students found to be ready for the interview should be sent directly from the teacher–coordinator's office to talk with the employer.

The fact that students are usually inexperienced suggests that they be instructed in regard to proper conduct during their first interview. The placement process, therefore, should include a preparation period.

The teacher–coordinator will find dramatization to be a most effective method. Role playing by students will help them to grasp the importance of presenting and conducting themselves properly in their first interview.

Preparation of the Employer for the Interview

The placement process should be an authentic experience. For this reason the employer should be cautioned to treat the student as he would any other potential employee who is applying for a job.

The employer should be requested not to accept or reject the student during the interview, but rather to withhold judgment until all students have been interviewed. Final judgment should be made jointly with the teacher–coordinator.

The employer should be informed that the interview will be the first opportunity to cooperate with the school in providing a realistic experience for the student. Success will be reflected by conviction on the part of students that they have actually been employed as a result of having successfully presented their own merits for the position. The preparation of the employer should terminate with making of a definite appointment for the student interview and with the request that the teacher–coordinator be notified as soon as possible after the interview.

Advising Student of Appointment for the Interview

The student should be advised of the appointment at once with the request to appear at the teacher–coordinator's office on the way to the interview. This contact with the student can be very brief, on the assumption that all students have been instructed thoroughly in regard to appropriate dress and grooming as well as conduct during the interview. At this office stop it should be necessary only to remind the students of the importance of appropriate presentation and to determine whether they are presentable.

All students should be instructed to contact the teacher–coordinator as soon as possible after the interview so that the results may be reviewed. It would be desirable for the teacher–coordinator to be aware of the student's reaction to the interview and the degree of his interest in being employed as a student at the training agency in question. It is quite possible also that the teacher–coordinator could satisfy questions in the student's mind that were not answered during the interview.

Multiple Interviews

If the employer would like to interview additional students before reaching a decision, or if for some reason the student is reluctant to continue the employment process, the teacher–coordinator should be prepared to send additional students for interviews. As a matter of fact, some teacher–coordinators have a policy of sending more than one student to be interviewed by each employer, with the number being determined by the number of applicants having the same occupational interest. For example, there may be four acceptable training agencies in dietetics, and five students with vocational interest in this occupation.

It may be good policy to arrange for all five to interview all four employers. An arrangement of this kind would make it possible for the employer actually to select the student, and to convey the impression that the student has successfully competed with others in being selected for the job. This policy tends to complicate the placement process, and consequently the teacher–coordinator may prefer to judge each case on its merits, and send more than one student in some instances, but not in others.

Good judgment based on knowledge of the employer and the student will obviate circumstances that might otherwise become problems. The employer should come to understand that any student recommended has been selected by the school as having aptitudes and vocational interests that compare favorably with the requirements of the job in question. One of the values of CE to employers, therefore, is that they can depend on the school to recommend only those students who are worthy of the investment they are required to make. The employer's judgment in the selection of the student should be based primarily on personal qualities as they relate to those of desirable and permanent employees.

Final Determination of Student Enrollment

After all interviewing has been completed and the teacher–coordinator has conferred with employers and students, their choices must be reconciled. This adjustment is a matter of judgment that must be exercised by the teacher–coordinator with the best interest of the student being the prime factor. This authority continues to implement the principle that the school must, in the final analysis, control the placement in order to ensure the placing of the right student in the right job.

The memorandum of training plan, which appears as Figure 7, should be a part of the placement process. Procrastination in executing this plan stands a good chance of creating problems that will defy satisfactory solution after the student has worked for a time beyond the deadline for the changing of schedules. The net result could be the entrapment of the students in situations they cannot escape, and a problem for the teacher–coordinator which cannot be resolved readily.

One of the basic requirements of federally reimbursed CE is that the students be "legally employed." The memorandum of training plan satisfies this requirement, although it is not considered to be a legal document. Using the community as a laboratory is based on individual agreements between the school and each cooperating employer. Only the signatures of the employer and agents of the school should be affixed to the agreement.

Figure 7   Sample Memorandum of Training Plan

(One copy due in State Office not later than end of first school month after school opens.)

This memorandum is for the purpose of outlining the agreement between the school and the employer relative to the conditions under which the student can be placed on the job. It, therefore, should not be interpreted by either agency as a legal document or any form of binding contract.

The _____ will permit _____
        Training Agency   Student

Sex: Male _____ Female _____ Age _____ Grade _____ to enter their

establishment for the purpose of gaining knowledge and experience as

_____   _____
       Occupation   OE Code No.

(It is understood that the occupation in which training is herewith being offered is one in which provisions of the wage and hour law *is* or *is not* applicable.)

1. This course of training is designed to run for _____ school year(s) with a minimum of FIFTEEN hours per school week required for the work experience and at least _____ period(s) in each school day required for related subjects.

2. A skeleton outline of the processes to be learned on the job and of related subjects to be taught in the school is presented on the back of this form and constitutes the major portion of the training program of this student.

3. While in the process of gaining occupational experience, the student will not be permitted to remain in any one operation, job, or phase of the occupation beyond the period of time that is necessary to become proficient.

4. The student while in the process of training will have the status of a noncompetitive worker neither displacing a regular worker now employed nor substituting for a worker needed by the training agency.

5. The compensation for this student shall be $ _____ per _____ .

6. All transfers, withdrawals, or dismissals shall be made jointly by the teacher coordinator and the employer.

_____   _____
         School   Employer

_____   By: _____
    Teacher–Coordinator

_____   Date: _____
School Superintendent or Principal

Distribution: One copy each to the employer, school superintendent or principal, teacher–coordinator, and state supervisor.

Figure 7 *(continued)*

This section should be filled in by the teacher–coordinator in conference with the employer of the student.

Outline of Job Processes	Outline of Related Subjects

Name of Student

I certify that satisfactory completion of the above program of training will justify granting _____ unit(s) of credit by this high school.

_____
Superintendent or Principal

Execution of the Memorandum of Training Plan

As final placement decisions are approached, the teacher–coordinator should seek a conference with the employer to complete the placement process, which, without exception, should include the explanation and execution of the memorandum of training plan. See Figure 7 for a memorandum of training plan currently being used in one of the states in which CE had its beginning.

Completion of the Placement Process

After full explanation and execution of the memorandum of training plan, the student should be advised of the effective date of employment and the hours of work each day and week. The student should also be given instructions relative to initial work experience, including the on-the-job instructor's name.

Official notice should be given to all concerned, including appropriate school officials, that the student in question is placed with a given firm and will be leaving school at a given time each day. A simple form should be designed upon which to transmit this message. The student's schedule should be finalized and approved by appropriate officials. After the memorandum of training plan is executed, copies should be distributed to the principal, the employer, and the State Department of Vocational Education, with a copy being retained for the files of the teacher–coordinator.

The new teacher–coordinator will probably be forced to complete the total process of the selection and the placement of students between July 1 and the deadline for the changing of schedules. Student selection and placement become a different problem after the initial employment period. As a matter of fact, the selection of students for succeeding years can be completed for the most part in preceding spring semesters.

Summer Placement

Summer placement should be considered a trial period for the student as well as for the employer. Problems arising during the summer will be indicators of incompatibilities that may militate against successful placement during the regular school year. On the other hand, successful relationships and work experience for the summer will strongly indicate that placement during the regular school year will be successful. The student who experiences an unsuccessful summer may be returned to the regular program without loss of time or credit.

Summer placement is recommended, but each case should be considered on its own merits. When it is found to be feasible, it should prove the best possible safeguard against placement errors.

The teacher–coordinator's summer-work schedule should allow time for sufficient attention to new students placed for summer tryout–work experience as a preliminary to placement as CE students. Contacts with students and their employers during this period will facilitate judgment relative to final enrollment in the following fall term. But if the teacher–coordinator's summer schedule does not allow time for minimum supervision, it would be wise to eliminate summer placements until supervision can be arranged.

Retarding Factors in Executing the Memorandum of Training Plan

The execution of the memorandum of training plan should be an integral part of the placement of students for training purposes. Earlier reference was made to the penalties of procrastination or failure to consider the memorandum of training plan as a necessary part of the placement process. A number of factors tend to compound the difficult nature of this task, any one of which may produce circumstances that would seem to necessitate postponement in order that other phases of the placement process might proceed without delay. Ironically no one is likely to object to such a postponement, and the first indication of delinquency probably would be notice of the due date for the fully executed instrument in a central office to which the school is required to report.

Several of the retarding factors mentioned above could be classified under the heading *time*. Perhaps the first of these would have to do with the time required to produce a sample schedule of processes for use as a guide in working with the employer in determining the scope of the work experience available to the student. If such a schedule is not available, a considerable research effort may be necessary to produce the occupational analysis from which the schedule of processes can be developed.

The complexity of the situation will depend upon the span of time over which conferences with employers can be spread. If the placement must be completed within two weeks after the opening of school, it would be extremely difficult to devote the necessary time to the placement process even if the employers' time could be made available. On the other hand, spreading the placement process over the period between May 1 and September 15 would provide ample time to complete the execution of the memorandum of training plan with a desirable degree of deliberateness. The maximum time available to the new teacher–coordinator probably would be between July 1 and September 15. This estimate is made on the assumption that the new teacher–coordinator's contract would be effective July 1.

The fact that employers are busy complicates the possibility of getting them to spend the time necessary to carry out the placement process properly. This pressure is especially evident during efforts to work with some of them at their places of business. The demand for their attention is often so insistent or they are so thoroughly pre-occupied that gaining and holding their attention is extremely difficult. After episodes of this kind, the employers may remain devoid of understanding of the educational nature of the program. Accordingly, employers may substitute preconceived notions of the part they are expected to play.

More will be accomplished and better attention will be given the problem by some employers away from their places of business. Other employers will be well enough organized to detach themselves from the demand of the moment to apply themselves to the matter of complet-ing the placement process. In any event, the success of the teacher–coordinator will depend to a great degree upon his ingenuity in setting up appropriate circumstances to structure and facilitate final placement conferences with all types of employers. If such conferences are suc-cessful, employers can be expected to regulate the work-experience phase of the program with paramount emphasis on the educational values to the student.

Typical Problems Involved in Student Placement

Problem 1 *Establishing safeguards to make sure that the right student is placed on the right job*

Human fallibility guarantees mistakes in the placement process. Naturally, the teacher–coordinator should exert every effort to keep such errors to a minimum and to correct those that are made as soon as possible. Although some errors are inevitable, failure to correct them is inexcusable. The employer and the student should not be left to suffer from an incompatible arrangement beyond a reasonable time.

A definite step-by-step procedure in placing students and the application of this procedure without exception will be extremely helpful in guarding against mistakes and in ensuring that no essential phase of the process is eliminated. This practice fortifies the teacher–coordinator's resistance to requests for exceptions.

The guidance procedures suggested earlier should provide an objective profile of individual students in terms of aptitudes and vocational interests. The teacher–coordinator should develop occupational descriptions in terms of success requirements. Equating these criteria from the standpoint of compatibility should be a relatively simple matter if they are properly recorded. The ingenuity of the teacher–coordinator in designing instruments for use in this process will be a success factor in the placement of students for educational purposes.

As suggested above, the placement process will be strengthened by the participation of guidance counselors. Such participation should provide a desirable degree of authenticity by virtue of the application of expertise in administering, scoring, and interpreting psychological tests given to potential CE students in an effort to identify basic aptitudes and vocational interests. This testing should bolster the confidence of the teacher–coordinator in dealing with employers relative to the qualifications of students being recommended for the type of work experience they have to offer.

The teacher–coordinator should be able to assure employers that the students being recommended have been skillfully selected in accordance with the compatibility of their aptitudes and vocational interest patterns with success requirements of the occupation in which work experience is available. Under such circumstances, student failures should result principally from personal characteristics found to be unacceptable rather than from incompatibility with occupational requirements.

In the final analysis, the student placement plan should be designed to include consideration of all germane factors, but should require that final judgment be exercised by the teacher–coordinator. This reservation is necessary to assure the placement of the right student on the right job, and to guarantee that the best interest of the student is served at the expense of all other factors in the placement process.

Problem 2 *Dealing with pressure from parents to place a son or daughter in the family business without regard for the personal qualifications of the student for the job*

On the surface, placements such as those suggested in this problem may seem to be desirable by casual observers and others who are not

81

properly informed about the program purposes and values. As explained earlier, however, such placements lack real work characteristics in employer–employee relationships and in the job responsibility which the student is normally required to assume. Besides, the student who really plans to become involved in a family business on a career basis is probably the exception rather than the rule. This fact strongly indicates that placements of this type stand a good chance of being ends within themselves rather than means to justifiable ends.

In all probability the best interest of the qualified student who requests placement in the family business and who has career interest in the occupation in question would be better served by placement in a comparable job over which the parents have no jurisdiction. The frequency of requests for the placement of students with parents as employers is evidence of the seriousness of this problem. As a matter of fact, it constitutes one of the most difficult situations with which the teacher–coordinator has to deal. For these reasons it is suggested that a very definite policy be established to prohibit the placement of students with parents as employers. To be successful, such a policy must be fully supported by appropriate administrative elements of the school and applied without compromise by the teacher–coordinator.

Problem 3   The tendency to accept placements based on agreements negotiated by employers and students

It would be much easier and less complicated to let nature take its course by letting students and employers come to agreement without interference from the school. But the teacher–coordinator who allows the program to degenerate to this point has abdictated the responsibility of guaranteeing that the best interest of the student will be protected at the expense of all other factors involved in the placement process. The teacher–coordinator who has difficulty in organizing time and effort is most vulnerable to this danger. There may seem to be no alternative because of deadlines, administratively established quotas, and demand for attention to other vital aspects of the program.

Succumbing to the temptation suggested above would have a devasting effect. As a matter of fact, complete capitulation would defranchise the program and make it unworthy of being called CE. There would be little probability that the school could exercise the kind of "job control" that is necessary to ensure the educational character of the work experience. Employers would tend to abide by their original arrangement with the student, and would resist any interference by the school. They would be entitled to expect students to discharge the responsibility for which they were employed without paramount regard for educational values. The net results of relationships of this kind would probably range from inadequate cooperation to complete separation of work experience from the influence of the school. The latter circumstances would place the school in an untenable position relative to its responsibility in protecting the best interest of the student.

It must be admitted that the solution to problems that could result from failure to foster basic principles in the student-placement process are likely to be extremely difficult. As a matter of fact, there seems to be only one way out, and that would be through the establishment of an authentic step-by-step procedure and its application without exception.

Problem 4 *The tendency to place students in school jobs*

Jobs within the school can be categorically eliminated as training agencies because they do not generally provide work environments realistically representative of the world of work. The fact that the employer will probably be an administrator or a faculty member perpetuates the teacher–student relationship as opposed to the essential employer–employee relationship inherent in job placements outside the school. The fact that students may perform essential services which the school cannot otherwise afford does not satisfy the principle that the best interest of the student must supersede all other values involved.

There is nothing wrong with students' performing services to the school through part-time jobs, but the resulting work experience does not meet the requirements of CE and does not merit the use of school time and the awarding of school credits. The addition of the CE program to the curriculum should not change the traditional method of handling typical student jobs always present. Many useful services are normally rendered to the school through part-time jobs such as secretaries, library assistants, and laboratory assistants.

The teacher–coordinator may find himself pitted against other elements of the school in discharging this responsibility of finally determining where students will be placed. The difficulty of such a position suggests that a definite school policy should be established either to eliminate the placement of students in school jobs, or to establish criteria to be used in considering each job opportunity on its merits.

There are circumstances in which it would be administratively wise for teacher–coordinators to be given the responsibility of handling all part-time school work. Such an arrangement should eliminate the possibility of competition or conflict between CE and any other part-time work experience program fostered by the school. The teacher–coordinator would continue to exercise the responsibility of finally determining who is qualified for placement and where placement will be made. Within this policy, students found not to be qualified for placement through CE could be placed through other part-time work plans that might be part of the school program. The policy regulating placement in such programs should stipulate that school credit will not be awarded, and should point out the conditions under which school time might be used for work.

Problem 5 *Reluctance of employers to sign the memorandum of training plan*

Employers who are attentative to the meaning of the memorandum of training plan may take exception to one or more of its items. For example, an employer may see the statement "All transfers, withdrawals, or dismissals shall be made jointly by the teacher–coordinator and the employer," as a threat to control of the business. If such a circumstance should develop, the coordinator must proceed very carefully in order to perserve the possibility of placing a student in an otherwise acceptable training agency.

The concept that the memorandum of training plan is simply a medium of understanding rather than a legal document should be carefully explained. If this does not remove the objection, it seems that the teacher–coordinator must resort to one of two alternatives. He or she may simply refuse to place the student without the employer's signature on the memo. The fact that the agreement is not legally binding, however, seems to present an acceptable compromise. If the employer will agree verbally to abide by the item in question and will sign the document with it removed, it is suggested that the objectional item might be marked out. It would probably be wise for the teacher–coordinator to clear such an action with administrative superiors before the placement of the student is fully consummated. It is further suggested that alterations in the memorandum of training plan should be exceptions rather than rules. Excessive alterations will tend to reduce the instrument to a point of no value.

Resistance to the signing of the memorandum of training plan may stem from other causes, such as a general reluctance on the part of businesspeople to sign any kind of a document that may in some way involve them with a federal agency. In any event, the coordinator must weigh the evidence at hand, acting at all times as the guardian of the student's best interest.

Suggested Activities

1. Prepare a listing of topical areas, with brief commentaries, which will completely describe the preparation of students for their first interview with potential employers.

2. Write a complete description of the placement process with emphasis on the introduction, explanation, and execution of the memorandum of training plan.

3. Describe the contribution that guidance counselors might make in the student selection process.

4. List and discuss briefly the various sources of the job processes to be recorded on the back of the memorandum of training plan. (See pages 76–77.)

5. Prepare a listing of related subjects suitable for recording on the back of the memorandum of training plan. (See pages 76–77, 196–197, and 203.)

6. Design a format for employers to follow in preparing job descriptions for use in the placement process.

7. Design a form for use in officially advising school officials, and other concerned individuals, of student placement. This form should include provision for recording the name and address of the firm in which the student is placed, the time of leaving the school each day, the total hours of work each week, the name of the on-the-job instructor, and other appropriate information.

chapter six

Visitation and Counseling

After the placement process is completed and the student is working in accordance with the memorandum of training plan, a system of visitation and counseling should be established. This activity is a vital part of the coordination process, and constitutes the basic link between the school and the cooperating employers.

There is a difference between visitation with purpose and just visiting. Employers are busy and for the most part do not have time to entertain visitors during work hours. For each visit there should be a reason worthy of the time required of the employer as well as of the teacher–coordinator.

Visitation Purposes

A number of legitimate purposes for teacher–coordinator visits to training stations are listed below with appropriate commentaries.

Employer Evaluation of Student Work Experience

A custom of the school requires that students be given a periodic grade indicative of the quality of work they are doing. In order to satisfy this custom, most CE programs require that employers evaluate the work of students at regular grading periods. Since this grading normally occurs at six-week intervals, the employer is called on for the evaluation report near the end of each six-week period.

Most employers are unskilled in the evaluation process and many of them would prefer not to grade the students at all. Others will give those students who are doing well A's and withhold judgment on those who are not doing so well. The tendency of most employers is to grade too high. In order to combat this tendency, the school must develop a qualifying process to keep the final grades of CE students in line. Such a process will be covered in detail in Chapter Eleven.

The fact that the employer is at a disadvantage in judging the quality of the student's work experience in accord with school policies constitutes a valid reason for the teacher–coordinator's visits near the end of each six-week period for the purpose of helping with the evaluation. During such visits, the teacher–coordinator should attempt to convince the employers that the best interest of the student will be served by a realistic evaluation. They should come to understand that through this evaluation there is opportunity to help the school identify areas where personal improvement is needed on the part of the student. As a general rule, employers will respond to tactful advice of this kind.

A sample progress report form representative of those currently in use in some states is shown as Figure 8. It should be in the hands of the employers near the end of each six-week period. If this form is consistently and properly executed, it becomes a permanent record of the employers' ratings of their student employees. As a general rule, employers prefer an instrument of this kind because its continuous nature affords an opportunity to review the previous six-week grades as a prelude to deciding what the current mark is to be. This review should contribute to consistency in grading.

Although the sample progress report form is largely self-explanatory, attention is called to the note "To the Employer." This short paragraph serves as a constant reminder of the purpose of the employer's evaluation of the student. This paragraph should be referred to as often as necessary to keep it paramount in the mind of employers as they judge the student. The reader should not be disturbed because the note is upside down, for the form is designed so that it will be properly positioned when folded for insertion into an envelope.

Attention is called to the listing of personality traits upon which the employer is asked to rate the student. Perhaps other traits should be included or should replace some of those on the list. The fact remains, however, that these 18 points provide an opportunity for the employer to render a comprehensive review of the student and to suggest, through the marking process, where personal improvement is needed.

The five blank spaces under Skills on the Job are provided for

Figure 8   Progress Report

SIGNATURE OF EMPLOYER

TERM	NAME OF FIRM	SIGNED BY	DATE
I			
II			
III			
IV			
V			
VI			

To the Employer:

Each normal individual possesses positive and negative qualities. The battle for supremacy is between these two forces. Individuals fail or succeed in life as their positive or negative qualities predominate. You, as an employer, are in a position to help us in our attempt to identify your trainee's undesirable traits and to help him or her replace them with positive qualities. Please take advantage of this opportunity by carefully marking this card. It will be in your hands once every six weeks of the school year.

PROGRESS REPORT
of

_____

Trainee

COOPERATIVE TRAINING IN DIVERSIFIED OCCUPATIONS
SENIOR HIGH SCHOOL

_____

TRAINING AGENCY

_____

OCCUPATION

88

Figure 8 *(continued)*

Please place a check under the column containing the letter grade which you believe that the trainee deserves. Code: A—Outstanding   B—Good   C—Average   D—Poor

PERSONALITY TRAITS	TERMS																							
	I				II				III				IV				V				VI			
	A	B	C	D	A	B	C	D	A	B	C	D	A	B	C	D	A	B	C	D	A	B	C	D
1. Personal appearance and bearing																								
2. Courtesy																								
3. Willingness to learn																								
4. Disposition																								
5. Physical vitality																								
6. Cooperativeness																								
7. Ability to take correction																								
8. Ability to follow instructions																								
9. Neatness in work																								
10. Thoroughness																								
11. Initiative																								
12. Dependability																								
13. Industry and effort																								
14. Enthusiasm																								
15. Judgment and common sense																								
16. Self-reliance																								
17. Attendance																								
18. Punctuality																								
SKILLS ON THE JOB	A	B	C	D	A	B	C	D	A	B	C	D	A	B	C	D	A	B	C	D	A	B	C	D
AVERAGES																								

employers to insert items which will enable them to evaluate the performance of students in areas which bear special significance to them or the type of work they represent. For example, an office manager may believe that accuracy, neatness, ability to spell, and technical ability are essential characteristics of successful secretaries.

On the other hand, the machine-shop foreman may believe that accuracy, speed, skill, ability to visualize, and technical knowledge properly characterize the successful machinist. Other employers may have different ideas relative to significant abilities of successful employees in their type of work. All employers should be requested to write in the points upon which they will evaluate the student with reference to specific job characteristics. In effect, this is asking employers to use the five spaces to describe their concept of a desirable employee.

Employers should understand how the progress report will be used. They should be advised, for example, that it will or will not be considered confidential. In the latter case, they will probably be more reserved in the marking process than they would if the report were not to be available to the student. It is suggested that the report would be more meaningful as a confidential instrument, and that it be marked "Confidential," thus assuring that it would be available only to school officials. The fact that the report would not be available to students under any circumstances would not decrease its value as a basis for counseling relative to need for improvement of job performance.

Working with employers in the evaluative process as a purpose of visitation should produce a number of valuable results. Among these would be the opportunity to maintain a continuous dialogue with employers relative to program purposes and values, and to keep the best interest of the student paramount in all judgments. In addition, the teacher–coordinator's ability wisely to counsel the student would be bolstered by a more intimate understanding of the bases upon which judgments were made by the employer.

Another value of working with the employers in the evaluative process is the opportunity to encourage them to judge students with an appropriate degree of sternness in comparison with successful workers. This comparison would combat a normal tendency on the part of the employers to excuse student deficiencies because they are "just high school students." Allowing this line of thought to influence the evaluative process would be to reward the student for deficiencies rather than to focus attention on the necessity for correction.

Although it would be desirable for the teacher–coordinator to have the opportunity to work with the employers in the evaluative process, it may not always be possible by virtue of the employers' choice. Even though they may be willing to discuss the progress report, they may prefer actually to negotiate the instrument in privacy or perhaps in conjunction with other members of the firm. If this decision should be the case, the teacher–coordinator should be prepared to leave a self-addressed envelope with the request that the report be mailed or else given to the student to deliver. In either event the envelope should be sealed in order to preserve the confidential nature of the progress report.

Acquainting the Employer with Directly Related Instruction

The fact that employers have little or no direct contact with the related instruction provided by the school suggests an excellent basis for training station visits. It is up to the teacher–coordinator to keep employers appropriately informed about the related instruction and to give them an opportunity to suggest special areas of study relevant to the type of work the student is doing. In such a conference, employers may be made aware of difficulties encountered by the school in providing directly related instruction, such as inability to acquire suitable reference materials. Employers may be able to donate technical books or trade journals or other appropriate documents not otherwise available to the school. If the problem is money, they may wish to purchase reference materials for their students.

In the final analysis, employer visits based on related instruction should result in a better understanding of what students are doing in the classroom. It may be necessary for teacher–coordinators to take significant evidence of the student classroom work with them on training station visits. Items such as the study guide, reference books, and completed assignments would serve as excellent topics for conversations with the employer as well as evidence of the character and the quality of the classroom work. A natural result should be to give the employer a better understanding of directly related instruction and its correlation with the work experience.

It may be advisable to ask employers whether they detect any evidence that students are attempting to apply the technical knowledge acquired in the classrooms to the solution of problems encountered on the job. Continuous reference to the relationship between directly related instruction and work experience will tend to preserve and

91

strengthen the educational nature of CE and to crystallize the role of on-the-job instructors as important members of the educational team.

Reconciliation of Job-Experience Reports

A general practice is to have each student record daily experiences on a job-experience report form. (See the sample form on pages 146–147.) A prime purpose of this form is to keep the teacher–coordinator informed of the nature and scope of the on-the-job experience. In addition, it serves as an instrument of correlation by providing daily indication of appropriate areas of study directly related to work experience. The authenticity of the daily job-experience report depends upon the integrity of its execution by the student. Without integrity, it has no value. On the other hand, understanding and acceptance of the purpose and the value of the job-experience report by the student should inspire sincere attention to its execution.

Suppose, for example, that a student reports day after day that work is applied primarily to the same job operations. The teacher–coordinator can logically assume that one of two circumstances is present, neither acceptable.

The student may not be recording daily job experience accurately by virtue of indifference or by deliberate intent to misrepresent the situation. The possibility that the student has not been properly instructed about correct procedure in making the report, or that the procedure is not understood, should not be overlooked. Another possibility is that the employer may have failed to move the student into new experience areas because of ability to produce skillfully in a single area. By yielding to this natural tendency, the employer is in violation of item 3 of the memorandum of training plan. This item states, in effect, that the student will not be retained in any one job or operation beyond the time necessary to reach proficiency in job performance.

In any event, a visit with the employer will be necessary to determine the reason for the unsatisfactory job-experience report. The employer should be asked to verify the truthfulness of the job experience the student has reported. If it is inaccurate as a result of failure to properly record the on-the-job experience, the teacher–coordinator should deal with the student.

If, on the other hand, the employer is found to be at fault, the teacher–coordinator should proceed with great caution. If the placement process was carried out properly in the beginning, the employer should immediately recognize this failure to provide a proper range and scope of job experience.

If for some reason the placement process failed to ensure the understanding and the acceptance of the memorandum of training plan, the problem becomes more difficult. Under such circumstances the employer may not be aware that holding students in areas where they are most productive constitutes a violation of the cooperative arrangement with the school. Employers, for example, could say that if they had understood this requirement, they would not have been interested in cooperating. This statement and other possible reactions of the employer could place the teacher–coordinator in a difficult position, with the distinct possibility that students may be forced to suffer from circumstances for which they are not responsible.

Encountering problems of this kind will measure the maturity of teacher–coordinators and their skill in dealing effectively with difficult situations. In such cases, a way must be found to reconcile the situation and save the training station, stabilize the attitude of the employer, and preserve the educational value of the work experience. The nature of the job-experience report will make it serve well as the purpose of an occasional visit with the employer and should provide a basis for meaningful and pleasant communication relative to important elements of the program.

Employer Evaluation of Completed Technical Assignments

The fact that the teacher–coordinator is not expected to be an expert in all occupational areas suggests that the employer might be called on to compensate for this lack of expertise in appropriate circumstances. The supervised and directed study method of teaching requires that each student have an individual daily assignment in an area of technical information related as closely as possible with on-the-job experience.

One function of the teacher–coordinator in applying this teaching technique is the evaluation of the completed assignments. It stands to reason that lack of technical ability would minimize the possibility of judging the accuracy and authenticity of information submitted by the students. One alternative would be simply to ignore accuracy and authenticity and to base the evaluation on other characteristics of the completed assignment. This practice might promote carelessness in choosing the content of the paper, thus resolving it into a meaningless combination of words. This travesty could occur without the knowledge of the teacher–coordinator if the completed assignment were not being read.

Another alternative would be to call on the employers to verify the answers to technical questions and the authenticity of the technical information in the completed assignments submitted by the students. It would be unwise to burden employers in this respect by calling on them too often. Making it the basis of periodic visits, however, should be in order. Employers may be proud to demonstrate technical knowledge, and students will prepare technical assignments with greater care if they know that their employers may evaluate them.

Student Problems as Bases for Visitation

There is no way to anticipate all of the students' problems nor is there a way to determine which problems will require one or more conferences with their respective employers. Some of the problems will result from human imperfections that CE is designed to identify and correct. It stands to reason, therefore, that the teacher–coordinator should not fail to apply corrective techniques with appropriate sternness at any time the student is guilty of conduct unbecoming to successful and desirable workers.

Problems of this nature will defy correction without the full cooperation of the employers. They must be prepared to require the same quality of job performance of students as they do from regular employees. The employer's cooperation should also include willingness to use the "job" as a means of correcting malfunctions of the student in other phases of schoolwork. Typical problems falling into these two categories would include failure to report for work without proper notice, personality clashes with coworkers, reluctance to accept correction or constructive criticism, job irresponsibility, failure to follow company policy, failure to observe safety precautions, absence from school but presence at work, reluctance to pursue classroom assignments, using the job as an excuse for failure in other subjects, and desire to drop out of school but to keep the job.

The employer may be reluctant to require job performance equivalent to that of regular employees in some cases. As a general rule, however, willingness to cooperate in this respect may be more forthcoming than it would be in cases where the employer is required to use the job to enforce conformance with school policies.

94

One of the most common offenses of maladjusted students is absence from school in the morning, but reporting for work in the afternoon. The fact that performance of this kind cannot continue to be tolerated by the school requires that a rigid policy designed to control such malfunctions be established jointly by the school and the employer. Such a policy should mandate that students failing to attend school in the morning are not permitted to work in the afternoon. Although some provision should be made for consideration of exceptional circumstances, the policy will have to be hard-nosed to be effective. It is obvious that a policy of this nature cannot be enforced without the cooperation of employers. They must assume the responsibility, upon notice from the teacher–coordinator, of refusing to let students work and of adjusting their pay accordingly.

Another problem of this nature may be illustrated by students who refuse to fulfill their responsibilities in other subject-matter areas, such as English, to the point that failure is imminent. The reason given as an excuse for failure is that there is not enough time to do the schoolwork because of job demands. In cases of this kind, the teacher–coordinator may decide that the students' best interest would be served by being removed from the job until deficiencies are remedied. This plan would require that employers deny students the opportunity to work during periods designated by the school with an attending loss of pay.

The employers' willingness to cooperate to the required extent will depend upon the original purpose in participating in the program. If the original intention was to make the cooperative student responsible for a specific job vital to operation of the business, resistance can be expected because absence of the student would affect production. On the other hand, if the student was employed in accord with item 4 of the memorandum of training plan, the employer could be expected to react favorably to such a request. This item provides that students will have the status of a noncompetitive worker, neither displacing a regular worker nor substituting for a worker needed by the training agency.

In other words, it should be possible for students to be removed from their jobs without vitally interfering with production. Although action of this kind may seem to be drastic, it can be depended on to be effective. The certainty of such action will serve as motivation to the entire class fully to discharge their responsibilities to the school.

This arrangement may seem to be in conflict with the basic vocational belief that work experience should consist of "useful and productive work." In the case of CE, however, the production should be supplemental rather than complementary to that of regular workers.

Students often seek enrollment in CE as a last resort in attempting to salvage their educational opportunity. This motive suggests that they are "dropout prone," for they may have previously considered dropping out of school but have not done so because of fear that they would not be able to find suitable jobs. Such students may see the job in which they are placed for educational purposes as an avenue to full-time employment in a desirable and compatible occupation.

Students with this tendency to drop out should confer with the teacher–coordinator so that the circumstances may be thoroughly examined. Here again the best interest of the student must be kept foremost in the minds of those who have a part in making the final decision. In all probability a conference with the employer should be arranged as the first order of business.

Ironically, item 4 of the memorandum of training plan may again be basic to employer attitudes in this matter. If, for example, a student is being offered an opportunity to work full-time in the job in which he or she is presently working part-time, it becomes obvious that item 4 has been violated, in that the student was employed in the beginning to perform a service vital to the business. If, on the other hand, full-time employment of the student would not eliminate the part-time job as an opportunity for the placement of another student, it could be assumed that the employer is not at fault.

The final decision should rest on the determination of whether the students' best interest would be served by remaining in school and delaying full-time employment until after graduation. However, other critical factors, such as family responsibilities, may enter into the decision.

Consequently, students may discount their own best interest in order to solve critical problems of immediate concern. When such temporary pressures influence the students, the teacher–coordinator may be unable to prevent them from making decisions that will inevitably be regreted.

CE students who leave school for full-time employment do not satisfy the purposes of the program. It must be said, however, that proper student-selection techniques and placement procedures may serve to launch potential dropout students into the world of work. There is a good chance that they may become useful and productive citizens, and whether or not their best interests have been served will depend on the circumstances involved in the decision to drop out, and on their ultimate success as full-time workers.

The foregoing student problems are indicative of the type of employer and school-related student malfunctions with which the teacher–coordinator should be prepared to deal. A conference with the student's employer is often needed to help solve these problems, but the need for face-to-face conferences does not discount the possibility of developing employer relationships of sufficient quality to justify the avoidance of occasional visits in favor of telephone calls when problems of minor importance are involved. The teacher–coordinator, however, should not resort to excessive use of the telephone at the expense of essential personal contacts with employers. The rapport with the employer and the measured judgment of the teacher–coordinator should be ruling factors in determining whether personal contact is necessary.

Introduction of School Administrators to Employers

School administrators should have the opportunity to visit students on the job and their employers. Such visits should serve to encourage administrative appreciation and awareness of the problems involved in operating the program. As a general rule, the employer will be flattered to be visited by an administrator and will welcome the opportunity to discuss CE. The successful school administrator will always be attentive to community feedback of this kind. The teacher–coordinator should find that visiting training stations jointly with the principal has sufficient value to justify periodic occurrence throughout the school year. Such visits should be limited to one per training station per school year, but they may be curtailed by the time the administrator has available for this purpose.

Need for Training of Employees

Another excellent purpose for visits with the employer could be to discuss the possibility of additional services that the school might make available. The teacher–coordinator, as an agent of the school, should examine any additional educational problems cooperating employers might have and the possibility of contributing to their solution. Such problems would have to do with training for those on the payroll, or for prospective employees.

The school should be equipped to deal with both of these problems through the adult phase of its vocational education program.

It is not suggested that the "typical reasons for employer visits" discussed above must all be employed within a given time, but they do indicate that valid purposes for contacts with employers are present in sufficient number and variety to eliminate purposeless visitation.

Visitation Record

One of the paramount questions in the minds of embryonic teacher–coordinators is: "How often should each student be visited?" The preferred answer they are hoping for is a pat formula or rule such as one visit per week, or perhaps three visits per six-week school term, but reducing visitation to a mechanical process would be an oversimplification and would tend to defeat its purpose. A tendency of this kind could result in scheduling visits at given times within given periods without regard to purpose or need. Visitation simply for the sake of visitation is a waste of time for all concerned.

There is no definite way of predetermining when or for what reason visits to employers should be made. Circumstances involved in the relationship between student and the employer will vary to the extent of defeating any attempt to place them in general classifications for visitations. At any given time, therefore, the intensity of the need for visitation may be different for each student. In the case of those who are well adjusted to their jobs with employers who understand and accept program purposes and values, there may be times when a visit is not advisable. Other students not so well adjusted to the job with employers who may not have completely fixed their philosophy concerning CE may need immediate attention through visitation.

Critical circumstances may develop in the case of some students demanding the immediate and continuing attention of the teacher–coordinator. Accordingly, the teacher–coordinator's judgment must be exercised in planning the visitation schedule in accordance with the intensity of need. Some students may require more visits than others during any given period.

This rationale is not intended to imply that visitation is not necessary for all training stations, but rather to suggest that the time and the frequency be based on judgment relative to the need in each case. It would be difficult to justify less than one visit per six-week school term for well-adjusted students. The frequency of visits should range from a minimum of one per six-week period to as many as are necessary to resolve adverse circumstances and to maintain awareness of the progress being made by students.

A method of recording the dates, the purposes, and the results of

Figure 9   Visitation Record

Purpose of Visit	Comments	Date

visits to training agencies should be developed. (See Figure 9.) A record of this kind will be of great value in keeping the visitation program properly structured from the standpoints of viability and variety of purpose. This record will help the teacher–coordinator to distribute the visitation time equitably among all training agencies and ensure that none be overlooked.

Figure 9 will serve for purposes of illustration, although the teacher–coordinator may prefer to design a visitation record form that is in accordance with local circumstances. In any event, the information required by the sample should be a part of the finally developed form. If the sample should prove acceptable, one should be prepared for each student and should be bound conveniently for handling. It may be more desirable to reduce the finished form to 5- by 7-inch cards for filing in a portable case. An improperly posted record would be of no value, for it would be misleading rather than helpful.

Values of Purposeful Visitation

There are many values that should accrue incidentally as a result of purposeful visitation, such as observation of the student at work, opportunity to sample attitudes of coworkers, opportunity to influence the thinking of the employer, receiving ideas and suggestions for related study, identification of needs for the student's personal improvement, awareness of the general attitude toward the student, awareness of the training-agency environment, continued alertness to the quality of the on-the-job training, and awareness of the general progress of the student.

The above list of values indicates what the teacher–coordinator should be looking for during visits. It could also constitute the criteria by which the quality of visitation is judged. Something relative to one or more of these items should be gained during each visit. If such values are not being realized, visiting techniques should be evaluated for the purpose of increasing efficiency.

Student Counseling

One of the prime values of CE is the opportunity to place high school students in real jobs in occupations in which they are qualified to succeed. The fact that this judgment is made before students are placed on jobs does not eliminate their inevitable need for encouragement, constructive criticism, and supervision as they attempt to overcome barriers and to solve problems encountered day by day on the job and at school. It is the responsibility of the teacher–coordinator to provide the leadership and the direction each student will need in varying degrees.

Intimate acquaintance with the training-station environment, the attitude and disposition of the employer, and the positive and negative characteristics of the student eminently qualify the teacher–coordinator to discharge this responsibility. Such qualifications should facilitate arbitration of differences of opinion or any other difficulty on the job or at school. The availability of these services should be helpful to the student in maintaining a sense of direction, and should provide the encouragement necessary to instill an abiding desire to acquire the personal qualities and abilities essential to success.

Although the teacher–coordinator may prefer to confine counseling to in-school and on-the-job problems, other problem areas, such as the home and boy–girl relationships, will probably become involved. The student will find it difficult to categorize problems to suit school-established classifications. Problems in any of these areas may well be the basis for failure to cope successfully with other problems. In the process of visiting training stations and in study of periodic employer-evaluation reports on students, the teacher–coordinator will identify important areas in which the student should make personal improvement.

These areas of deficiency will serve as excellent points of departure for much of the student counseling, which, if properly received, may initiate personal-improvement programs. The correction of faults identified by employers should eventually change unacceptable individuals to desirable employees.

Bases for Student Counseling

The counseling process should be based on the teacher–coordinator's knowledge and understanding of the student–employer relationship and the current status of the student relative to other facets of the total environment. The counseling process may include discussion of the employer's evaluation of work experience, consideration of personality clashes with employer or workers, commendation for any successful accomplishments, being a good listener to real or fancied problems, encouragement to excel, discussion of personal improvement program, helping to crystallize an image of desirable employees, establishment of personal values and ethical standards, and cultivation of recognition and respect for the dignity of work.

Since student counseling will probably be initiated during the directly-related-subjects period, it will be given appropriate treatment in Chapter Eight. It has been briefly discussed at this point to suggest that the counseling process may be based primarily on information gathered in training-station visits.

The Visitation Process

It has been emphasized that successful training-station visitation is normally based on purpose inspired by current circumstances. Consequently, the schedule of visits should be planned carefully in accordance with the urgency of employer–student problems and other conditions of school–employer relations.

The following analysis is recorded to indicate the basic elements of training-station visits, not to imply that visitation is a mechanical process, but rather to outline its essential parts. Efficient teacher–coordinators will perfect their own visitation pattern, being very careful to avoid fragmentation of the process.

Preparing for the Training-Station Visit

The first step in preparing for a visit to a given training station should be to check the visitation record for the purpose of reviewing the date, the purpose, and the results of previous visits. (See Figure 9.) First consideration should be given to the possible need to follow up significant aspects of prior visits.

A review of the purposes of previous visits may suggest an appropriate purpose to assign to the current visit. Such a review will also eliminate the possibility of repetition of purpose. Setting the purpose of the visit in this way will facilitate orderly procedure in the remaining phases of the preparation.

The purpose of the visit will determine which materials, if any, should be assembled. Such materials may include study guides, completed study assignments, reference books, and other materials that might augment the potential of the visit.

Preliminary consideration should be given to questions or suggestions to be mentioned in conversations with the employer to inspire improvement of the on-the-job environment. The experienced teacher–coordinator may find mental notes to be sufficient, while inexperienced individuals may find it to their advantage to prepare a written list of leading questions. Diplomacy and tact are essential during the visit.

Making the Visit

If the visit is to be by appointment, contact should be made to determine when the employer will be available. The teacher–coordinator should arrive promptly and be prepared to proceed with the interview. An invitation to have a cup of coffee may be in order, but should not be pursued unnecessarily if the employer is not enthusiastic about it. It is desirable that the conversation be conducted in a setting that will enable the employer to give undivided attention to the matter at hand. Very little will be accomplished in open areas within hearing of others, or within reach of the telephone. Getting the attention of a busy employer sometimes presents a very difficult problem. Accordingly, it may be necessary to seek a conference at a location apart from the place of business.

Post the Visitation Record

Immediately upon returning to the office, the teacher–coordinator should post the visitation record. Special care should be exercised in recording the date, the purpose, and the results of the visit, together with any additional information beneficial for future reference. Under no circumstances should this information be left to memory. The intensity and the variety of responsibilities tend to eliminate a dependable memory of significant details involved in training-station visitation.

Counseling the Student

The visitation process will be completed when notes are prepared for use in student counseling at the first opportunity. The intensity of the need for counseling will vary with the purpose and the results of the visit. If the purpose was to work with the employer in adjusting a problem, counseling would be mandatory as soon as possible.

Teacher–coordinators who have difficulty in planning and organizing their activities will be most vulnerable to the tendency to fragment the visitation process. Such individuals tend to visit spasmodically without specific purpose, and to procrastinate. Although the characteristics referred to just above were assigned to failure-prone teacher–coordinators, they are also representative of difficulties experienced by qualified and hard-working individuals in fully consummating the training-station-visitation process. The problem, therefore, is to overcome the natural or imagined barriers and obstacles.

Typical Problems in Visitation and Counseling

Problem 1   *The equitable distribution of visitation time among training stations*

A natural tendency of teacher–coordinators is to seek environments in which they feel most comfortable and to avoid those where they are uncomfortable. For this reason unorganized and unplanned visitation will inevitably involve an inequitable distribution of visits among training agencies. A determining factor in the frequency of visitation is the manner in which the teacher–coordinator is received. If the reception is warm and friendly, the urge to return will be strong; but if the employer is difficult to contact and the teacher–coordinator is given as little attention as possible by those whom he is able to see, the urge would be to avoid as many future contacts as possible.

Ability to identify with training-station environments will also strongly affect the natural desire to visit training agencies. For example, a male teacher–coordinator might have very little interest in beauty culture and ladies' "ready-to-wear" sales. For different but equally impelling reasons, a female teacher–coordinator might be uncomfortable in occupational areas such as sheet metal and pipe fitting.

Training-station visitation must be planned and regulated to overcome the natural tendencies suggested above, and to ensure equitable distribution of visitation time in accordance with the intensity of the problems involved. This need accounts for the recommendation that an accurate record of visitation be kept to note dates, purposes, and results, and that it be reviewed consistently as a prelude to the planning of visitation schedules. This approach will enable the teacher–coordinator to arrange visits according to student needs, as opposed to aimless visitation according to subconscious urge. Training-station visitation is a basic operation of CE and should be executed in a businesslike manner without being affected by personal desires or tendencies.

Problem 2   *Helping employers in evaluating work experience*

The integrity of CE depends to a great extent upon the employers' evaluation of the students' work experiences. If their marks are realistically based on quality as compared with successful workers in comparable occupational fields,they should constitute authentic guidelines for the development of acceptable skill and knowledge as well as personal improvement. If employers overlook or excuse student deficiencies, their evaluative marks will be misleading and will serve as retardants to the students' development. Students should be encouraged to request that they be given realistic evaluation so that they may know where improvement is needed. Sincere students properly selected and placed will accept realistic evaluation marks as prime guidelines in their success formula and will profit from them.

Another target of the teacher–coordinator's efforts to educate employers should be to develop consistency in the evaluative process. The attempt to reconcile the employer's marks with the grading system of the school would be facilitated if an A from one employer meant about the same as an A given by other employers.

If, for example, some employers award students an A for dependability even though they have been absent several times without reason, while other employers award their students A only for perfect work attendance, a definite inequity is present. In the first case, the students' absence from work may be excused because they are considered to be "just high school students" and as such cannot be expected to be as responsible as adult workers. It can be assumed that the second group of employers base their evaluations on comparisons with what they expect from regular employees and that unauthorized absences would have been reflected in the evaluation marks.

By being exacting, the employer contributes to the development of good work habits. The first student may be encouraged to underestimate the importance of being at work every day, and may accordingly develop a bad habit that delays adjustment to the world of work. Such divergence in the meaning of a grade is fraught with misunderstanding and disappointment. The integrity of the school will be affected and the work experience of those involved will be permanently misrepresented. In the final analysis, it is obvious that the best interest of the student is served by the greatest possible consistency in the evaluation of work experience according to the standards used in the judgment of regular employees.

Problem 3 Effecting two-way correlation of work experience and related instruction

The term *correlation* as it is used in the statement of this problem means relating directly related instruction as closely as possible with work experience. The term *two-way* suggests that correlation is a joint responsibility, in that the school should relate technical instruction to job experience and the employer should provide opportunity for its application on the job. The school discharges its responsibility for correlation in the related-instruction classroom through the application of techniques to be discussed in Chapter Eight.

Working with the employer in the development of an environment which provides encouragement and opportunity for the application of related technical knowledge to the solution of on-the-job problems is an important function of visitation. The beginning may be in the designing of a mutually convenient method of keeping the employer informed about the content of the directly related instruction. The process of informing the employer should pave the way for suggestive questions from the teacher–coordinator such as the following:

1. Have you noticed a tendency on the part of your trainee to apply or declare technical knowledge?
2. Are there ways of encouraging the student to become concerned about the "why" as well as the "how" of the job?
3. Would it be objectionable to seek ways to reward the student for technical dexterity?
4. Would it be feasible to raise technical questions in the course of job performance, such as "How is a transformer constructed and what are its functions in the electrical transmission system?" Such a question originating on the job should provide motivation for the study of the matter in the classroom.
5. How is recognition for the application of technical knowledge involved in the process of job-experience evaluation?
6. Would it be in order to call in the student occasionally for general counseling on the combination of skill and technical knowledge as an avenue to success?
7. Could the on-the-job instructor be encouraged to champion the opportunity to gain technical knowledge at school as an opportunity not to be taken lightly?

Implementing the suggestions implied in the questions above should be basic to the establishment of highly desirable on-the-job environments essential to the unexcelled educational opportunity CE should provide. The teacher–coordinator should devote an appropriate amount of time counseling with each student about suggestions supplemental to those made to the employer concerning the development of desirable on-the-job environments. The student properly selected and placed should readily respond to suggestions implied in the following questions:

1. Have you found any relationship between your related technical study and your work experience?
2. Have you found opportunities to apply your technical knowledge to the solution of on-the-job problems?
3. How do you account for the fact that your employer has given you an average rating on technical knowledge?
4. Do you and your on-the-job instructor discuss the technical aspects of the job or the operations you perform?
5. Have you talked to your employer about the importance of technical knowledge to employment opportunity and subsequent advancement after graduation from high school?
6. Are there workers at your training station who have a high degree of manipulative skill but very little or no technical knowledge? What future do these individuals have?
7. Who is the most successful person you know in your occupation? How do you account for this success?
8. In your estimation, what are the prime values that accrue to the individual as a result of the achievement of a high degree of skill, both manipulative and technical?

The teacher–coordinator should find that the time devoted to the encouragement of employers and students to become interested in the acquisition and the application of technical knowledge as it relates to work experience will pay dividends in terms of increased educational values. The three essential ingredients of success in this endeavor are properly selected and placed students, employers who understand and accept their responsibility relative to the purposes and values of CE, and qualified teacher–coordinators sincerely committed to the accomplishment of program purposes. The absence of any of these ingredients will tend to defeat success.

Problem 4 *Adjusting intolerable job-related circumstances*

Scrupulous attention to good and acceptable practices in the student selection and placement process will reduce the incidence of unacceptable circumstances relative to the cooperative arrangement between the school and the employers. Properly selected students placed in occupational circumstances receptive to their total being will generate desirable rather than undesirable relationships.

The well-placed students' enthusiasm to acquire skill and knowledge

107

essential to success will overcome negative factors that could otherwise develop into serious problems. But when an undesirable situation does arise, procrastination on the part of representatives of the school in facing up to placement errors will contribute to the ultimate loss of training stations. This danger, of course, is one of the greatest hazards of CE. The program cannot operate without sufficient numbers of qualified training stations. The loss of one or more each year would have an insidious effect on the program.

In addition to problems resulting from errors in placement, other intolerable circumstances may develop as a result of students' failure to accept and discharge their responsibilities as trainees. This problem is often the net result of accepting students without regard for the characteristics essential to satisfactory disposition of job responsibilities. The lack of integrity, dependability, and other important character traits will almost surely produce problems that may become acute enough to defeat the cooperative arrangement between the school and the employer before satisfactory adjustments can be made.

Hopefully, however, problems of this nature will develop gradually rather than suddenly, thus providing time to effect personal improvement programs on the part of involved students. The employer's acquiescence to rehabilitation for a delinquent student will depend upon the type and the intensity of the deficiency and the employer's nature, in each case. If, for example, the problem had to do with failing to report for work regularly and on time, most employers could be expected to be cooperative with efforts of school officials to apply corrective measures.

On the other hand, most employers will exhibit less patience with student problems involving theft or other forms of dishonesty. The natural tendency of the employer would be to discharge a student employee upon discovery of dishonesty. This natural tendency, however, may be tempered by the mutually agreed upon memorandum of training plan, which stipulates that the adjustment of on-the-job problems be made jointly by the employer and the teacher–coordinator.

Abiding by this agreement would require the employer to report the student's personal ineptness or character deficiency to the teacher–coordinator and then to proceed jointly in determining how the problem can be resolved. The employer should not be forced to suffer beyond a reasonable point in circumstances of this kind. As a matter of fact, the school is obligated to protect employers against compromising circumstances by virtue of their willingness to cooperate. Accordingly, school officials must not hesitate to remove the student when all other means of adjustment have been exhausted.

When removing the student from the job becomes necessary, it should be justifiable as serving the best interest of the student. The student will be less embarrassed to be removed from the job by school officials, with the possibility of being placed on another job, than to be fired by the employer for dishonesty. Removal by the school might provide an opportunity for rehabilitation without negative effects, whereas being fired by the employer could result in permanent damage to the student's reputation.

Job-related student problems may place employers in positions considered to be untenable and consequently prompt withdrawal from CE rather than risk recurrence of similar intolerable circumstances. The fatal nature of employer attitudes of this kind justifies the establishment of aggressive school policies designed to eliminate circumstances conducive to their development.

Problems such as those described above would be accentuated in circumstances where the teacher–coordinator fails to establish liaison of sufficient intimacy with training stations to result in awareness of on-the-job problems. Two conditions may account for such failure: aloofness from training agencies and too few visits to them, and inadequate or ineffective visits.

The teacher–coordinator may dislike the environment of some training stations to the extent that insufficient visitation occurs to establish the type of relationship essential to the adjustment of on-the-job problems. In either event, CE will be in jeopardy until visitation policies and conduct are improved and strengthened.

For example, let it be said again that school officials are justified in establishing aggressive policies to cultivate the confidence of the employers in their cooperative relationship with the school, and to eliminate circumstances conducive to misunderstanding and distrust. Such policies should ensure the continuing operation of CE by virtue of the availability of qualified training stations.

Problem 5 *Effective counseling relative to job-related problems and the need for personal improvement*

The teacher–coordinator should recognize the necessity of developing relationships with students which are based on mutual confidence and respect. Far too often advice will go unheeded until the students decide that the teacher–coordinator respects them as individuals and is personally interested in them. Once this ideal relationship is achieved, students can be expected to seek opportunities to discuss their school and job-related problems; and they will be receptive to constructive criticism and suggestions for personal improvement.

The teacher–coordinator, having gained the confidence of the student, may find it difficult to confine counseling to school and job problems because of critical personal problems of paramount concern to the student. Problems may range from critical relationships with parents or other members of the family to financial difficulties. The teacher–coordinator, although probably not qualified to deal successfully with such problems, should not hesitate to be a good listener.

At an appropriate time, such problems should be referred to qualified sources of counseling, such as the school counselor or the local minister. Under no circumstances should teacher–coordinators offer advice that they are not qualified to give. The students may be unwilling to confide in the persons to whom they are referred, in which event additional effort should be made to find acceptable sources of counseling.

The teacher–coordinator's concern is justified because the student's educational progress and personal development will depend upon the satisfactory solution of personal problems as well as those related to the educational program. Consequently, following up to ensure adequate counseling is advisable. In effect, the teacher–coordinator becomes a counselor on counseling.

Counseling students about their need for personal improvement could involve circumstances sometimes considered embarrassing. For example, a male teacher–coordinator may find it difficult to advise female students that their cosmetic use, hair styling, length of skirt, wearing of hose, health habits, or cleanliness are out of character with the work environment of their training stations. Although it may be wise to seek help from female faculty members, or vice versa in the case of a female teacher–coordinator, the type of rapport discussed above should permit this type of counseling.

Students will be inclined to be receptive if they are convinced that the advice is being offered sincerely in their best interest, without regard for the sex of the counselor. Sincerity in this case means that the teacher–coordinator actually does have a real interest in each student. Such an interest cannot be faked. Total rejection of counseling efforts can be expected to result from feigned interest and concern.

Suggested Activities

1. After a study of the listing of the personality traits and job skills on the student progress report form on pages 88–89, redesign the form and its content to incorporate personal ideas and provisions for anticipated local circumstances.

2. Design a policy relating to school and job absenteeism of CE students for presentation to school officials for consideration and approval prior to the opening of school the first year CE becomes a part of educational program.

3. The visitation record form on page 99 includes the basic elements of the visitation process. After thorough consideration of the form and its use, redesign it to include personal ideas and innovations.

4. Using the progress report on pages 88–89 as a point of departure, compose evaluative criteria for employer use in determining a grade for each of the eighteen personal traits listed on the form.

5. Compose a statement of policy designed to cultivate employer confidence in the cooperative relationship with the school involved in CE.

chapter seven

Organization and Effective Utilization of Representative Advisory Committees

Vocational education is basically more sensitive to its environment than are other facets of education. This sensitivity is especially evident in the case of CE. The fact that vocational education in all its forms is designed to "prepare individuals for successful entrance into and progress in the world of work in chosen occupations" produces two very important areas of sensitivity.

One of these has to do with the need of contemporary high school students, who will not enter college, to be prepared for employment in occupational areas in which they are qualified to succeed. Another closely related area of sensitivity involves the vital need of the community for a dependable source of qualified workers to enter economically important areas of employment. In the final analysis, these two needs can be equated because emerging high school graduates who will not enter college need to be prepared for employment in jobs available in, or within reasonable proximity of, their home community.

It becomes obvious that intelligent operation of vocational education programs will require an intimate knowledge of the employment opportunities in the service area of the school as they relate to the career interests of high school students. Community familiarity of this nature is extremely difficult for the school to achieve through its own resources. It becomes necessary, therefore, to devise a medium through which satisfactory community liaison can be established and maintained.

The most satisfactory approach to this problem has been found to be the application of the following basic principle, which is in accord

112

with the intent of all federal legislation for vocational education: All vocational education programs should function under the counsel and advice of representative lay advisory committees.

Such lay groups should constitute the kind of liaison the school must have with its geographic service area in order to be fully aware of its basic needs and how well they are being met. In addition to the general advisory committee, each occupational area should be served by as many craft or occupational committees as are necessary to assure proper standards in course content, equipment, facilities, and all other essential environmental factors.

The term *representative* in the above statement of principle has two connotations which should be understood by those who are responsible for the selection and utilization of general advisory committees. The first of these is that such committees should include equal representation from employer and from employee factions of the communities which they represent. The second connotation is that the selected membership of the advisory committee should formally represent the organization or other segment of the community from which it comes. Under no circumstances should advisory committee appointments be made on a basis of personal friendship without regard for official community affiliation.

Functional Characteristics of General Advisory Committees

The operation of lay advisory groups should be an integral part of the vocational education program plan to the extent that their functions are programed as essential steps in basic operational procedures. Far too often the advisory committee becomes inactive almost immediately after it is appointed. This neglect usually occurs when institutional representatives responsible for the appointment and working with such committees see no real reason for their existence other than the fact that they are required by an agency to which the institution is responsible. The attitude of school administrators can be expected to improve when they come to understand and accept the principle that lay advisory committees have no administrative responsibility or authority. They are established for the sole purpose of giving school officials the benefit of their counsel and advice concerning the current needs for vocational education in the service area of the school.

There is very little chance that an advisory committee can function effectively if those in charge do not sincerely want its advice and counsel. The same authority that required the original appointment of the advisory committee may also require that certain utilization procedures be exercised, such as a given number of meetings per year or perhaps formal approval of equipment lists or programs of study. Any counsel or advice offered under such circumstances will be rejected by school officials beyond its necessary utilization as an essential part of official reports and records. The advisory committee can be expected to sense the lack of enthusiasm and sincerity on the part of school officials, with resulting resentment and ultimate failure to function effectively.

The advice of general advisory committees and craft or occupational committees must be carefully considered and used when it is applicable and is not in conflict with institutional policy or acceptable educational practice. When the advisory committee becomes assured that the school officials are sincerely interested in its advice and that it will be used when it is applicable within the bounds of institutional policy and good educational practice, positive response can be expected.

School officials should spare no effort to express appreciation for the services rendered by advisory groups. The members should be made to feel that they are needed and that they are making a vital contribution to the educational program of the institution.

Legal Requirements

Although the use of lay advisory committees has been in accord with the intent of all federal legislation for vocational education, it was not legally required until the passage of the 1968 amendments of the Vocational Act of 1963. This federal act establishes and funds federal and state advisory councils and fixes their areas of function. The federal law does not require the utilization of local advisory committees in the operation of local programs of vocational education. State plans for vocational education, however, should mandate the use of local advisory groups in the operation of reimbursed local programs.

Advisory Committees for CE

The general advisory committee normally has the primary purpose of providing advice relative to the operation of total programs of vocational education in local, regional, or state school systems. In an advisory system of this type, vocational education in specific occupational areas would be served by craft or occupational committees representing the occupation in question in each case.

The term *craft* usually refers to occupations that can be apprenticed or that require the development of a high degree of manipulative and technical skill. Other occupations that cannot properly be characterized in this way are normally referred to as *occupations*, thus accounting for the phrase *craft or occupational committee*.

The interest and concern of craft or occupational committees are occupationally specific in that the membership is composed of individuals representing a single occupational area. The prime purpose is to identify and foster acceptable occupational environmental standards. A committee of this kind also provides an intimate contact with the craft or occupation it represents. There follows a full description of the general advisory committee as it should be organized and utilized in the operation of CE.

General Advisory Committee for CE

All vocational education programs should function under the counsel and advice of representative general advisory committees in order that their purpose and function may be based firmly on authentic and current needs of the geographical area served by the school. In the case of CE the concern of the general advisory committee is general as its activities relate to the community, yet specific to the extent of dealing with specific occupational environmental problems.

The function of the general advisory committee in connection with CE organized to serve specific occupational areas such as distribution and office occupations assumes a character similar to that of the craft or occupational committee in that only one general occupational area is involved in each case. The function of the general advisory committee for CE would include:

1. Consideration and evaluation of occupations to be included in the program, according to criteria established by the school.
2. Consideration and approval of training stations according to criteria established by the school.
3. Aid in selection and placing students.
4. Assistance in developing community relationships.

5. Assistance in community occupational study to determine the type and quantity of vocational education needed.
6. The recommendation of craft or occupational committee members who are qualified to deal with specific occupational problems.
7. Serving as a buffer between the school and various segments of the community in the solution of relationship problems.
8. Serving as a feedback medium from community to school.

Membership of General Advisory Committees

The definition of membership given earlier in this chapter applies to this committee in that it should include official and equal representation from employee and employer factions of the community. Accordingly, the number of employer representatives should be balanced by an equal number of employee representatives.

The general advisory committee should include representation from other elements of the community, such as professional organizations. A good membership composition would include equal representation from employer, employee, and professional groups. Hence, the smallest possible membership would consist of one from each group. The membership can increase to desired size, but care should be exercised in maintaining proper balance.

The general advisory committee should be kept as small as possible, for it will be found that small committees are generally more productive than large committees. Membership ranging from five to eleven is ideal and normally large enough to cope with the problems of CE.

The most productive advisory committee member is usually a person already heavily involved in civic affairs. This fact indicates a type of person dedicated to community service. Such individuals can be depended on to adjust their schedule to make themselves available. This suggestion is offered to counter the tendency of the inexperienced teacher—coordinator to look for individuals who "have time to serve" without interfering with other civic responsibilities.

The fact that individuals are not involved in public service is prima facie evidence that they do not wish to be involved and that they are not likely to respond to the opportunity for advisory committee membership, even though they may accept the appointment. Possible exceptions to this rule may be young citizens who have not found, but are looking for, compatible avenues of community service. Individuals of this type may be found in organizations such as the junior chamber of commerce. Labor organizations or other employee groups can be requested to recommend young men and women who are searching for an avenue of community service.

Frequently, the younger person will be able to identify more rapidly and completely with innovative plans such as career education and CE than can older and more conservative individuals who have weathered the storms of community development through difficult periods. The latter are prone to maintain the status quo and to judge education by criteria established when they were in school.

Public education has traditionally lagged behind contemporary needs, and alert school officials welcome all the help they can get from younger committee members who possess empathy with youth and who are receptive to the changes required to meet contemporary challenges. The suggestion that ambitious young people may prove to be productive advisory committee members is not meant to discount the value of seasoned community servants, for their wisdom and experience are indispensable in dealing with problems inherent in CE. Perhaps the best solution would be to temper committee membership with a sensible balance between ambitious youngsters and those who are more experienced. High priority should be given to parents of high school students.

It is doubtful that a method of selecting committee members could be devised that would guarantee perfect committee performances; but the greater the care in the selection, the greater the probability of excellence in performance. Newly selected committees will almost surely include some members who will fail to respond to committee responsibilities.

To guard against having to live with nonproducing members beyond reasonable periods, all appointments should be made officially for only one year. This time limit will provide an opportunity to replace non-producers at the end of each school year, while those who have served satisfactorily should be reappointed. This policy will serve to strengthen the advisory committee from year to year.

The school should be represented on the committee by the teacher–coordinator and by the superintendent of schools or a designate on a nonvoting basis.

Step-by-Step Procedure for Selecting Committee Members

1. Secure administrative approval.
   The superintendent of schools is responsible and accountable to the

community for the public educational program. It is the superintendent's prerogative, therefore, to establish operating policies and procedures. Under no circumstances should an advisory committee of any kind be established without administrative approval.

2. Seek official recommendations for committee membership from appropriate organizations.

a. *Employee representatives*: There may be a central labor committee in each jurisdictional area which will represent all locals. This committee provides a good entree to organized labor and is an excellent medium through which to transmit requests for recommendations. The same approach is applicable to other employee organizations, except that the contact would probably be directly with the organization rather than through a central committee.

In seeking recommendations from all organizations the type of individuals desired and their functions should be made clear. Ask for multiple recommendations from which a given number will be selected. Such recommendations should be made without the knowledge of the recommendees in order that selection may be made freely by school officials.

b. *Employer representatives*: If there are specific organizations representing employers, the request for committee-member recommendations should be transmitted through an appropriate officer or committee. Following the procedure suggested above, request several recommendations from which a given number will be selected. If such an organization is not present in the community, request for recommendations can be presented to an appropriate committee of the local chamber of commerce.

c. *Professional representatives*: Professional organizations comparable to those for employers and employees may not be present in all communities. In their absence it is suggested that an in-school committee composed of the superintendent of schools, the principal of the school in which the program will operate, and the teacher–coordinator select professional committee members. A committee of this kind can be expected to look with favor upon professional persons who have demonstrated friendship with the school.

3. Investigate individuals recommended.

After recommendations are received, the teacher–coordinator should initiate a methodical investigation of each individual according to the qualities suggested above. It will be advisable to contact as many people as necessary to determine which of those recommended are best qualified.

4. Make appointments official.

When the process has been completed to the satisfaction of all concerned school officials, the superintendent should make the appointments official and advise the appointees accordingly. The official appointment should be made in a letter in which the conditions of the appointment and the functions of the committee are briefly described. The letter should clearly indicate how the appointee can make the acceptance or rejection a matter of record within a given period of time.

5. Advise recommending agencies.

After receiving the acceptance of appointees, the recommending organization should be advised in writing of those finally selected as committee members with the request that they be officially designated at their next meeting.

6. Release news.

The first step should be the preparation of a news article for release from the office of the superintendent. This article should briefly describe the purpose and the function of the advisory committee, with emphasis on those individuals who have been appointed to membership. The local newspaper may be requested to give the story a prominent location in an early edition.

Circumstances To Be Avoided

School officials should guard against the presentation of problems or questions, to the committee, to which administrative solutions already have been found. In effect, the school would be asking that the committee "rubber-stamp" action that has already been taken rather than requesting advice on the proper disposition of current problems. The committee can be expected to resent and resist being used in this way.

The most desirable type of committee member probably will be a community leader, with the net result that the time given to the committee will be that required for meetings. For this reason school officials should not ask for advice on matters requiring extensive study. When such matters become of paramount importance, the "legwork" should be done by the school before presentation to the advisory committee.

Statistical information should be interpreted so that the committee may judge without extensive study. When school officials are not qualified to render authentic interpretations of the statistics or data in question, it may be necessary to call in consultants with the necessary expertise to make the presentation to the committee.

School administrators should avoid carefully the presentation of matters of an administrative nature to the advisory committee. School officials, including the school board, cannot delegate or share their administrative responsibility for the school. The presentation of such problems would violate this principle and invite a type of action inconsistent with the purpose and intent of the advisory committee.

The type of questions or problems which could lead to the passing of formal resolutions by the committee should be avoided. The origination and passage of resolutions is closely related to legislative power and could prove to be a satisfying experience for some elements of the committee. This tendency would be especially noticeable in the case of those members representing the more aggressive organizations. Unbridled committee action of this kind could result in embarrassing circumstances for the committee, the school, and the community.

Perhaps the greatest hazard in working with a lay advisory committee is a letdown after the "honeymoon" is over. A lack of problems considered to merit the attention of the committee could result in an insufficient number of meetings to maintain the interest of members. Still worse would be the holding of meetings without adequate plan or purpose. The committee will quickly sense lethargy of school officials, and their own concern for committee responsibilities will decrease correspondingly. If it develops that a scheduled meeting does not really have a purpose of sufficient caliber to justify the time and effort required, it should be postponed. It would be far more constructive to call off the meeting than to hold one that would fail to satisfy minimum expectations of the committee members.

Defining the Role of the Advisory Committee

The value of the service a representative advisory committee can render depends heavily upon its understanding and acceptance of the role it is designed to play. A clear statement of the limits of the advisory committee's function should be included in the original request for recommendations, and should be a part of the invitation to potential members.

The function of the committee should also be restated and discussed at the first meeting and should be included on the agenda of subsequent meetings as often as necessary to cultivate committee awareness of its functional limitations. Skillful school administrators will avoid difficulty by finding diplomatic ways of emphasizing the advisory nature of the committee's function without being offensive to its members.

Emphasis should be placed on the importance of individual participation in committee activities. An agenda for all meetings should be sent to all committee members to give them an opportunity for prior consideration of the major problems to be discussed. The suggestion should be made that the disposal of most of the problems will depend upon the understanding and knowledge that the committee members have of CE and the contribution it is designed to make to the total educational program of the public school. In this respect the committee members should be encouraged to familiarize themselves with basic program information in brochures prepared for distribution at the first meeting. The agenda for each meeting should allow time for the discussion of questions relative to this information.

Committee members should be admonished to cultivate open minds in dealing with questions and problems presented to it by school officials. The basic criterion upon which decisions are based should always be the best interest of the student. The vested interests of other concerned elements of the community should be superseded by this cause to the end that it will always be the ruling factor in committee consideration.

All advice and counsel to school officials should be based on a consensus of the total committee rather than on an individual opinion expressing a minority view. For this reason, it should be suggested that the members refrain from expressing personal opinions on current issues outside committee meetings before a consensus has been reached. Such restraint will promote committee solidarity and unanimity in all actions.

Committee members should be encouraged to keep the organizations they represent informed about their participation as members of the advisory committee. The results of committee deliberations should be presented at appropriate times so that such organizations will be reasonably informed about CE and the contribution their representatives are making.

Programing Advisory Committee Action

Pressure brought on by deadlines and other responsibilities involved in CE contribute to delinquency of school officials in making the best use of advisory committees. In addition, the general unwieldiness of lay groups presents the necessity of planning well in advance of any action expected. School officials are not often allowed to enjoy the luxury of advance notice of the problems presented to them for solution. Nor can many of their problems be postponed until an advisory committee can be called into session.

For these reasons the advisory committee cannot be expected to participate heavily in the solution of day-by-day problems, but rather to be involved primarily with vital aspects of CE prevalent during given periods of the year. For example, the selection and review of occupations and training stations to be included in the program should take place prior to the opening of school. A series of meetings for the purpose of seeking the advice of the advisory committee should be given a definite place in the sequence of steps included in the process of evaluating and selecting occupations and training stations. Such meetings can be tentatively scheduled well in advance and could occur about the same time each year.

The fact that the committee participation is programmed as a definite part of the selection and evaluation process assures the best chance for its effective utilization. Other vital aspects of CE should be made the subject of subsequent committee meetings throughout the year. A program of work of this nature will produce results of much higher caliber than can possibly be expected where no plan of operation is prepared. After preparing a preliminary draft of a program of work, the teacher–coordinator should present it to the administrative superiors for consideration and approval. After administrative approval, the program should be presented to the advisory committee at the earliest appropriate time.

Craft or Occupational Committee

There will be times when the combined technical knowledge and ability of the general advisory committee and school officials will fall to satisfy all the technical needs of CE. When this need is evident, the general advisory committee should recommend a craft or occupational committee, composed of from three to five members, to meet this need.

Study guides normally are available for the use of students in the most popular occupational areas, but may not be available in other areas. It may become necessary, therefore, for the teacher–coordinator to call on a craft or occupational committee to help in the development

122

of an occupational analysis as the first step in the development of the study guide. This action would be normal procedure because the teacher–coordinator is not expected to be competent in all occupational areas. The teacher–coordinator is expected, however, to be adept in the utilization of advisory groups in securing the necessary information.

The first step in the development of a study guide is a given occupational area, therefore, should be the assembling of an ad hoc craft or occupational committee for the time necessary to develop the basic occupational analysis. The teacher–coordinator should be qualified to apply this information in the process of completing the study guide.

Another need that can best be met by a craft or occupational committee is the provision of technical advice relative to the content which should be included in special courses for adult workers in given occupational areas. The teacher–coordinator may become aware of the need for such courses incidentally in the performance of the coordinating functions, or from the results of an occupational study of the community. An appropriate craft or occupational committee will be the best source of information relative to course content and other technical aspects of the occupation in question. Such a committee should also be helpful in finding a qualified teacher for the course.

Another potential service of the craft or occupational committee is in helping to open up occupational areas for the placement of students. Help of this kind is frequently needed in some communities in the skilled occupations. For example, a certain local labor organization may categorically refuse to accept students in the skilled trade over which it has jurisdiction. A craft committee representing this skilled trade should be helpful in relieving this situation.

Other needs for craft or occupational committees will vary from community to community. The teacher–coordinator should not hesitate to ask the general advisory committee to recommend such a lay group at any time a need for its service arises.

It is suggested, however, that committees of this type be given temporary assignments and that they be dismissed upon completion of their work. It is not normally necessary or desirable that the craft or occupational committee be formally organized or elect officers. The teacher–coordinator should preside and make all assignments. The qualified teacher–coordinator will be skilled in working with lay committees, and will be well versed in drawing information from the artisan, and in bringing it to bear on the purpose at hand.

Pitfalls in the Utilization of Lay Advisory Committees

The pressures under which teacher–coordinators and school administrators work render them especially vulnerable to a number of hazards inherent in normal relationships between school officials and lay advisory committees with which they are working. In order to guard against becoming involved in unfortunate circumstances which can result from the violation of certain basic principles, the following listing of general precautions is offered:

1. Do not procrastinate in putting acceptable committee recommendations into practice. If delay is necessary, the committee should be advised of the reason.
2. Do not fail to give the committee the administrative support it needs to carry out its assignments.
3. Do not allow advisory committees to become administrative in their functions.
4. Do not become involved in labor–management controversies. The fact that it is strongly recommended that employees and employers be equally represented is not meant to imply that the advisory committee should be the victim of labor–management problems. It simply means that there should be a balance in the influence of the two factions in recommendations made to the school.
5. Do not fail to keep the committee informed concerning the program they are attempting to serve. Members quickly sense reluctance on the part of school officials to take the committee into their confidence.
6. Do not fail to respect the time limitations of committee members. Failure to call meetings far enough in advance to give members sufficient time to adjust their schedules is unfair and will prompt absenteeism. Failure to begin meetings on time or allowing them to drag on and on is inexcusable.
7. Do not take the advisory committee for granted. It should be remembered at all times that committee members have made professional and personal sacrifices in order to make themselves available to serve on the advisory committee.

These suggestions do not depart from basic principles which are a part of the operational pattern of successful leaders. Individuals who are functioning successfully in leadership roles in schools will employ these principles and many more, without being prompted, in their relationship with advisory committees.

Typical Problems in Utilizing Advisory Committees

Problem 1 *Securing administrative support in the selection, the organization, and the utilization of a representative advisory committee*

The school administrator may sincerely question the need for, or the advisability of, an advisory committee. This doubt may stem from the conviction that another lay group in addition to the Board of Education would present unnecessary problems. For the most part, however, the successful school administrator can be expected to have an open mind and to be receptive to evidence supporting the need for advice and counsel in the operation of CE.

The request for approval to organize a representative advisory committee should be based on its merits. The fact that the State Plan may require the utilization of advisory committees as an integral part of the operation of reimbursed vocational programs may force acquiscence but will not change or improve administrative attitude. As a matter of fact, the school administrator will resist control of this nature by an outside agency. This tendency places major responsibility on teacher–coordinators in that administrative response to proposals to establish advisory committees will probably vary in accordance with the sincerity and enthusiasm with which they are presented. If teacher–coordinators are thoroughly sold on the need for lay advisory committees, they should be able to elicit favorable response from their administrative superiors. On the other hand, if they are not enthusiastic they will find little difficulty in cultivating administrative doubt which they may have inspired.

If the teacher–coordinator manages to transmit the idea that the committee is not necessary, but that it is legally required by the state department of vocational education, the chances of administrative cooperation in the selection and utilization of a representative advisory committee will be poor. A committee organized under such circumstances would be forced to function in a hostile environment without adequate leadership from the teacher–coordinator and without essential administrative interest and support.

Problem 2 *Teacher–coordinator fear of inability to cope successfully with a representative advisory committee*

The membership of a representative advisory committee should be composed of community leaders who have demonstrated interest and ability in some area of community service. The stature and caliber of such a group merits capable leadership from the school the committee has been created to serve. Fear of leading such a group could stem from

125

the uncertainty of personal ability to dominate the committee to the extent necessary to provide effective leadership.

The individual not properly prepared to assume the responsibilities of coordination by virtue of education and experience is most vulnerable to the crippling effect of fear of this kind. The difficulty could stem from several sources, among them immaturity, timidity, poor educational background, and inexperience. From whatever source the inability stems, it could jeopardize the proper and efficient utilization of a representative advisory committee.

If deficiencies such as those suggested above result from inexperience rather than from a basic "incurable cause," an administrative stand-in should be provided at points where inexperience places the teacher–coordinator at a disadvantage. Wise school administrators can continue this practice as long as necessary without damaging the potential of the fledgling teacher–coordinator on the supposition that the latter is well versed in what should be done but inexperienced in performance.

If the deficiency stems from an incurable source, there is little hope that time will solve the problem. This dilemma serves to emphasize the importance of the initial selection of the teacher–coordinator in accord with the qualifications described in Chapter One. Areas of deficiency which show up after employment produce the necessity of administrative judgment as to whether they stem from inexperience or from sources which normally resist corrective efforts. Dealing promptly and courageously with this problem will be in the best interest of all concerned, including the teacher–coordinator as well as present and future generations of the youth of the community.

CE can never be any stronger than the teacher–coordinator, and can be expected to be a vivid reflection of his weaknesses, sometimes at the expense of his strengths. On the other hand, early recognition of deficiencies as a result of inexperience, with attending provision of compensating arrangements, will allow the fledgling to develop in a way that will fully vindicate the administrative wisdom exercised.

Problem 3 *Orientation of the representative advisory committee and keeping it informed*

The representative general advisory committee has been described as being composed of individuals of experience and stature in some areas of community service. These qualifications tend to ensure the ability to serve effectively as committee members but do not imply understanding of the nature of the responsibilities of this committee. Therefore, it is immediately obvious that an initial phase of committee operation must be devoted to the orientation of its members. Failure in this respect will leave the committee at a distinct disadvantage.

The committee that is not properly oriented will tend to set its own course of action in accordance with self-assigned purposes or those resulting from misinformation. It was suggested earlier that a brochure be prepared to explain committee functions and responsibilities, and that it be emphasized in early contacts with members. The process of committee orientation, however, must not be allowed to end with this initial effort, which cannot be expected to make more than a superficial impression on committee members.

The desired depth of understanding and appreciation of the responsibility of advisory committee membership will only result from knowledge and appreciation of the purposes and the educational values of CE. It is, for example, just as important that members understand and accept the educational values and characteristics of the program as it is for employers and school officials to do so. Here again the problem is obvious, but the solution may be difficult.

To begin with, the committee members should not be expected to glean the necessary understanding and appreciation from special brochures and other printed material. Such information will be helpful and should be made available, but it must be richly supplemented to accomplish the desired results. Effectively supplementing printed materials will tax the ingenuity of the teacher–coordinator and other school officials. The well-qualified and sincerely dedicated coordinator, however, will recognize the necessity of thorough committee orientation and will make every effort to bring it about.

After successful orientation is accomplished, it will be necessary to devise a plan to keep the committee informed systematically about the CE program as it functions in the school.

Problem 4 *Avoiding malpractices in utilizing general advisory committees*

Some of the most common hazards are included in the following listing:

1. The selection of committee members on the basis of friendship to school officials rather than according to their official affiliation with the community.
2. Ignoring the committee after its organization as a reaction to being legally required to include it in the vocational programs.
3. Failure to program the action of the advisory committee as an integral part of basic program procedures.

4. Circumventing the necessity of holding formal committee meetings by making periodic calls on individual committee members asking for individual opinions or advice on current problems.

Individual opinions expressed outside the committee meeting are not acceptable in lieu of the consensus resulting from committee action. Asking committee members to react to problems as individuals is unfair and fails to satisfy the purpose for which the advisory committee was established.

5. Holding the number of meetings below the level of the minimum required for meaningful committee accomplishments.

6. Setting membership limitations above recommended maximums, thus creating an unwieldy body too large to function efficiently.

Problem 5   Establishing and maintaining a satisfactory program of work for the general advisory committee

It stands to reason that a productive program of work for the general advisory committee would of necessity have to follow the successful elimination of malfunctions such as those described in Problem 4. Success in this respect will depend heavily upon the effectiveness of the leadership the teacher–coordinator can bring to bear in working with the administrative superiors and other school officials.

The following guidelines should be helpful in designing a program of work for the representative general advisory committee:

1. Establish a calendar of activities fixing approximate dates for meetings to deal with anticipated problems and activities. The calendar should include meetings to deal with problems such as committee orientation, consideration and approval of occupations and training stations to be included in the program, review of student placements, midterm progress report, annual report, placement and follow-up report, and community occupational study. Additional meetings to deal with unanticipated problems should be called when necessary.

2. Present the proposed calendar of events to appropriate administrative officers for consideration and approval.

3. Place a copy of the calendar, after administrative approval, in the hands of all concerned school officials, and distribute copies to committee members at first opportunity.

4. Follow the approved program of work with the least possible deviation. An agenda should be prepared for each meeting as far in advance as necessary to provide time for distribution to committee members and to school representatives who will attend.

128

Problem 6 *Finding ways and means of appropriately recognizing the services of the representative general advisory committee*

School officials may find themselves at a loss, at times, for ways and means of appropriately expressing appreciation for the services of the advisory committee. The same acts or expressions often repeated become ineffective and eventually suggest insincerity. It becomes necessary, therefore, that representatives of the school design a multiplicity of ways to recognize and to express appreciation for advisory committee services. The following suggestions should be helpful in accomplishing this task.

The superintendent of schools or the president of the school board should periodically attend advisory committee meetings. Although their presence and perhaps an expression of appreciation will be worthwhile, it is far more important that they show familiarity with the services of the committee and its value to the school.

No opportunity should be overlooked to include the names of committee members in school publications such as official bulletins, brochures, and publicity releases to newspapers and professional organs. Public addresses by school officials may include references to the advisory committee and its members. Such reference is especially appropriate in speeches to local civic and professional organizations.

One committee meeting during the year, perhaps the last one, could be a luncheon or a banquet. The program could be an "Annual Report on CE" with specific advisory committee services highlighted. Guests should represent all facets of community leadership and the board of education as well as the press and the local radio and television stations.

Another opportunity that should not be overlooked is the inclusion of advisory committee members on the guest list of the annual employer–employee banquet. The program should include recognition of the advisory committee.

There are other ways of recognizing and showing appreciation which should be employed judiciously by school officials. Such resourcefulness should eliminate the repeated use of shallow expressions which tend to become meaningless.

Suggested Activities

1. Prepare an agenda for the first meeting of the general advisory committee. Follow each item on the agenda with a brief statement of justification.

2. Prepare a small brochure depicting the purpose, role, and responsibility of the general advisory committee.

3. Design a plan for general advisory committee orientation relative to purposes and values of cooperative education and the contribution it is designed to make to the overall educational program.

4. Elaborate on the following statement: "The qualified teacher–coordinator is skilled in working with lay committees, and is well versed in drawing information from the artisan and in bringing it to bear on the purpose at hand."

5. Compose a statement, for administrative consideration and approval, justifying the appointment of a representative advisory committee for CE. Build the statement around such items as purpose, composition, importance, responsibility, and role.

6. Develop a program of work for a CE representative general advisory committee for a school year. Incorporate all areas of concern requiring advisory committee attention.

Part III

Teaching
Related Subjects

Introduction to Part III

A major responsibility of the school in cooperative education is classroom instruction designed to provide (1) technical information related as closely as possible to work experience, and (2) generally related information which will contribute to good citizenship on and off the job.

The first of these instructional areas is referred to as "directly related instruction"; the second area is designated "generally related instruction." The relative importance of these two types of instruction has been a subject of debate since the inception of CE. Some argue that technically related information is more important because of its complementary value in the development of job skills. Others will argue that job skill and job intelligence have little value for the individual who is void of the personal characteristics essential to getting and holding a job. Each school of thought may influence the emphasis placed on each type of instruction or perhaps the total exclusion of one in favor of the other. The well-versed teacher–coordinator, however, will be hard-pressed to discount the value of either type of instruction, but will tend to champion the value of both and to make an equitable distribution of time and effort between them.

Unfortunately, some states have not seen fit to establish content or time requirements for related instruction in CE, thus leaving the responsibility of determining what and how much will be taught to the discrimination of the teacher–coordinator or perhaps a local curriculum committee. For this reason a great divergence in what is taught and in the distribution of time may be found among programs from community to community. Content and time distribution policies established through central agencies should strengthen related instruction and eliminate the determination of its limits by teacher–coordinators or other local school officials.

The quality of related instruction is a dependable gauge of the total quality of CE. If it is strong, other vital aspects of the program can be expected to be strong also, because its vitality stems from the strength and quality of other parts of the program. For this reason it is not probable that the related instruction could stand alone in strength while other vital phases are conspicuously weak. On the other hand, strength in all of these areas will tend to generate strength in the classroom.

The effect of inadequacy in vital elements of CE may not be so pronounced in the generally related phase of the classroom instruction, because it is designed without specific occupational connotations. The emphasis is on the general needs of all workers in effecting satisfactory adjustment to the world of work and in the assumption of responsible roles of citizenship on and off the job.

Rationalization of the potential dilemma suggested above may account for emphasis on generally related instruction at the expense of directly related instruction, or the elimination of one or both areas in favor of a less difficult method of applying classroom instructional time. The related instructional phase of CE is a prime characteristic which distinguishes it from part-time work-experience programs or other arrangements which simply permit students to work part-time while going to school.

Chapter Eight is devoted to directly related instruction purposes, methods, materials, equipment, and evaluative processes. The treatment is in sufficient scope and depth to develop an understanding and appreciation of this important area of instruction.

Chapter Nine provides in-depth treatment of generally related instruction, including its nature and purpose, methodology, appropriate areas of instruction, and evaluative procedures.

Chapter Ten treats club work as the third instruction phase of CE. This designation is justified on the basis that meetings are frequently held during related instructional periods, and that club activities serve as excellent teaching vehicles for some areas of instruction. Some states have attached sufficient value to youth organizations for CE students to justify making them a requirement for reimbursable programs.

Chapter Eleven has to do with testing and grading in all areas of CE.

134

chapter eight

Directly Related Instruction

The purpose of directly related instruction is to provide CE students with technical information correlated as closely as possible with work experiences. This type of information has to do with the "why" of work experience and is basic to intelligent job performance and progress. The student who acquires appropriate technical knowledge and learns to apply it to the solution of problems encountered on the job should be able to project his thinking into higher occupational levels. This ability satisfies the second half of the definition of vocational education stated earlier, as follows: "The purpose of vocational education is to prepare individuals to enter successfully and make *progress* in chosen occupational areas."

Essential Elements of Directly Related Instruction in Diversified CE

The Related-Subjects Classroom

The cost and scarcity of classroom space practically eliminate the chance of a classroom being assigned for the sole use of a CE class. The necessity of sharing classroom space with other classes, therefore, creates the probability of problems and conflicts. For example, CE requires bookshelves in which to store occupational reference books, periodical racks for the storage of odd-shaped paperbacked materials, and pigeonhole arrangements for the storage of individual student notebooks and study guides. These fixtures, together with other classroom equipment normally used in directly related instruction, render a shared classroom vulnerable to the carelessness of other teachers and the curiosity of students in other classes. As a general rule, the molestation of reference materials is serious enough to eliminate the possibility of maintaining the necessary quality of filing and storage. In addition to this danger, the loss of books and other forms of references tends to be prohibitive.

The dilemma described above does not eliminate the necessity of classroom sharing, but it should inspire a special classroom design to compensate for the inadequacies of regular facilities. Such a classroom (see Figure 10) could be produced by remodeling conventional space in an existing building. It is probable, however, that the best opportunity would come with the designing of new school buildings which are a part of the future of most progressive communities. It is suggested, therefore, that teacher-coordinators and other school officials be alert to such opportunities.

Attention is called to the following characteristics of the CE classroom. Viewing the floor plan from right to left, the first section is divided into three specialized areas, designated I, II, and III.

Area I is an office for the teacher-coordinator and is partitioned with glass to allow for viewing of the classroom area. This view provides opportunity for the counseling of students while the directly-related-subjects class is in progress. Direct access is also provided to the corridor, making it possible for the teacher-coordinator to use the office while other classes are being conducted in the classroom.

Area II is devoted to the housing of bookshelves, periodical racks, and pigeonhole arrangements for the storage of notebooks and study guides. (See Figures 11 and 12 for fixture suggestions.) There are two doors, which facilitates the flow of students in and out at the beginning and ending of each class period. These doors can be locked to eliminate the entrance of students from other classes that will share the classroom.

Area III is a closet for the storage of instructional equipment. This closet can also be locked when the CE class leaves the room.

Area IV is a classroom area that can be shared with other classes without conflict or complications.

The dimensions included on the floor plan are minimal. They should be increased to the greatest reasonable extent within the available floor space. The CE classroom should be larger than the conventional classroom, if possible, in order to accommodate activities peculiar to related instruction.

136

Figure 10 Sample Cooperative Education Classroom

A: closet door 2'8" × 6'8"
B: closet door 2'8" × 6'8"
C: library door 2'4" × 6'8"
D: library
E: accordion door 2'6" × 6'8"
F: office door 2'6" × 6'8"
G: classroom door 3'0" × 7'0"
1: office desk
2: office desk chair
3: file, 2- to 4-drawer
4: table and chair, secretarial
5: notebook and reference book storage
6: magazine rack
7: bulletin board
8: chalkboard
9: seating, student
10: study tables
11: lectern
12: coordinator's desk and chair

137

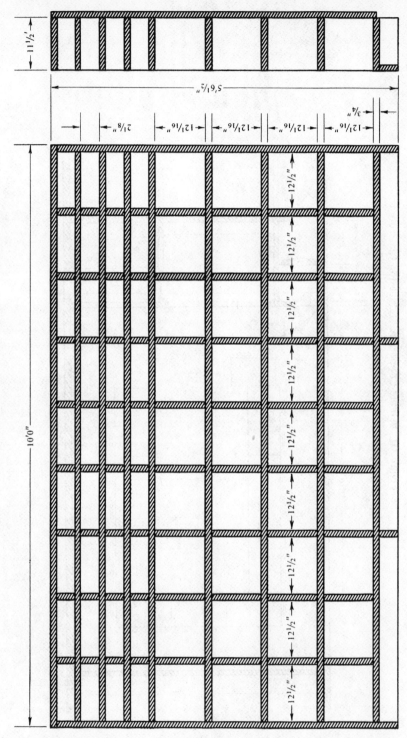

Figure 11 Suggested Notebook–Study Guide–Reference Storage

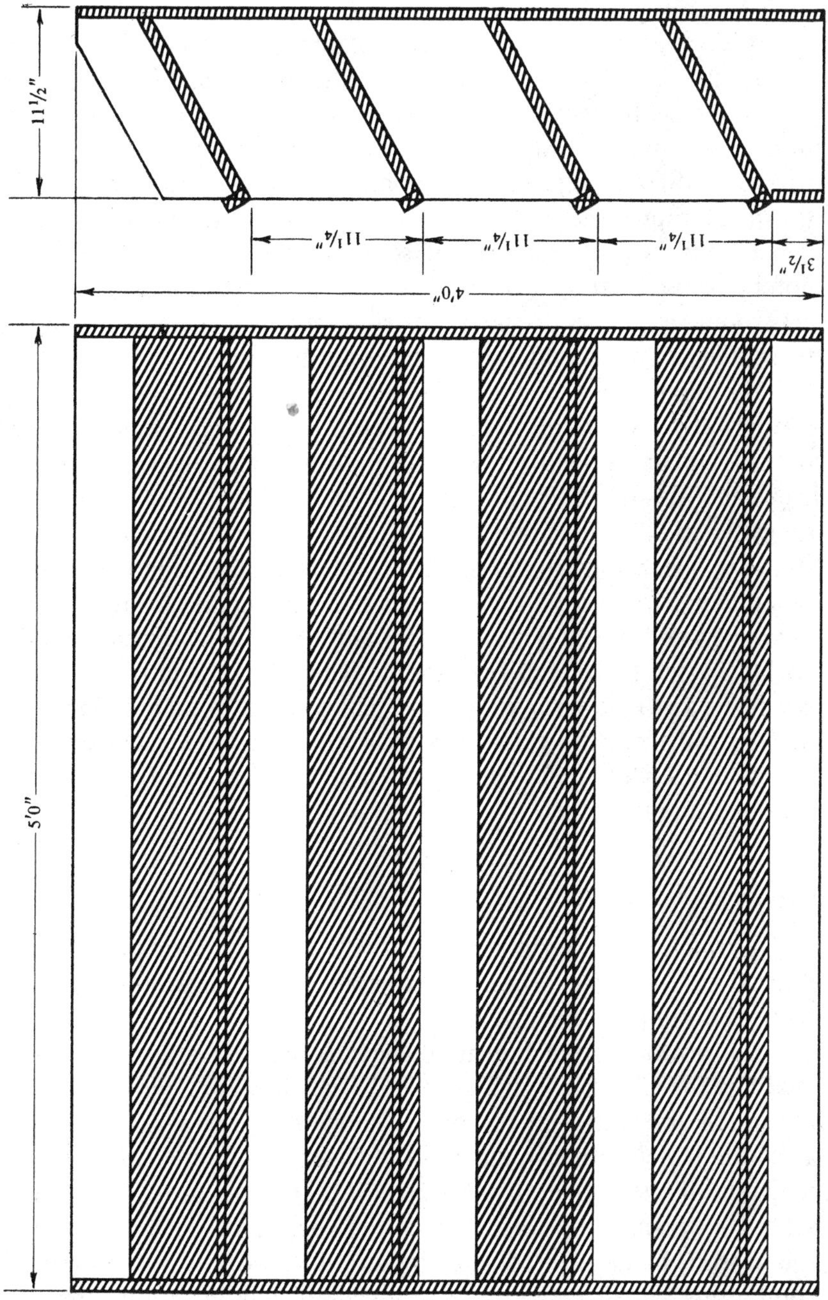

Figure 12 Periodical and Journal Rack

11¹/₂"

11¹/₄"

11¹/₄"

11¹/₄"

3¹/₂"

4'0"

5'0"

Classroom Furniture

It is sometimes difficult for school administrators to understand and justify the insistency of teacher–coordinators that the related-subjects classroom be furnished with tables and chairs, as opposed to conventional classroom furniture such as tablet-armed chairs and desks. The nature of directly related instruction is such that students are required to spend much of their time in working on individual assignments which may require the use of several reference sources as well as a notebook and study guide. The use of tables as suggested in the classroom floor plan provides sufficient tabletop space to accommodate these items, whereas the tablet-arm chair does not.

The flexibility of table and chair arrangements is highly desirable in related-subjects activities. The conference-type arrangement, shown on the floor plan, lends itself well to directly related instruction and is an especially desirable arrangement for generally related instruction. At times it may be desirable to effect table arrangements to separate students according to occupational interest or to adapt the room for other activities. From these suggestions it becomes obvious that the flexibility and multiplicity of table and chair arrangements would be a decided asset to related instruction. The climaxing attribute probably would be the ease with which the tables could be stored along the wall or removed from the classroom to accommodate extracurricular activities such as club meetings or open house for faculty, parents, and various student groups.

Classroom Location

A principle proved important to CE is that the classroom should be located in the same general area as are other classrooms in the high school building.

New vocational–technical educational centers often offer tempting facilities for CE. Accepting such facilities, however, violates the principle stated above in that it would remove the program from the general areas in which other high school classrooms are located. The class schedule of the cooperative student will be attuned to the regular high school program rather than that of the vocational–technical center. For this reason, being located separate and apart, often beyond convenient commuting distance from the high school building, would be a handicap rather than an advantage, even though the facilities are superior.

140

Reference Materials

The quality of directly related instruction depends upon the availability of appropriate reference books and other materials in each occupational area in which students are placed. Reference books are the tools of directly related instruction, and their absence would create circumstances for the teacher–coordinator similar to that of a shop teacher attempting to teach woodwork without the necessary tools. Directly related instruction cannot be provided without appropriate amounts and types of reference materials.

Securing Reference Materials Federal funding provided by the 1968 Amendments of the Vocational Act of 1963 eliminates the financial difficulty public schools may have had in obtaining suitable and appropriate reference materials in sufficient quantities. Funds should be available for such purchases in most states through state departments of vocational education. Inadequate or improper reference materials in the contemporary related-subjects classroom, therefore, suggest malfunction or negligence on the part of the local teacher–coordinator and other school officials, in that they have failed to assess their needs and file them through appropriate channels.

The stature of the occupations included in the CE program has a great deal to do with the availability of suitable reference materials. If, for example, the occupation in which a given student is placed does not require a learning period of sufficient length and intensity to merit being included in the program, it is unlikely that sufficient directly related reference materials will be in existence. This difficulty can be illustrated by the placement of a student in a job such as "bag boy" at a local grocery store. Directly related instruction for such occupational areas would have very little substance and would leave most of the time allocated for it to be dissipated in some other fashion. Individuals who are normally classified as good students could become problems in circumstances of this kind.

On the other hand, dozens of books, periodicals, and occupational journals could be made available to students placed in occupations which require suitable learning periods. The probability that funds will be available from local, state, and federal sources leaves only the exertion of the necessary effort on the part of local teacher–coordinators and school officials to ensure that ample instructional materials will be available. Such effort would consist primarily of determining needs, locating sources, determining costs, and budgeting accordingly.

Annual budgets should provide funds for the purchase of reference materials for new occupations periodically added to the program, the replacement of material lost or worn out, and the enrichment of materials in all occupational areas.

Funds should be budgeted in sufficient amount to purchase at least three good reference books for each occupation in which placements are to be made. Multiple copies of reference books will be needed in the more popular occupational areas in which several students may be placed. For example, the placement of five students in a single occupational area would require enough copies to assure the availability of reference sources at all times. The placement of one student as a laboratory technician, on the other hand, would require the purchase of a minimum of three reference books.

Technical reference books should be richly supplemented by materials available from a number of sources, such as the Government Printing Office, Washington, D.C. Bulletins, brochures, and periodicals are available in many forms in many occupational areas at low cost. There is also a wealth of free material that can be found by the alert teacher–coordinator.

Care should be exercised in selecting reference materials within the reading-ability range of CE students. Technical books, which are principal sources of information for fields such as electricity and electronics, are often written at reading levels far above that of the average high school student.

Storage of Reference Materials Reference books should be stored in the classroom area where directly related instruction will be carried on, or in specially designed space adjacent to the classroom. (See the suggested plan for bookshelves, Figure 11.) They should be arranged alphabetically accordingly to occupations. For example, books in occupational areas beginning with A may be placed in the upper left-hand corner of the book shelving, books in areas beginning with B may be placed immediately to the right, and so on. Filing books in this fashion should make them easily assessible to students at all times. The necessity of assessibility eliminates the feasibility of storing reference books at points away from the classroom, such as the school library.

Getting students to return books to their proper places may become a problem. The following suggestions should be helpful in this respect:

1. Arrange books in the desired order and position in each section of the bookshelves.

142

2. Give students time at the end of each period to replace properly the books they have been using.
3. Appoint a student committee to monitor the replacement of books at the end of each period.
4. Do not allow students to leave books and other materials on tables or at any other location in the classroom.
5. Do not permit students to remove reference materials from the classroom.

The filing of paperbacked periodicals, pamphlets, and magazines presents a much more difficult storage problem. The principal difficulty stems from the odd shapes and sizes of such materials. The suggested rack, illustrated in Figure 12, offers possibilities but fails to overcome many of the difficulties inherent in such storage. A student committee appointed to monitor the storage process should be helpful and might well develop a satisfactory storage system.

Classroom Supplies

Writing materials, including notebook covers, notepaper, and writing instruments, are normally provided by each student according to his or her needs. The desirability of uniformity in size, shape, and color to facilitate identification and storage and to satisfy other unique characteristics of directly related instruction may prompt the establishment of specifications to be followed in the purchase of these materials. For example, it may be specified that each student secure two $8\frac{1}{2}$- by 11-inch three-hole notebook covers, one black and the other red; a supply of notepaper to fit these covers; and two ballpoint pens. The uniformity of this material can be further ensured by providing the school bookstore, or business establishments handling school supplies, with appropriate specifications far enough in advance to provide time for stocking.

It is normally the responsibility of the school to supply an appropriate study guide for each student and to make available the reference sources to which it is keyed. The availability of study guides and attending reference sources should be considered as important factors in the selection of occupations to be included in the program. The advisability of placing students in occupational areas for which study guides and reference materials are not available is highly questionable. A possible exception to this policy could be an occupation providing ample reference materials, but for which a study guide has not been developed. In this event the teacher–coordinator should develop a procedural instrument suitable for student use in supervised and directed study.

Supervised and Directed Study

Supervised and directed study may be defined as a method of teaching that requires each student to have a self-contained, individual assignment each day that is not necessarily related to the assignment of any other student. The burden of acquiring the desired information is on the student under the supervision and direction of the teacher–coordinator. Techniques and procedures are usually devised to aid the student and teacher in selecting the assignment and the accomplishment of its objectives.

The probability that embryonic teacher–coordinators may have more difficulty in relating with this method of teaching than with more conventional methods which are applicable to CE prompts its thorough treatment in this chapter. (See the teaching technique beginning on page 162.) A more casual treatment of directly related instruction in occupationally specialized programs begins on page 164.

The supervised and directed study method of teaching is uniquely applicable to the directly related instructional phase of diversified CE because it provides opportunity for students to have individual assignments each day directly correlated with their work experiences.

Individual Assignments

The fact that individual daily assignments are necessary does not mean that they must be new or different each day. It does mean, however, that the assignment of any given student does not necessarily relate to the assignment of any other student. The practicability of a new assignment for each school day is ruled out by the fact that many of them will require several class periods for completion.

Daily assignments may be recessed in favor of new assignments necessitated by variation in work experience. The recessing of an assignment in progress is often justified by virtue of the student's need for introductory information in a new work-experience area. The amount of time to be applied to the new assignment before returning to one in recess is a matter of judgment on the part of the teacher–coordi-

144

nator. It will also be necessary that the teacher–coordinator determine the number of recessed assignments each student may hold in varying stages of completion. There may be a time when the student would not be permitted to take on a new assignment until the backlog of recessed assignments was reduced.

Correlation

Teaching through the supervised and directed study method makes it possible to offer the technical information needed at the time the student is most receptive to it.

This receptiveness will be at the highest level during the time the student is physically involved in the work experience with which the technical information is concerned. It necessarily follows, therefore, that the greatest possible correlation should be maintained between work experience and directly related study. The more removed assignments are from work experience, the less effective and the more academic they become.

To illustrate the type of technical information most appropriate for students, let it be assumed that the on-the-job experience of an auto-mechanics cooperative student involved a problem with the condenser in the ignition system with which he is working. Modern testing equipment would quickly indicate that the condenser was not functioning properly. Standard practice would dictate that it be replaced through a relatively simple manipulative procedure.

All of this may be done without knowledge of or concern about the construction of the condenser or its function in the ignition system. The CE student should, however, upon his return to the related-subjects classroom the next morning, follow through by recording the job on his weekly job-experience report form as "Tested, removed, and replaced an ignition condenser." (See Figure 13.) The assumption continues that this job experience might then become the subject of the directly related assignment and serve as the key to the use of the automotive study guide in the pursuit of technically related information.

After selecting from the automotive section of the bookshelves reference books which contain information concerning the condenser, the student proceeds with his study in accordance with instructions included in the assignment.

Students placed in areas such as food service, farm mechanics, distribution, business and office, health care, industrial, and service occupations would follow essentially the same procedure. They would

Figure 13   Sample Weekly Job-Experience Report Form

Student's Name	Occupation	Employer

SECTION A

WORK EXPERIENCE ON JOB	M.	T.	W.	T.	F.	S.	TOTAL TIME
1.							
2.							
3.							
4. *Tested, removed and replaced ignition condenser*	1¼						
5.							
6.							
7.							
8.							
9.							
10.							
11.							
12.							
TOTAL HOURS FOR WEEK							

SECTION B

DAYS	TIME IN	TIME OUT	TOTAL DAILY	
Mon.				
Tues.				Date (Monday)
Wed.				
Thur.				Amount of
Fri.				Pay Earned
Sat.				
	TOTAL HOURS			

146

Figure 13 *(continued)*

SECTION C: ASSIGNMENT SHEET

MONDAY:

Date _____   Job No._____

Subject: _____

References:_____

_____

_____

TUESDAY:

Date _____   Job No. _____

Subject: _____

References: _____

_____

_____

WEDNESDAY:

Date _____   Job No. _____

Subject: _____

References:_____

_____

_____

THURSDAY:

Date_____   Job No. _____

Subject:_____

References: _____

_____

_____

FRIDAY:

Date _____   Job No._____

Subject: _____

References:_____

_____

_____

SECTION D: COMMENT

_____

_____

_____

_____

_____

be concerned with the recording of their work experiences of the previous day on the job-experience report form (Figure 13), and using it as the key to determining their daily assignment.

The technical nature of the information involved in each case lends prestige to the necessity of correlation. The student is much more apt to grasp its significance and understand its application if subjected to it during or near the time of actual involvement on the job.

There may be circumstances that would justify the placement of difficult technical assignments under the supervision of a teacher in appropriately specialized areas when satisfactory arrangements can be made.

Weekly Job-Experience Report Form

The sample job-experience report form shown in Figure 13 is typical of those used for reporting the work experience of CE students. The fact that it is a form usually provided by the local school, as opposed to an official state form, presents the opportunity for the application of personal ingenuity on the part of the local teacher–coordinator in developing a special design to suit local conditions. Regardless of the alteration of design, however, the basic elements of the form should be retained. A new form should be issued to each student each week.

Section A is conveniently designed for the recording of daily work experience of CE students. This on-the-job experience for each day of the week should be recorded in appropriate spaces—with the exception that jobs repeated during the week should not be recorded a second time. The amount of time devoted to them should simply be placed in the column headed by the day of the week on which the experience occurred.

It would not be practical for the teacher–coordinator to require students to be overly concerned about the accuracy of the time recorded for each job. It is important, however, that an accurate record of the jobs encountered each day be maintained.

It becomes obvious that the proper execution of Section A will provide a résumé of weekly work experience of the student in terms of the different jobs experienced, together with the approximate time devoted to each of them. If the student should repeat a job on more than one day during the week, the total time devoted to it could be determined by totaling the times recorded for each day. This total should be placed in the total column at the extreme right of Section A.

The times recorded for other jobs encountered during the week should be extended in the same fashion. The weekly totals of time devoted to each job would serve as a dependable basis for periodic summaries which would yield valuable information, including the total amount of time devoted to each job during the period in question. This information could be presented to the student at his graduation exercises in the form of a certificate which would certify the time devoted to each job included in the schedule of work experiences, which is normally jointly determined by the teacher–coordinator and the employer at the beginning of the training period.

Section B is provided for the recording of the time of arrival at work and the time of leaving, together with the total hours worked daily and per week.

Section C provides a system through which the student can keep a record of study guide assignments attempted each week together with the references read. Although use of this section of the form may be considered as optional, it has value for the student as well as for the teacher–coordinator.

Section D provides an excellent opportunity for the student to record instances where he has found an opportunity to apply technical information gained in the classroom to on-the-job circumstances. He should be instructed to use continuation sheets if necessary. Good response here should merit recognition and reward.

Although the design of the weekly job-experience report form may be varied according to the ingenuity of the teacher–coordinator and local circumstances, its use is vital. To fail to require daily reports would be to sever the school's contact with the daily work experience of each student.

In addition to being an instrument of correlation, the job-experience report serves as a constant indicator of the nature and scope of on-the-job experience. Its value as a source of purposes for employer visitation is described in Chapter Six.

The Study Guide

The fact that supervised and directed study requires that each student have an individual assignment each day immediately poses the question as to how and by whom the assignment will be made. This responsibility obviously rests with the teacher–coordinator. Although the discharge of such a responsibility is possible, it tends to usurp an inordinate amount of the teacher–coordinator's time and probably would exclude the possibility of devoting appropriate effort to other responsibilities.

As a result of experience with early forms of the study guide, a format has evolved which partially corrects initial faults. This modern instructional aid is developed in three parts, samples of which are described as follows.

Part I. Occupational Analysis, Progress Record, Assignments, and Bibliography

Part I should include an analysis of the occupation in which the student is placed, combined with a progress record form. The analysis may be made to serve as an index to student assignments (sometimes referred to as classroom jobs). There follows in Figure 14 a suggested format for such an instrument.

Part I, which includes an assignment for each job recorded in the analysis, should be bound separately from Parts II and III. It should be issued to the student for his personal use.

Progress Record The progress record, which is combined with the job analysis as shown in Figure 14, illustrates one method the student can use in keeping a perpetual record of on-the-job and classroom progress. There follows a brief description of the procedure students should follow in negotiating this instrument.

When introduced to a new job the student should, upon his return to the classroom, place a line across the square ☒ opposite the name of the job in the job analysis, in the column headed "Progress." This entry will indicate to the teacher–coordinator that the student is in the process of learning how to do the job. As soon as the student is able to perform satisfactorily without instruction but still under supervision, the first line should be crossed ☒. When the job can be performed proficiently, the entire square should be shaded ■.

If this record is kept for each job, the column headed Progress will become a bar graph of the on-the-job experience. The dates of first introduction to the job and when the point of proficiency is reached should be respectively recorded under Begun and Proficiency.

The date that the classroom assignment in the study guide is completed and handed in should be recorded in the space opposite the name of the assignment in the job analysis, in the column headed Date Completed.

If the entire progress record is kept up to date as suggested above, it

Figure 14   Format for an Occupational Analysis and Progress Record

JOB NO.	TYPE OF JOB	JOB PERFORMANCE			REF. READING
		Prog.	DATE		DATE COMPLETED
			Begun	Prof.	
	Major divisions of the occupation in question, with attending jobs to be performed by the CE student, should be listed in this space. The total analysis will include as many pages as are necessary to record all the jobs included in the experience range which the student is expected to accomplish.		*Progress in the classroom and on the job should be recorded in this space as indicated below.*		
	Job worked on previous afternoon	⊠	10-7		10-17

Figure 15   Sample Format for Study Guide Assignment

ASSIGNMENT TITLE _____

ASSIGNMENT NO. _____

I. REFERENCES

(Available and appropriate references with indicated points of study will be listed in this space.)

II. PRESENTATION

Read and study carefully all references. Reread as many times as necessary those areas of information that are difficult for you to understand. Ask your teacher–coordinator for help when needed.

As you study, be especially attentive to, and take notes on, information pertaining to the following topical areas:

(Topical areas germane to the assignment title will be listed in this space as a guide for the student's study.)

III. APPLICATION

Write a summary of the information you find in your study concerning the preceding topical areas. Suggest as many applications to your job experience as you can think of. Ask your teacher–coordinator to help you make these applications.

IV. THE TEST

When you believe you have mastered the content in the assignment, ask your teacher–coordinator for the TEST.

Answer all questions carefully and fully. Solve all problems that may be included in the TEST. Do this without the aid of your reference books or notes and in accordance with instructions from your teacher-coordinator.

V. RE-TEACH

Questions that you cannot answer correctly will be indicators of informational areas you should restudy. Keep in mind that this technical information has value for you *only* as a part of the knowledge which *you* can apply to on-the-job circumstances. Confer with your teacher–coordinator concerning areas you need to restudy.

VI. THE COMPLETED ASSIGNMENT

When the assignment is completed, turn it in according to the teacher-coordinator's instructions.

152

Figure 16   Sample Format for Bibliography

Basic Reference Books
(Books to which the study guide is keyed will be listed in this space.)

Supplemental References
(Reference materials which will provide opportunity for additional reading and study for those students who should have supplemental assignments will be listed in this space.)

Note to the Teacher–Coordinator
(The bibliography in the study guide is an authentic source of reference book titles needed for the occupational area in question.)

---

will be an accurate indication of the progress on the job and in the classroom. It should be mentioned at this point that the student's understanding and acceptance of the importance and value of the progress record will have a great deal to do with its integrity.

Referring again to Figure 14, the indication is that the student under consideration has not reached the proficiency level in job performance but has progressed to the point of doing the job under the supervision of his on-the-job instructor. Although the classroom assignment was completed and turned in on 10/17, more experience is needed before job proficiency can be claimed. It can be assumed, however, that the student is technically well versed by virtue of having satisfactorily completed the research and study assignment.

Assignment The heart of directly related instruction in diversified cooperative education is the individual assignment which can be correlated with daily work experience. Figure 15 is a sample format for an assignment sheet which includes complete and detailed instructions for the student to follow. The study guide should include an assignment for each job included in the analysis.

Bibliography Each study guide should carry a bibliography including references to which it is keyed. A sample format for a study guide bibliography is shown in Figure 16.

Part II. The Test

The teaching process is not complete without a test to indicate the degree of learning which has taken place. For this reason all assign-

Figure 17 Sample Format for a Study Guide Test

ASSIGNMENT TITLE _____

ASSIGNMENT NO. _____

   I. True–False. Mark all questions T or F according to your best judg-

      ment. (Correct all statements marked F.)

         1. _____   (A minimum of 10 true–false state-
                                     ments pertaining to the subject
         2. _____   matter included in the assignment
         3. _____   should be recorded in this space.)

         4. _____

         5. _____

         6. _____

         7. _____

         8. _____

         9. _____

        10. _____

  II. Multiple Choice. Indicate the correct statement by placing the appro-

      priate letter in the spaces provided directly to the right of the question

      number.

         1. _____   (A minimum of 5 carefully de-
                                     signed multiple-choice questions
         2. _____   pertaining to the subject matter in-
         3. _____   cluded in the assignment should be
                                     recorded in this space.)
         4. _____

         5. _____

 III. Essay Questions

                 (Each study guide test should in-
                 clude at least one essay question in
                 order that students will be required
                 to express their thoughts in writ-
                 ing.)

Figure 17 *(continued)*

IV. <u>Problems</u>

> (At least one problem should be
> included in each test. Such prob-
> lems should require, in their solu-
> tion, the application of technical
> information acquired through su-
> pervised and directed study coupled
> with on-the-job experience.)

Note: Study guide tests will vary in length and type of questions and in
accordance with the nature of the subject matter included in the
assignment.

ments should include a test representative of the research and study the student is required to do. Satisfactory performance on the test should be a dependable indication that the student has mastered the technical information essential to intelligence job performance and future progress. The teacher–coordinator should not hesitate to require restudy of those technical areas in which weakness is indicated.

The sample format for a study guide test in Figure 17 is illustrative of the kind of test that might be given to the student after he has completed the research and study required by an assignment. The test should not be in the student's possession until he calls for it according to instructions. This stipulation indicates that Part II should be pre-pared in loose-leaf form so that individual tests can be issued when necessary.

The sample format for a study guide test in Figure 17 suggests that questions be designed to examine the extent to which the student has understood and retained the technical information included in the assignment. Students normally prefer questions in modern forms such as true–false, multiple choice, and matching.

They tend to believe that questions of this type will eliminate the subjective judgment or opinion of the teacher relative to the correctness of the answers. The elimination of the necessity of judgment in the evaluation process would be helpful to the teacher–coordinator in the light of his probable lack of technical efficiency in some of the occupational areas which are represented in the class. In any event the test should include at least one question which would require the students to express themselves in writing in terms of information gained from classroom study and on-the-job experience.

155

The principal difficulty in the use of objective tests resides in the fact that they can be used only one time, thereby necessitating that they be maintained in multiple copies in order to assure availability at all times. Consequently, the binding of objective tests into a single volume is impractical, whereas essay questions bound in this fashion could be effectively used many times.

Part III. Answers

Part III of the study guide should be a bound volume of answers to all questions included in all assignments. It should be properly coded to facilitate the identification of any desired listing of answers. It should be designed for the use of the teacher–coordinator only and should not, under any circumstances, come into the possession of the student.

A sample answer sheet is shown in Figure 18. The design of this instrument reduces the checking of the test to a simple process.

Student Use of the Study Guide in Supervised and Directed Study

Upon entering the classroom, the student should immediately post the daily job report form. (See Figure 13.) It is very important that this record of the work experience be kept consistently and that it be as accurate as possible. It should serve as the teacher–coordinator's daily contact with the work experience of the student. The student should be taught to make the record as meaningful as possible. To do so he must carefully identify and record new experiences as well as those previously introduced. The student who is not impressed with the importance of this information will tend to allow the report to become vague and meaningless.

If the work experience recorded on the daily job report is new, it could serve as the clue to the classroom assignment for the day. The student should confer with the teacher–coordinator in determining whether or not a new assignment should be initiated, or whether the assignment in progress should be continued. In either event, the first step in the use of the study guide is the determination of which on-the-job experience will serve as the basis for the current assignment.

If it is to be a new assignment, the next step would be to search the analysis (see Figure 14) for the job in question or one reasonably similar to it, to serve as the key to the appropriate assignment. After

Figure 18   Sample Answer Sheet for Format Study Guide Test

ASSIGNMENT TITLE _____

ASSIGNMENT NO. _____

I. True–False

   1. __F__

   2. __T__

   3. __F__

   4. __F__

   5. __F__

   6. __T__

   7. __T__

   8. __T__

   9. __T__

 10. __F__

II. Multiple Choice

   1. __a__

   2. __c__

   3. __d__

   4. __b__

   5. __c__

III. Essay Questions

     (The answers to essay questions
     may be written in this space or ref-
     erences may be given as to where
     answers may be found.)

locating the appropriate job the student should turn to the assignment indicated by the job number in the analysis.

The third step in the use of the study guide by the student would be to follow the instructions included in the assignment. (See the sample assignment in Figure 15, page 152.)

Initial Classroom Concerns

Teaching students how to conduct themselves in the directly-related-subjects classroom, which may differ drastically from the conventional classroom to which they are accustomed, is a most important initial teacher–coordinator responsibility. The normal departure from conventional circumstances is primarily in the areas of fixtures and equipment, teaching methods, and the degree of freedom that may be accorded the student. Students may be prone to interpret a reasonable degree of freedom to converse with other students and to leave their seats for legitimate purposes as the removal of all classroom restrictions to which they have been accustomed. If the results of such misinterpretations are allowed to go unchecked, chaotic conditions are certain to develop in the classroom.

It becomes necessary, therefore, to deliberately teach the student how to assume and discharge the responsibilities which accompany the informal environment of the directly-related-subjects classroom. Students may be permitted to be the master of their own conduct to a limited extent, if it can be done without disturbing other students who are in pursuit of similar objectives in their respective fields of interest. A properly conditioned CE class could conceivably achieve a classroom environment which would resemble the order and quietness which normally prevail in a well-managed library. The fact that ideal circumstances seldom prevail, however, suggests that the teacher–coordinator should be prepared to deal with conditions less than the ideal.

Experienced teachers will support the principle that it is easier to relax classroom requirements than it is to withdraw privileges and freedoms that have been permitted for a period of time. For this reason it is strongly suggested that the inexperienced teacher–coordinator establish a stern code of classroom conduct with the intent of relaxing it, in appropriate time, within the limitations imposed by the desired classroom environment. Accordingly, the initial classroom conduct probably should not differ greatly from that of the conventional classroom from which the students came, and the degree of relaxation possible will depend upon the classroom personality of the teacher–coordinator.

There are certain factors of classroom control which should be considered carefully by the teacher–coordinator before entering the classroom for the first time. Such consideration should include decisions relative to requirements to be imposed as well as the conduct to be expected. The new teacher–coordinator who anticipates initial re-

158

quirements and definitely determines what will be expected of the student should achieve initial classroom success. On the other hand, failure in this respect will almost surely result in failure to cope successfully with initial classroom problems.

Classroom Control Factors in Supervised and Directed Study

The recommendation that a minimum of the first ten related-subjects periods at the beginning of the school year be devoted to orientation (see p. 198) provides opportunity to teach the student what is expected in the classroom as well as other facets of the program. Successful presentation of the orientation unit should leave no doubt in the mind of the student about what is expected in personal conduct in the classroom and on the job. The test administered to the students upon completion of the orientation unit should be written evidence that they know what is expected of them. This test should be a matter of record in the students' personal files.

Being sure that the students understand what is expected of them is the first requisite of good discipline. Students who break codes of conduct which they understand are exceptions rather than the rule and should be dealt with accordingly.

Prime classroom control factors which should be carefully considered to the extent of preconceived decisions relative to requirements and expectations are included in the following list:

1. Entering the Classroom
   Upon entering the classroom students should be encouraged to assume an attitude of respect for the dignity of the classroom, which would include proceeding to their seats in a "businesslike manner" by way of the storage area to pick up study guide, notebooks, and reference materials.
2. Seating Arrangement
   Allowing students to select their own seats in the classroom may prove to be satisfactory, but it is more likely to satisfy personal desires at the expense of essential elements of good classroom environment. It is suggested, therefore, that seats assigned alphabetically will be more conducive to satisfactory seating arrangements.
3. Daily Routine
   Upon being seated, the student should promptly proceed, without

disturbance, in the fulfillment of the daily routine. This may involve the following:

a. Filling out the job experience report.

b. Continuing research and study.

c. Writing of summary paragraphs representative of the highlights of the reference materials involved in current study.

d. Restudying notes taken during the period of study.

e. Taking a study guide test.

f. Restudying informational areas in which weakness was demonstrated on the test.

g. Following special teacher–coordinator instructions.

4. Required Work for Each Student

The amount of work to be required of each student frequently constitutes one of the most difficult problems with which the teacher–coordinator has to deal. Students tend to expect specified and unified assignments, as a result of their experiences in conventional high school courses. In combating this situation, the teacher–coordinator should develop an assignment system which:

a. Will not require that a specified number of assignments be completed in a given time.

b. Will cause each student to treat each assignment on its own merits with reference to the amount of research necessary to fulfill its requirements.

c. Will compensate for individual differences through recognition of quality versus quantity, sincerity of purpose, application of technical information to job circumstances, and all other appropriate means.

d. Will include a method of scoring which will tend to evaluate the amount and quality of work done rather than the number of assignments completed or the time involved. It is suggested that a point system be developed which would assign numerical value to each assignment in accordance with the amount of study and research necessary to satisfy its requirements.

e. Will include other provisions that may be conceived by the teacher–coordinator which will cause students to proceed at their own best rate of speed with emphasis on the personal value of the information gained in the solution of problems encountered in the world of work, rather than upon the completion of any given number of assignments.

5. Classroom Freedoms Versus Responsibilities

The student should be taught that each classroom freedom carries with it a responsibility. Willingness to accept the responsibility should determine whether or not the freedom will be granted. Areas in which the question of freedom usually arises include the following:

a. Freedom of movement in the classroom. As a general rule, a reasonable degree of freedom of movement may be permitted if students can be taught to individually assume the responsibility of preserving the dignity of the classroom and respecting the rights of other students to pursue their assignments without being disturbed.

b. Freedom of conversation with other students. Freedom to converse with other students concerning areas of mutual interest which are involved in current assignments is sometimes granted. Although there may be some justification for a classroom policy of this kind, it should be understood by the inexperienced teacher–coordinator that students are generally prone to abuse such a privilege. It should also be recognized that monitoring the conversations to determine if they are legitimate would not be possible. The suggestion is, therefore, that conversations between students in the related-subjects classroom be reduced to that normally permitted in the conventional classroom. Compromising beyond this point will defy acceptable classroom controls.

6. Student Attitudes

The attitude of the student will largely determine the value received from directly related instruction. Attitude will also tend to regulate conduct. It is obvious, therefore, that teacher–coordinators should concern themselves with the cultivation of appropriate student attitudes. The following suggestions may be helpful:

a. "Sell" the concept that related technical information has value in the solution of problems encountered on the job.

b. Be sure that students know what is expected of them.

c. Have a clearly defined and well-organized plan of classroom procedure.

d. Be enthusiastic and sincere in all student relationships.

e. Be fair, firm, and friendly in the enforcement of classroom policies.

f. Predetermine what students are expected to do and firmly require that it be done.

g. Demonstrate personal interest in each student.

h. Plan your work, and work your plan.

7. Studying for Other Courses in the Related-Subjects Classroom

Whenever the importance of related technical information occupies a low position on the scale of values, the student is prone to attempt to use the class time for other purposes. The most common abuse of this nature is the use of class time to prepare for other classes, such as English. As a matter of fact, students, when left to their own devices, will often plan to use their related-subjects class time for this purpose.

The inexperienced teacher–coordinator will find it difficult not to be permissive in this respect, especially when the student presents a reason that seems to be justifiable. Acquiescence, even though it be reluctant, will tend to spawn more and better reasons each day, to the ultimate end that the related-subjects classroom will become a study hall by default.

8. Housekeeping
   CE students frequently enjoy sharing the housekeeping responsibilities inherently involved in the related-subjects classroom, such as:
   a. Removing paper and other materials from tabletops and floors.
   b. Checking and arranging books in library shelves.
   c. Checking and arranging materials in periodical racks.
   d. Checking and adjusting windows and shades.
   e. Arranging tables and chairs.

   If housekeeping duties such as those suggested above become a part of the classroom routine, a roster or other device should be designed so as to cause each student to be assigned for equal amounts of time to each duty.

9. Ending the Period
   An appropriate amount of time should be allowed for students to replace reference materials, study guides, and notebooks, perform housekeeping duties, and return to their seats for formal dismissal.

Teaching Techniques in Supervised and Directed Study

Teaching successfully through the supervised and directed study method requires that the teacher–coordinator apply a number of techniques inherent in the process. There follows a brief discussion of the most vital of these techniques:

1. Circulating the Classroom
   The teacher–coordinator should spend an appropriate portion of the instructional time in circulating the classroom for the purpose of:
   a. Being available when needed by the student.
   b. Being continuously aware of what the student is doing at all times.
   c. Assurance that all students are pursuing their assignment as opposed to other inappropriate activities.

2. Helping Students Determine Assignments
   Although students should be taught how to determine their own

daily assignments, their decisions should be closely supervised and approved by the teacher–coordinator. Judging whether or not an assignment that is in progress should be continued or a new one initiated should be a teacher–coordinator responsibility. It is through this process that the teacher–coordinator determines that the classroom study is properly correlated with work experience. This function should be largely consummated at the beginning of the period.

3. Helping Students Interpret Technical Information

CE students may have difficulty in reading some of the technical materials included in their assignments. It becomes necessary, therefore, that the teacher–coordinator be immediately available to help the student interpret the material being read.

4. Causing Students To Be Constructively Engaged at All Times

Perhaps the teacher–coordinator's greatest expertise rests in his or her ability to cause students to apply themselves effectively in the related-subjects classroom. It is within this realm that classroom discipline problems develop primarily in the case of students who have no desire or interest in acquiring technical information related to an occupation in which they have no career interest. Students who are placed in occupations compatible with their aptitudes and career interests are not likely to present problems of this nature. The fact remains, however, that the teacher–coordinator must find ways and means to preserve a classroom environment which is conducive to effective pursuit of individual assignments.

Definite policies relative to classroom activities should be established in the beginning with special reference to the use of class time to prepare for other classes and other inappropriate activities. There can be no compromise in the enforcement of policies of this kind. Study for other classes must not be permitted.

5. Counseling Students

An appropriate amount of the teacher–coordinator's class time should be devoted to counseling students relative to problems they have encountered in school or on the job. The amount of time devoted to counseling should be controlled by the urgency of the need on the part of students. Here again, the teacher–coordinator should be sure that counseling sessions are conducted out of hearing range of other students, perferably in complete privacy.

6. Oral Testing

Perhaps the greatest lesson CE students should learn is that the purpose of directly related instruction is to give them an opportunity to find, interpret, master, and apply technical information in the solution of job-oriented problems. They should accept the fact that related technical information has no value until it becomes a

163

part of their knowledge. In this respect they must come to understand that studying, taking notes, writing summaries, handing in completed assignments, and taking tests are means to this end rather than ends within themselves.

An effective way to check the retention of related technical knowledge is through individual oral testing. The certainty that such tests are coming is as effective as the test itself. This is particularly true if the resulting marks enter strongly enough into the determination of final grades. Oral test questions should be based on completed assignments which the student has turned in at least ten days prior to the date selected for the test.

Ability to answer the questions orally should be a dependable indication of the retention of technical information acquired in supervised and directed study. The oral test should be based on answers previously given to questions on study guide tests. The grading process should take place simultaneously with the administering of the test with the full knowledge of the student.

Students should be selected for the oral test at random in order that none will know when their time is coming. They should not be given opportunity to prepare for the test so that the answers to questions will be a true reflection of their knowledge.

The teacher–coordinator should be sternly fair in administering the oral test to the end that students will come to respect it as an opportunity to reflect their ability to retain and apply the technical knowledge they have gained through directly related study.

Related Instruction in Occupationally Specialized Programs

As stated earlier, this book deals with basic principles and methods applicable to CE wherever and in whatever form it is found. An exception to this generalization may be variation in the methodology in directly related instruction in those programs involving specialized occupational areas. Although the purpose of directly related instruction in such programs should be the same as that in the diversified occupational approach, the similarity of on-the-job experiences may render group instruction possible and desirable in basic areas of technical information. The principles of selling, for example, may be basic to most areas of distribution, thus well adapted to group instruction.

However, the need for technically related information in occupationally specialized programs cannot be entirely satisfied through the use of group techniques at the total expense of individual instruction correlated with work experience. As a matter of fact, to disregard the relationship between directly related instruction and work experience violates a basic principle of CE and relegates much of what is taught to academic status (theoretical without having an immediate bearing). The time inevitably comes when each student has need for technical information unrelated to the needs of other students. Failure to provide opportunity to acquire such information through individual instruction or study robs the student and tends to divorce the instruction from the work experience.

Perhaps the best solution would be to effect an appropriate compromise between group and individual instruction through the equitable assignment of instructional time to each form of instruction in accordance with local circumstances. If, for example, five periods per week are scheduled for related instruction, two periods might be devoted to individual instruction through supervised and directed study correlated with work experience, with the other three periods being devoted to group instruction in technically related subjects. Circumstances may justify reversal of this arrangement, or changing it to a more appropriate time allotment. In either event, however, neither form of instruction should be entirely excluded in favor of the other.

Teacher–coordinators who are preparing themselves for employment in programs involving specialized areas such as business and office occupations should become fully oriented in specialized forms of related instruction through teacher-education courses in their area of interest. Such courses should follow a study of this book and should deal in depth with related-subjects teaching methods and techniques, and the development and use of instructional materials.

The purposes and characteristics of generally related instruction should be the same in all CE programs. Teaching methods and techniques, therefore, should be approximately the same in occupationally specialized programs as in those embracing multiple occupational areas. For these reasons Chapter Nine is applicable to all forms of CE.

The remaining portion of this section is devoted to brief commentaries on related instruction in occupationally specialized cooperative educational programs.

Trade and Industrial Education

The directly related instructional phase of CE in trade and industrial education is conducted primarily through the supervised and directed study method. This is necessary by virtue of the diversification of the occupations in which students are placed. Chapter Eight, therefore, is entirely applicable to the directly related instruction in trade and industrial education.

Distributive Education

Cooperative education in distributive occupations may be defined as an educational plan which provides opportunity for high school juniors and seniors to acquire skills and knowledge in this specialized occupational area for which they have appropriate aptitudes, vocational interest, and personal qualities. This is accomplished through part-time work experience in selected local business establishments, under the supervision and control of the school, and related instruction in the related-subjects classroom.

All facets of this book are applicable to CE in distributive occupations as defined above, with the exception of some phases of directly related instruction. The probability that job placement in distributive education will, for the most part, be concentrated in occupational areas involving retailing, salesmanship, and marketing lends prestige to teaching in these and similar subject-matter areas through group methods and techniques without too much concern for the necessity of correlation with work experience. This conclusion is based on the assumption that classroom instruction can justifiably be designed to develop initial competency in these areas with secondary concern for technical information related to the principal products involved in daily sales experiences on the job.

The basic principles of selling and merchandising are applicable to the process of selling automobiles, insurance, articles of clothing, and so on. In other words, basic technically related information in distributive education becomes generally related information in the sense that it is of general interest and value to all students without regard for its relationship with specific work environments. Subject-matter areas such as retailing, selling, and marketing, therefore, can be taught in the same manner as are generally related subjects.

The preceding rationale may be acceptable as long as it does not exclude consideration of the inevitable need of students for information directly related with their own work experiences. The time comes, for example, when the student who is engaged in insurance selling needs specific technical information on insurance which is not related to the needs of other students. Accordingly, an equitable portion of the related instructional time should be devoted to individual instruction through supervised and directed study or other methods such as the "project."

Preparatory Courses

It is generally conceded that the work experiences phase of CE in distributive occupations would be strengthened if knowledge and a degree of skill in areas such as retailing, selling, and marketing could be acquired prior to job placement. Federal legislation strongly supports this school of thought through the authorization of the expenditure of federal funds for the "Project Method of Preparatory Instruction" in distributive education. Rigid standards are not established by law and the result has been a variety of operational patterns.

Perhaps the most logical of these approaches places preparatory courses in retailing, selling, and marketing at the tenth- or eleventh-grade levels as prerequisites to CE in the eleventh or twelfth grade. In this fashion the project method can serve effectively as a tool in the instructional process to combat the academic tendency which plagues preparatory courses when they are divorced from the influence of work experience. Such courses are strengthened when the project laboratory becomes an integral part of the instructional process.

Preparatory distributive education, which involves simulated work experience in a project laboratory, can be institutionally self-contained on approximately the same basis as other vocational preparatory courses which meet the traditional requirement that at least one-half of the school day be devoted to useful and productive work. Accordingly, at least three periods of a six-period school day should be devoted to appropriate study and related projects in the project laboratory. The environment produced in the project laboratory should approximate, to the greatest possible degree, that in which the student will subsequently work. All experience should be as near the real thing as possible in order that students may obtain a reasonable orientation to the world of work as they prepare for entry-level employment upon graduation from high school. A course arrangement could parallel CE with the project laboratory substituting for the on-the-job work experience.

A difficulty frequently experienced by teacher–coordinators in distributive education is the problem of compensating for double standards in enrollment policies which may result from any number of local circumstances. In such cases admission to preparatory courses may not be limited to students who have vocational interest in the instruction.

Consequently, such courses will fail to serve as effective feeders to CE or to prepare students for entry employment after graduation from high school. Under these circumstances instruction in preparatory courses may be reduced to an academic form which has little or no preparatory value for that which is to follow. On the other hand, enrollment policies for distributive education preparatory courses which compare favorably with those for CE in this field would cast students in tryout roles designed to feed those with proven qualifications into culminating programs of CE, or into entry employment in appropriate areas of distribution. This process would tend to eliminate those students who fail to measure up at appropriate points in the developmental process.

The Project Method

The project method should not be considered by distributive education teacher–coordinators as a new technique. As a matter of fact, this method of teaching was highly developed in vocational agriculture, home economics, and trade and industrial education following its conception and introduction by William Heard Kilpatrick in 1917. The principal responsibility of distributive education, therefore, has been the adapation of the project method to teaching in the field of distribution. In so doing, the principles and philosophy which were developed in other areas of vocational education should have served as effective guidelines in the adaptation process.

The properly conceived project in distributive education combines classroom instruction with supervised and coordinated individual or group activities or laboratory experiences which are germane to the occupational areas in which students are preparing for employment, without the utilization of actual work experiences. As a general rule, the project will be strengthened if simulated laboratory activities can be supplmeneted with actual work experience for given times and purposes.

Business and Office Cooperative Education

This program may be defined as an instructional plan which provides opportunity for high school juniors and seniors to acquire marketable skills and knowledge in business and office occupations, for which they have appropriate aptitudes, vocational interest, and personal qualities. All of this preparation is accomplished through part-time work experience in selected local establishments which require office personnel in the conduct of their businesses, and related instruction in the school. The similarity of this definition with that recorded earlier for distributive education implies strong compatibility between the two programs, which may account for the fact that they are administratively combined in some state departments of vocational education.

All areas of this book are applicable to business and office education, with the exception that a portion of the directly related instruction may be accomplished through group instruction. Here again the similarity of work experiences may justify group instruction in basic technical areas, such as typewriting, shorthand, filing, and so on. As was the case in distributive education, these areas of instruction tend to become generally related subjects because they are of general interest and value to all students regardless of the type of office in which they are getting their work experience.

These subjects can be successfully taught through group instructional methods without too much concern for their relationship with current work experiences. As is the case in all forms of CE, however, an appropriate portion of the instructional time should be devoted to the acquisition of technical information directly related to each individual's work experience. This balance may be accomplished through supervised and directed study, as described in this chapter.

The basic generally related information needed by students in business and office education should not differ from that in other occupational areas. For this reason Chapter Nine should be entirely applicable.

Throughout the development of CE in business and office occupations a frequent practice has been to delay placement on the job until the senior year. This delay may be necessary to provide time for potential CE students to take the preparatory courses in basic areas such as typewriting, shorthand, filing, and accounting. An arrangement of this kind may be more necessary in business and office education than in other areas because the employer, in many cases, will not be able to help the student to develop these essential skills.

The lawyer, for example, may be skilled in dictating letters but have no knowledge of shorthand or how to use the typewriter. By the same token, the retail merchant may have records to keep but little knowledge of recordkeeping. The fact that this will probably be true in all job areas in which business and office students are normally placed suggests that such skills be held as prerequisites to job placement. Entering CE as juniors may be possible if these subjects are available in the freshman and sophomore years. Difficulty in making such arrangements, however, frequently delays CE in business and office occupations until the senior year.

Other Specialized Occupational Areas

Cooperative education is applicable, in its modern concept, to other specialized occupational areas included in state departments of vocational education, such as agriculture, health, and home economics. As has been the case in the specialized occupational areas previously discussed, all aspects of the subject matter included in this book are applicable to these areas, with the possible exception of the methods employed in directly related instruction.

The fact that each of these areas has its own peculiarities from the standpoint of occupational diversification suggests that there may be opportunity for variation in the methods utilized in directly related instruction. In some programs the similarity of work experiences may justify the use of group instructional techniques. Here again the teacher–coordinator should be cautioned that such methodology should not be employed to the total exclusion of individual instruction needed to satisfy the inevitable need of each student for specific technical information directly related to and correlated with work experience.

The fact that such needs will not be currently related to those of other students produces a classroom situation requiring individual instruction, which can be accomplished through supervised and directed study or similar methods (see p. 144). Vocational agriculture, in its modern concept, is extended by definition to include all occupations compatibly related to agriculture. This definition extends CE potential in agricultural occupations to include occupational areas almost as diversified in nature as in trade and industrial education. Given programs of CE in vocational agriculture, therefore, may be sufficiently diversified to make supervised and directed study the prime method of instruction in its directly related phases.

Typical Problems in Directly Related Instruction

Problem 1 *Maintaining the correlative relationship between daily assignments and work experience*

Although the method of determining directly related assignments which has been suggested is philosophically sound, it becomes somewhat academic in the light of actual circumstances which frequently develop to create exceptions to the rule. It was stated earlier that daily classroom study should include technical information concerning the work experience of the preceding day. This suggestion will serve satisfactorily if the school can control on-the-job experience to the extent of holding it in a given area of concern until the directly related information is exhausted in the classroom.

Unfortunately, however, such control would be in conflict with another program characteristic in that the job experience can be expected to vary in accordance with the production schedule at the place of employment. The normal expectation, therefore, would be that the work experience may change from day to day, thus invoking the need for new related technical assignments before the one currently being pursued is completed. Exceptions to such circumstances would occur in highly specialized places of business, where the job experience can be confined to given areas for given periods of time.

The real problem is that in attempting to literally follow the principle that directly related instruction should be correlated with on-the-job experience could cause the student to shift attention too quickly from one area of technical information to another to permit mastery in any area. It becomes necessary, therefore, that the teacher–coordinator serve as the judge in determining the number of technical areas in which the student should maintain unfinished assignments and when new assignments are in order.

The complicated nature of the relationship between related study and work experience makes perfect correlation difficult to achieve. The more nearly the related technical instruction approaches perfect correlation, however, the stronger and more appropriate it will be. It is the ability to effectively apply the techniques involved in the supervised and directed study method of teaching, including correlation, that places the teacher–coordinator in the class "master teacher."

Problem 2 *Coping with individual differences in the directly-related-subjects classroom*

The carryover from conventional classroom procedures can be expected to cause students to request that they be given specific production quotas required to earn a given grade. For example, they may ask, "How many assignments are required per week to earn an A?" or "Is it necessary to complete an assignment each day?" The nature of these questions suggests that students can be expected to view assignments in the directly-related-subject class as ends within themselves rather than as a means of acquiring technical information which can be applied in the solution of problems connected with their work experience.

It may be difficult to explain that the assignments included in the study guide are not standardized in terms of the amount of time required. Some may be finished within one or two periods, whereas others may require several periods. For this reason it is not feasible to measure student classroom performance in terms of the number of assignments completed within any given period of time. Students should be cautioned not to be concerned about the number of assignments completed by other students because the amount and difficulty of the study and research involved in any series of assignments will vary to the point of destroying any possibility of a fair comparison.

Students should be instructed that it is their responsibility to work consistently at "their own best rate of speed" until each assignment is completed, without regard for the amount of time required or the number of assignments completed during any given period. They should be encouraged to accept the fact that the evaluation will be based on "quality and quantity" of work rather than on the number of assignments completed.

It was suggested earlier that ability to read well would be a valuable asset to the student in directly related instruction. As a matter of fact, the student's production in the classroom will vary in accordance with reading ability. Good readers should find themselves able to master the related technical information without difficulty. On the other hand, the poor reader may become the victim of a dilemma in attempting to read the technical content included in the assignment. At best, efforts to satisfy the assignment will be reduced to a slow and laborious process.

The probability that poor writing ability will accompany poor reading ability will further complicate the instructional process. It may also be assumed that students burdened with these deficiencies will be the victims of defensive attitudes developed as a result of the circumstances to which they have been subjected throughout their school life. Accordingly, the poor reader is in a problem area which must not be ignored by the teacher–coordinator. The poor reader who is left to his own devices may simply sit through directly-related-subjects classes, feigning study without disturbing other students. The attitudes mentioned above, however, may cause the student to develop into a discipline problem.

If the CE class includes poor readers, it stands to reason that some means must be developed to compensate for their deficiency. Creating a classroom situation which will satisfy this need will tax the ingenuity of

172

the teacher–coordinator. However, success in this endeavor will pay dividends in terms of student accomplishments which they would not have otherwise achieved.

Problem 3   *Adjusting to the deficiencies of the study guide in directly related study*

The development of study guides suitable for use in supervised and directed study is a tremendous undertaking. As a matter of fact, the task is so comprehensive and costly that no publishing company has accepted the responsibility for massive publications in this field.

The fact that there is no general agreement relative to the most desirable study guide format has produced a great divergence in the study guide forms that have been developed. This variation, coupled with the occupational spread usually found in a typical diversified cooperative education class, may produce the necessity of using several study guide forms. This diversity brings about classroom problems in that procedures and requirements have to be equally diversified, thus operating against a uniform approach to supervised and directed study in any given related-subjects classroom.

A persistent problem in the use of study guides is the tendency to consider them to be useless when major references are unavailable. The teacher–coordinator should counter this tendency by teaching the students the basic elements of research, including how to find, master, and use information for a given purpose. They should come to understand that the possession of this ability is a prime mark of an educated person, and will contribute heavily to their progress after graduation from high school. Success in this teaching effort will enable the students to proceed from the topical areas suggested in the study guide assignment without concern for the absence of specific reference sources. Study guide developers should refrain from keying assignments to specific chapters and page numbers. In lieu of specific keying, emphasis should be placed on the development of a comprehensive bibliography to serve as a guide in securing a broad variety of reference materials.

The fact that many study guides may not include a sufficient number of assignments to occupy the student for the entire training period requires that a system of developing supplementary assignments be devised. Such a system may be restricted to the efforts of the teacher–coordinator, or it may be designed to include the efforts of students. As a matter of fact, it could be a profitable experience for students to develop supplemental assignments in their occupational areas of interest. Accordingly, the student would be required to master the technical information involved to the point of being able to develop the test.

Experienced teachers will agree that the ability to compose a good test question is based on complete understanding of the subject matter to which it refers. For this reason the development of supplemental assignments should have student values superior to those of original assignments included in the study guide. The stronger students can be expected to cope successfully with this assignment. The poor reader, however, will experience difficulty and will need assistance from the teacher–coordinator, or perhaps from the more capable students in the class.

Problem 4 *Coping with classroom problems resulting from improper or inadequate student enrollment and placement policies*

It was stated earlier that vocational education can be given successfully only to those who want, need, and are capable of profiting from the instruction. Accordingly, those enrolled in CE without the preceding qualifications may contribute unacceptable behavior in the directly-related-subjects classroom. Their conduct may reflect reactions such as indifference, insistence upon inappropriate classroom activities, reluctance or refusal to pursue assignments, or negative attitudes toward school and work.

Such reactions are inevitable on the part of those students who find themselves involved in a situation which requires earnest concern and dedicated application, as opposed to their basic intent simply to work part-time for reasons other than to satisfy career purposes. Attempts to correct resulting circumstances through disciplinary action may well prompt varying degrees of classroom rebellion. Students may not accept efforts to force them to become concerned about uninteresting technical information related to occupations in which they have no career interest.

The seriousness of the situation will depend upon the number of students involved. If, for example, the majority of the students in the class were in this category, the teacher–coordinator would, in all probability, have to accept one of two alternatives: either remove the rebels from the class or capitulate to a classroom environment entirely out of character and unacceptable in CE.

Such a classroom situation may be characterized as follows:

1. Students seldom voluntarily become involved in appropriate classroom activities.
2. Excessive conversation among students.

3. Boisterousness to the extent of classroom disruption.
4. Insistence upon the use of the period as a study hall.
5. Excessive movement in the classroom with attending disturbance.

Accepting any combination of these circumstances will constitute loss of control of the classroom at the expense of those students who are sincerely concerned about acquiring technical information related to their work experience. Although a strong autocratic personality may control a classroom situation of this kind, there would be little chance of correcting it until a student selection and placement policy is established which will reasonably ensure that qualified students be admitted and that they be properly placed. The cooperative education class largely composed of qualified students would make rebelling students the exception rather than the rule.

The hopelessness of classroom environments resulting from faulty student selection and placement policies should not be confused with similar circumstances which will inevitably result from the teacher–coordinator's inability to cope satisfactorily with supervised and directed study for whatever reason. Such an individual will tend to allow unacceptable circumstances to develop even in classes with enrollments which include a preponderance of qualified students. Qualified as well as unqualified students will be prone to take advantage of classroom permissiveness and indecisive action on the part of the teacher–coordinator.

Enrollment policies will seldom be perfected to the point of assurance that 100 percent of the students admitted to CE will want, need, and be capable of profiting from the instruction. It behooves the teacher–coordinator, therefore, to be prepared to cope with less than perfect circumstances in the directly-related-subjects classroom.

Problem 5 *Leaving students unattended in the directly-related-subjects classroom*

Attention is called to this problem to alert inexperienced teacher–coordinators to the necessity of their presence in the classroom at all times if they expect to attain and maintain acceptable classroom circumstances. The informality of the directly-related-subjects classroom, as compared with that of the conventional classroom, produces a mutliplicity of instances where the teacher–coordinator has the choice of performing teaching responsibilities or engaging in other activities prompted by personal impulses.

For purposes of illustration, let it be assumed that a CE class has entered the directly-related-subjects classroom and is apparently busily involved in the routine which it has been taught to follow. This produces the opportunity for the teacher–coordinator to apply the teaching techniques listed on pages 162–164, or to succumb to the temptation of engaging in personally inspired activities, such as:

1. Visiting the principal's office.
2. Conferring with the counselor or other faculty members.
3. Making telephone calls.
4. Visiting the teacher's lounge.

By capitulating to the urge to satisfy these or similar impulses, teacher–coordinators lose the opportunity to fulfill their teaching responsibility in the classroom, and by so doing encourage students to disregard their own responsibilities. The assumption that teacher–coordinators can discharge classroom responsibilities in absentia is erroneous. As a matter of fact, they cannot control, or even be aware of, what goes on in their absence. The suggestion is, therefore, that the teacher–coordinator's presence in the directly-related-subjects classroom is essential at all times. This statement is made in the face of the possibility that teacher–coordinators may aspire, with time and experience, to achieve a relationship with students which would inspire loyalty in sufficient intensity to guarantee meritorious classroom decorum with or without their presence. Teacher–coordinators are cautioned that such a student–teacher relationship is seldom achieved and certainly cannot be depended upon in early teaching experiences.

Suggested Activities

1. Prepare a lecture on "Two-Way Correlation" for presentation in CE directly related instruction. Include an explanation of the use of the job-experience report form (Figure 13) as an instrument of correlation.
2. After a thorough study of the study guide in its three parts (pp. 149–157), prepare one or more lectures on how it should be used in directly related instruction.
3. Taking into consideration the initial classroom concerns (pp. 158–162), write a detailed description of the student decorum expected in the classroom. Include definite policy relative to such items as movement in the classroom, conversations between stu-

dents, study for other courses, and other forms of disturbing activities.

4. Design a chart or other suitable instrument upon which information can be recorded that will compare the presentation of directly related information in a diversified CE class and an occupationally specialized class in distributive education. Build the instrument around the five teaching steps on page 189.

5. Prepare a detailed classroom routine in diversified CE directly related instruction. Include all routine teacher–coordinator and student activities, beginning with students entering the classroom and ending with their exit.

6. Develop an assignment device which will cause each student to be assigned for equal amounts of time to each of the five housekeeping duties as they are recorded on page 162.

chapter nine

Generally Related Instruction

It is said that a vast majority of those losing their jobs do so because of unacceptable personal traits and characteristics rather than inability to do the work. The fact that numerous studies provide statistical evidence to support this statement is ample justification for devoting an appropriate portion of the classroom instructional time of CE students to efforts combating this area of deficiency. Ignoring the need for this instruction may place the school in the position of preparing young people for jobs that they may not be able to secure and hold by virtue of unacceptable personal characteristics. The relative importance of generally related instruction as compared with directly related instruction, therefore, is dissipated in the light of the necessity for both. Excess ability in either area will not compensate for lack of ability in the other.

Although generally related instruction should be occupationally oriented, it does not specifically relate to given occupations. On the contrary, it deals with the common elements of all areas of employment, thus rendering it of general interest to all students.

Purposes and Values

Citizenship Development

The importance of ability to recognize and adapt to the human elements of the on-the-job environment should not be underestimated.

178

Beginning workers are faced with all sorts of attitudes on the part of those with whom they come in contact on the job. Some may be hostile or indifferent, while others may be friendly and receptive. Behavior patterns should have been developed to compensate for the negative attitudes to which beginning workers are subjected, as well as to recognize and graciously accept those of a positive nature. A prime purpose of generally related instruction is to equip beginning workers with the sensitivity and social skills essential to the discharge of the responsibilities of on-the-job citizenship.

Successful identification with and adjustment to the world of work are prerequisites to good citizenship in the community in which the worker lives and works. Another important purpose of generally related instruction, therefore, is to provide the young worker with the knowledge and civic skill essential to good community citizenship.

Human Relationships

Understanding why people act as they do, when they do, is a valuable asset to beginning workers in their personal relationships with individuals at all levels. They should be equipped to recognize and compensate for the way those with whom they come in contact habitually react to negative as well as pleasing environmental circumstances. They should understand that getting along with people on and off the job rests in their ability to anticipate and understand their reactions to given circumstances. "Winning friends and influencing people," therefore, depends upon ability to capitalize upon and compensate for the habitual reaction patterns of those with whom one works, rather than the projection of an image of self-importance. An additional purpose of generally related instruction, therefore, is to equip the beginning worker with the psychological skills essential to the development of good human relations.

Personal Development

One of the greatest services the public school can provide for its students is to cause them to focus constructive attention upon themselves. Skillful teaching and effective leadership should cause students to become vitally interested in identifying their strong, weak, desirable, and undesirable personal characteristics. They should develop interest in the elimination of negative and the accentuation of positive personal traits. Students should come to understand that man fails or succeeds in life as positive and negative qualities predominate. It becomes a major responsibility of the school, therefore, to help the young worker to solve these vitally important personal problems. It would be impossible to place a monetary value on successful teaching in this area other than to equate it with the wealth of success as opposed to the poverty of failure.

Inspiring concern on the part of young people about themselves is relatively ineffective without appropriate follow-through media which will enable the individual to initiate and pursue a personal improvement program. It behooves the teacher–coordinator, therefore, to devise a variety of personal improvement plans in order that students will have a choice in the procedure they will employ. The story of Benjamin Franklin's efforts to improve his personality is always interesting to young people and should be a source of personal inspiration.

Work Habits and Attitudes

The desirability of any worker to the employer will vary in accordance with the caliber of work habits and attitudes. Unusual skill and knowledge may be of sufficient importance to cause the employer to overlook, for a time, poor and undesirable work habits. It can be expected, however, that the individual who is poorly equipped in this respect will be replaced at the earliest feasible opportunity. The beginning worker should be thoroughly aware of the importance of good work habits and should be required to consider carefully the basic elements thereof. Cooperative education provides unexcelled opportunity to practice and perfect good work habits before graduation from high school. Although the responsibility is divided between the school and the employer, the school is not relieved of the responsibility of inspiring concern on the part of students and the establishment of circumstances which will cause them to do the following:

1. Develop respect for the dignity of work through characterizing the job as an avenue of service to society.
2. Cultivate character traits such as loyalty, integrity, sincerity, and dependability, to the end that proper and appropriate attitudes will be developed.
3. Evaluate coworkers and superiors in terms of desirable and undesirable work habits and attitudes.
4. Select and practice desirable characteristics identified in the work-habit patterns of successful workers.

Basic Characteristics of Generally Related Instruction

Generally related information for CE students is classified as knowledge essential to the well-being of all workers, regardless of the occupational area in which they are engaged. This instruction will normally be confined to approximately 40 percent of the related instructional time, or two class periods per week.

The methods employed in the teaching of generally related information are similar to those applied in the teaching of conventional high school subjects. The nature of the subject matter and its relationship with actual circumstances in the world of work, however, produce opportunities to apply teaching techniques in greater variety than are usually applied in the conventional classroom.

It has been found that generally related information can be presented effectively in units especially prepared to satisfy specific needs of CE students. Each unit should be designed to equip them with a portion of the knowledge, understanding, and appreciation they need to successfully enter and make progress in their chosen occupational areas.

The following specific characteristics will describe generally related instruction in more detail.

Students Do Not Normally Have Textbooks

Adapting generally related instruction to the specific needs of cooperative students practically eliminates the probability that appropriate content will be available in a single volume. For this reason students do not normally have textbooks. This situation, aside from occasional special assignments, relieves the student of the necessity of preliminary study and preparation for generally-related-subjects classes. By the same token, the total responsibility for transmitting information to students is vested in the teacher–coordinator. The efficiency of this transmission of knowledge rests in wise selection of subject matter, thorough preparation, and the methodology employed. This arrangement continues to satisfy the principle that related-subjects classes should be organized and designed so as not to require outside preparation or study. This departure from traditional requirements is offset by the relevancy of the subject matter to the world of work, which presents students with daily opportunity to try out the principles taught in the classroom.

Classroom Activities (Students)

The absence of textbooks and the necessity for study and preparation for generally-related-subjects classes place great importance on student activity in the classroom. Such activity can be expected to vary in accordance with local conditions and the differences in teacher–coordinator concepts of what constitutes desirable and acceptable procedure.

The following student activities are typical in the generally-related-subjects classroom:

1. Entering the Classroom
   The classroom entrance should be virtually the same as that suggested for directly related instruction, with the exception that the student should pick up only those items from the storage area that will be needed in generally related instruction.
2. Participation in Classroom Activities
   After the daily job-experience report is posted, students should promptly prepare themselves to participate in the classroom activities scheduled for the day. This may include the following:
   a. Rapt attention to teacher–coordinator presentations, accompanied by the taking of full and meaningful notes
   b. Entering into class discussions
   c. Reporting on special assignments
   d. Relating and applying information to on-the-job circumstances
   e. Taking interim or unit tests
   f. Participation in any other classroom activity the teacher–coordinator may have scheduled
3. Housekeeping
   Keeping the classroom in order is just as important an appendage of generally related instruction as it is of directly related instruction. It is suggested, therefore, that the same policy be applied (see p. 162).
4. Ending the Period
   The probability that generally related instruction may not involve as much individual activity as does directly related instruction may reduce the amount of time required for "end of the period" activities.

Applicable Teaching Methods

The inexperienced teacher–coordinator frequently fails to recognize the necessity for the thoroughness of preparation required for the effective teaching of units of generally related subject matter. The probability that the content areas involved will not have been an important part of the educational background makes extensive reading and study an important part of adequate preparation. This need focuses attention on the absolute necessity of adequate reference sources for each unit to be taught.

The nature of generally related instruction is such that some significant details should be anticipated well in advance of the scheduled time for presentation of any given unit. Such details could include the selection and scheduling of special speakers and films, the preparation of pass-out materials, and the making of special student assignments. This lends prestige to the "program of work," which will be discussed later in this chapter. (See Figure 21.)

There follows a listing of typical methods and techniques which may be applied in the teaching of generally related subjects.

Lecture

The teacher–coordinator should plan his or her teaching to involve as many of the senses as possible. This suggests that lectures should be richly supplemented by the use of audiovisual aids, to the end that the students' opportunity to involve their senses in the learning process will be increased.

The fact that the sense of sight is many times more effective in its contribution to learning and retention than is hearing alone suggests that it should be employed to the greatest possible extent. If other senses can be brought to bear, the learning process should be enhanced accordingly.

Lectures should be designed to inspire class participation through discussion, asking and answering of questions, and the application of the subject matter to practical situations.

Speakers from Business and Industry

Speakers should be selected from business and industry in accordance with the subject matter being taught at the time of their visit. They should be asked to confine their remarks to relevant areas. For example, a personnel director from a local business or industry might be asked to speak on "What the Employer Expects from Beginning Workers" in connection with the teaching of the unit on employer-employee relations.

Students should be prepared for such presentations and should be encouraged to actively participate by asking questions after the speaker has completed the talk. It may be advisable to help students to compose, in advance, questions they will ask.

Students should also be taught to properly receive and appreciate their visitors. This would include giving them their undivided attention, asking questions at the appropriate time, and expressing appreciation. This is excellent experience for students and makes a good impression on the visitor. The inexperienced teacher–coordinator is cautioned not to expect students to perform satisfactorily without being thoroughly prompted in advance.

Special Reports by Students

Generally related instruction should include at least one special report per student per semester. Although such reports should be prepared for presentation to the class, some of them may be of sufficient quality to merit presentation to other groups in and out of the school. It may be appropriate, for example, to arrange for one or possibly two students to present their reports to a local civic club or perhaps a generaly assembly at school.

Although the subjects for student reports should correlate with current units of instruction, special occasional assignments may be made from such special topical areas as:

1. My job as an avenue of service to society.
2. The problems of society routinely solved through my job.
3. What it takes to get to the top in my occupational area of interest.
4. Qualities of success I have observed in my superiors at work.
5. Instances of the application of technical knowledge gained in the classroom to the solution of on-the-job problems.

Advance dates should be established for special student reports in order that correlated assignments may be made early enough to provide adequate preparation time.

Let it be assumed, for purposes of illustration, that a number of special assignments are made and scheduled for presentation during the teaching of the unit "Personality Development." The subjects of these reports may be selected from such topical areas as:

1. The importance of personality to success in the world of work.

184

2. Which personal characteristics of my boss contribute most to his success.
3. Personality as a reflection of character.
4. The basic elements of personality.
5. A plan for personal improvement.

It stands to reason that students will need help from the teacher-coordinator in the preparation of assignments of this nature. Suggestions should be made relative to sources of information and the format to follow in the preparation of the report. Students should be encouraged to draw materials for the report from their work experience to the greatest possible extent. As a matter of fact, the special report could serve as a medium through which the student is encouraged to identify certain elements of the work environment that may not otherwise receive attention.

Definite requirements should be established for special reports relative to the length of the presentation, the use of notes (do not allow the reports to be read), and the form in which the report will be turned in.

Panels and Symposiums

The symposium and the panel discussion (which are both more applicable with second-year students) are frequently confused, because they present similar physical appearances. They will both normally include a chairman and a number of coparticipants who will be seated behind a table on a stage facing the audience.

Similarity ceases at this point, however, in that the symposium is defined as a group of prepared written or spoken comments which describe different points of view concerning the subject matter under consideration. The chairman introduces the speakers, who in turn present their prepared statements. The plan requires that the audience listen to the presentations and then make up their own minds concerning the issue at hand.

The panel discussion, on the other hand, is normally composed of a comparable number of individuals each of whom are the possessors of special knowledge and expertise in the areas to be discussed. Such individuals do not prepare a formal statement but do prepare themselves to discuss various aspects of the problem from the standpoint of their special knowledge or experience.

As a general rule, the first part of the discussion is carried by the chairman, who orients the panel as well as the audience in regard to the questions to be discussed, introduces the panel members in terms of their qualifications to participate, and establishes the rules which will control the discussion. If audience participation is intended, the means by which it may be done should be clearly explained by the chairman.

After the orientation process is completed, the chairman will usually get the discussion under way by raising a question pertinent to the issue at hand. A panel member may be asked to react or it may be left open to reaction from any member of the panel. In either event the desired result is a lively discussion between panel members through the chairman. Additional questions should be introduced by the chairman as they are needed to keep the discussion alive.

For the sake of emphasis, let it be said again that although the panel and symposium take the same physical form, they are entirely different in action, which may, in the final analysis, accomplish the same purpose.

The Conference Method

The conference method (most applicable as a method of problem solving in second-year student groups) may be successfully applied if individuals composing the conference group have had mutual experiences. For example, a class of second-year CE students will have had mutual experiences in the realm of employee–employer relationships which will enable them to contribute to the solution of problems in this area. The mutual experiences of conferees are determiners of the subjects in which the conference method may be justifiably employed.

The success of the conference method will depend heavily on the ability of the teacher–coordinator (conference leader) to draw out, evaluate, and integrate student responses based on their own work experiences. The conference leader must employ tactics to inspire active participation in the discussion of questions and case problems related to typical on-the-job environmental factors, and must correlate, harmonize, and unify the combined reactions of the group in the solution of the problem or the answer to the question at hand.

In effect, the conference is the reverse of the lecture, in that the conference leader causes the class to tell what it knows rather than to present subject matter to it.

As a general rule, the major function of conference leaders is to control the discussion and preserve the serenity of the conference. They seldom express an opinion but rather serve as a medium through which the collective judgment of individuals can be summarized, pooled, and applied to the solution of problems. They reserve the opportunity for each conferee to contribute from personal experience to the solution of the problem under discussion.

Role Playing

Dramatization through role playing is frequently a most effective method of teaching, especially when the topical areas to be dealt with can be physically demonstrated in the classroom with enough reality to properly represent valid situations.

Role playing in areas germane to current generally related units of instruction may include such topical areas as:

1. Job interviews.
2. Making and receiving introductions (including the handshake).
3. Good versus poor health habits.
4. The effects of good versus undesirable personal traits.
5. Relating employee expectations to an employer (diplomatically).
6. Soliciting the help of a friend in the development and carrying out of a personal development program.
7. Acquainting a fellow employee with a handicapping personal trait or deficiency.

The teacher–coordinator may find it profitable to dramatize certain elements of directly-related-subjects classroom decorum through the assumption of the role of the student in:

1. Entering the classroom and proceeding to assigned seats.
2. Movement during the class period.
3. Performance of housekeeping duties.
4. The storage of materials at the end of the period.
5. Leaving the classroom upon being formally dismissed.

Buzz Sessions and Discussion Groups

The use of buzz sessions, discussion groups, and similar techniques are useful devices in providing opportunity for individual participation in the formulation of answers to questions or the solution of problems. Although such techniques are normally considered to be most applicable to large groups, the probability remains that application may, at times, be feasible in supplementing lectures and other methods which are utilized in generally related instruction. Let it be assumed, for example, that the teacher–coordinator poses certain questions during or at the end of a lecture. In a subsequent class meeting, these questions could be attacked by dividing the class into small groups and assigning the questions for discussion. Each group should be instructed to be prepared to report its conclusions to the entire class after a given amount of time. Each group should elect a chairman and recorder as the first step. The responsibility of the chairman will be to lead the discussion of the assigned topics. The recorder will record pertinent contributions. The chairman will summarize and report the findings of the group to the class.

The application of techniques of this kind will often inspire responses from individuals who would normally remain silent, thus encouraging total participation. The teacher–coordinator will find that judicial utilization of small-group techniques in applicable forms will often produce results which may not otherwise be achieved.

Lesson Planning

The importance of planning each lesson to be presented as a part of generally related instruction cannot be overemphasized, especially when the method to be employed involves the transmission of information to the class, with special reference to the lecture. The use of a definite procedure will contribute to lesson planning in an orderly fashion. The sample lesson-planning procedure shown in Figure 19 should be suggestive to the teacher–coordinator in the development of a plan suitable to his or her own purposes.

Although some variation of the planning process is permissible, the basic steps of teaching should continue to constitute the framework around which the lesson is developed. The sample lesson plan shown in Figure 20 illustrates application of the suggested lesson-planning procedure in the planning of a lecture on employer–employee relations. The outline of instruction should be expanded to the extent necessary to provide the aid needed by the teacher–coordinator in presentation.

Figure 19   Suggested Lesson-Planning Procedure

I. Preparation of the Learner (Motivate)
   A. Give the student reason for wanting to know what you propose to teach.
   B. Outline and emphasize student values.
   C. Relate what you will teach to something already known.
   D. Relate to that which has been taught before.
   E. Tell how it relates to that which is yet to come.
   F. Provide other appropriate incentives which are designed to appeal to basic motives to the end that the learner will be ready to receive that which is about to be taught. Until this attitude develops, the remaining steps of the lesson will be ineffective. (See Problem 4, page 206.)
II. Presentation (Tell)
   A. After adequate preparation, present the information.
   B. Be sure to present it in logical sequence.
   C. Do not try to present too much at one time.
   D. Encourage questions so you will know that the learner is listening.
   E. Emphasize key points by repeating as many times as necessary.
   F. Always teach from notes; do not read to students.
   G. Frequently, this step can be combined with step III.
III. Demonstration (Show)
   A. When feasible, combine this step with step II, Presentation (Tell).
   B. If a job is being taught, *show* the learner *how* to do it.
   C. When teaching technical information, give examples of how it applies or contributes to job performance.
   D. Use mockups, charts, and all other applicable aids in demonstrating.
   E. Ask questions and encourage the learner to do likewise.
   F. Repeat the demonstration as many times as necessary.
IV. Participation (Do)
   A. The learners have been told and shown—Now let them do it!
   B. If informational topic, let the learner illustrate its application.
   C. Let them repeat the process until learning has been accomplished.
   D. Supervise the *doing* closely, being sure to correct mistakes.
V. Test (Check)
   A. Administer an appropriate test to verify student learning.
   B. Re-teach if necessary.

Figure 20   Sample Lesson Plan

Subject: Employer—Employee Relations

Topic: What the Employer Expects from the Employee

Objectives:

1. To Emphasize the Importance of Employer Expectations of the Young Worker
2. To Acquaint the Student with Basic Employer Expectations

Preparation of the Student to Receive the Instruction—Motivation:

1. Reminding the Class That First Impressions Are Lasting
2. Telling Appropriate Stories Illustrating Proper and Improper Initial On-the-Job Conduct
3. Explaining the Importance and Value of Knowing and Understanding What the Employer Expects of Employees

Presentation and Application:

Outline of Instruction	Teaching Aids—References
I. What the Employer Expects A. Cooperation 1. With the employer 2. With coworkers 3. With customers 4. With others involved in daily work	A suggested reference: *Succeeding in the World of Work*, by Kimbrell and Vineyard, McKnight Publishing Company, Bloomington, Ill., 1970.
B. Integrity 1. Honesty the best policy 2. Some forms of dishonesty: a. Habitual tardiness b. Unjustified absence c. Slowing down d. Fudging on quiting time e. Soldiering f. Stealing from company property	List various forms of dishonesty on the chalkboard or by use of an overhead projector.

190

Outline of Instruction	Teaching Aids—References
C. Following instructions 　1. Compromise not acceptable 　2. Failure to follow instructions	Relate several cases involving failure to follow instructions.
D. Acceptance of constructive criticism 　1. Criticism contributing to improvement 　2. Profiting from, rather than resenting 　3. Difference between constructive and destructive criticism	Explain fully the difference between constructive and destructive criticism.
E. Dependability 　1. Arriving on time each day, a little early if possible 　2. Working with or without close supervision 　3. Knowing responsibility and discharging it without fail 　4. Typical results of failure to be dependable	Ask students to give examples of all forms of irresponsibility (list them on the chalkboard for discussion).
F. Loyalty 　1. Not complaining about company faults to friends 　2. Keeping company information confidential 　3. Supporting and defending your company	Explain fully what is meant by "confidential information." Ask students to relate incidents of disloyalty they have observed (mention no names).
G. Sincerity 　1. Sincere interest expected 　2. A lack of sincere interest resented by employers 　3. Willingness to learn 　4. Application of technical	Relate cases depicting insincerity with attending results.

191

Outline of Instruction	Teaching Aids—References
knowledge acquired in the classroom to job situations	Emphasize the use of technical knowledge on the job.
H. Respect for the integrity of work	
1. Excellence in work rewarding	Emphasize the avenues of success through the work ethic of America.
2. Work honorable	
3. Work necessary	
4. Workmanship a source of pride	This is an important topic. Get the strongest individuals available to help impress students with the "integrity of work" at all levels.
I. Maintenance of physical ability to work	
1. Your health your own responsibility	
2. Responsibility to develop good health practices, including proper eating and sleeping habits	Pass out a list of good and poor health habits. Discuss each of them.
3. Getting doctor's care when needed (don't blame your boss)	Emphasize the importance of the worker's accepting responsibility for his own health.
4. Absence on account of illness is just as costly to the employer as that for any other reason	

Test:

1. Why is it important for the student to know what the employer has a right to expect?
2. List and discuss briefly three of the most important employer expectations.
3. Explain how the student should react to unjust criticism.
4. What should the student do when in doubt about what is expected?
5. Comment briefly on the following statement: "The avenue of success in America is through excellence in work."

Preparing a Program of Work

The preparation of a program of work for the school year will enhance the effective teaching of generally related units of instruction. The fact that such units are not self-contained, in their most effective form, requires advanced planning to accomplish a number of their most essential features.

Selecting and Scheduling Units of Instruction

Perhaps the most important function of the program of work is causing instructional units that are to be taught to be selected and scheduled before the school year gets under way. This scheduling is the key to all the preliminary planning that should be done, including the acquisition of the necessary reference materials.

Scheduling Audiovisual Aids

The value of films and other audiovisuals in the teaching process has been established. The fact that such films, for the most part, will have to be acquired from a variety of sources requires that a date be established for their use and that they be ordered far enough in advance to assure their availability at the desired time. Films shown out of sequence with the unit of instruction to which they relate have little value and certainly do not satisfy their purpose in helping to teach the unit in question.

Scheduling Special Speakers

Special speakers should serve essentially the same purpose as other teaching aids in the teaching process. Appropriate presentation dates, therefore, are important. The industrial personnel director mentioned earlier, for example, would be out of place and ineffective in the talk on "What the Employer Expects from Beginning Workers" (see p. 183) if it were presented during the time that a unit was being taught on a subject unrelated to employer expectations. In addition to preserving the germaneness of this relationship, speakers can be selected and invited far enough in advance to permit them to arrange to be present and to make the necessary preparation.

Scheduling Student Reports

The program of work should provide a medium through which special student reports can be scheduled at appropriate times. Assignments can be made as far in advance as necessary to allow ample preparation time. Here again, attention should be given to the preservation of germaneness of the report to the unit with which it relates.

Lesson Scheduling

The amount of time required for each unit will depend upon the number of lessons each includes. Accordingly, the content of all units to be taught should be divided into lessons in order that approximate time elements may be determined. If, for example, the unit on employer–employee relations were divided into eight daily lesson plans, it necessarily follows that it, together with the ten periods assigned to orientation, can be completed within the first six-week period. Subsequent units may be scheduled so as to coincide with six-week terms if feasible. Such a time schedule would adapt well to the traditional school year, which involves six 6-week terms.

Sample Program of Work

Figure 21 shows a two-month excerpt from a sample program of work for related instruction. This sample should be helpful to the teacher–coordinator in developing the program-planning instrument. September and October were selected to illustrate the scheduling of the orientation unit and the first unit of generally related instruction. The process demonstrated in these two months can be continued throughout the nine months of the school year.

The sample-program-of-work excerpt establishes the first day of school as being Monday, September 4. This date should be adjusted in accordance with the opening date of the school in question. The first ten related-subjects periods are assigned to orientation, with the orientation test set for Friday, September 15. The unit on employer–employee relationships is scheduled to be introduced on Monday, September 19. From this point on, the generally-related-subjects period is divided so as to provide space for the scheduling of special activities or the use of special teaching aids.

For example, a special speaker is scheduled for Tuesday, September

194

26, and a film for September 28. The fixing of these dates suggests that the film can be ordered far enough in advance to assure its arrival at the appointed time. By the same token, the selection and invitation of the speaker can be appropriately accomplished. The unit is scheduled to be completed in eight lessons, ending on Thursday, October 12. The unit test will be given on Friday, October 13. A new unit on personality development is planned to be introduced on Monday, October 17.

The program of work should be completed for the entire school year far enough in advance of the opening date to provide the time necessary to do the specific planning essential to successful teaching. All dates involved in the program of work should be coordinated with the official school calendar.

It is obvious that a different program of work will be needed for second-year students, who are scheduled separately from first-year students.

Suggested Areas of Instruction

The content areas to be included in generally related instruction should be selected on the basis of the common needs of CE students. Although some variation may be expected, the general informational needs will be approximately the same. This similarity does not eliminate the probability, however, that individual differences will still be around to complicate the teaching process.

The great importance of the orientation period prompts inclusion of the following, relatively full, outline of the content, which should be included for best results. This outline should be expanded and developed into a minimum of ten lesson plans before its presentation is attempted. The teacher–coordinator should prepare very carefully in order that there may be no doubt left in the minds of students as to what is expected of them in school and on the job. Definite policy decisions should be made, before teaching begins, in all areas having to do with classroom and on-the-job decorum, together with a determination of the criteria and method by which the student will be judged. These elements should be clearly defined and fully explained during the orientation period.

The instruction in the orientation unit should serve to get the student started in work in school and on the job with a minimum loss of time and in a manner to make desirable progress in both areas. It should be pointed out that the teacher–coordinator must study through

Figure 21 Sample Program of Work

SEPTEMBER

MONDAY	TUESDAY	WEDNESDAY	THURSDAY	FRIDAY
				1
4 ORIENTATION	5 ORIENTATION	6 ORIENTATION	7 ORIENTATION	8 ORIENTATION
11 ORIENTATION	12 ORIENTATION	13 ORIENTATION	14 ORIENTATION	15 ORIENTATION TEST
18 DIRECTLY RELATED INSTRUCTION	19 LESSON 1: EMPLOYER–EMPLOYEE RELATIONSHIPS	20 DIRECTLY RELATED INSTRUCTION	21 LESSON 2: EMPLOYER–EMPLOYEE RELATIONSHIPS	22 DIRECTLY RELATED INSTRUCTION
25 DIRECTLY RELATED INSTRUCTION	26 LESSON 3: EMPLOYER–EMPLOYEE RELATIONSHIPS Special Speaker	27 DIRECTLY RELATED INSTRUCTION	28 LESSON 4: EMPLOYER–EMPLOYEE RELATIONSHIPS Film	29 DIRECTLY RELATED INSTRUCTION

OCTOBER

MONDAY	TUESDAY	WEDNESDAY	THURSDAY	FRIDAY
2 DIRECTLY RELATED INSTRUCTION	**3** LESSON 5: EMPLOYER-EMPLOYEE RELATIONSHIPS Student Skit	**4** DIRECTLY RELATED INSTRUCTION	**5** LESSON 6 Conference	**6** DIRECTLY RELATED INSTRUCTION
9 DIRECTLY RELATED INSTRUCTION	**10** LESSON 7: EMPLOYER-EMPLOYEE RELATIONSHIPS Special Student Reports	**11** DIRECTLY RELATED INSTRUCTION	**12** LESSON 8: EMPLOYER-EMPLOYEE RELATIONSHIPS Conference on Problems	**13** Unit Test on EMPLOYER-EMPLOYEE RELATIONSHIPS End of First Six- Week Term
16 DIRECTLY RELATED INSTRUCTION	**17** LESSON 1: PERSONALITY DEVELOPMENT	**18** DIRECTLY RELATED INSTRUCTION	**19** LESSON 2: PERSONALITY DEVELOPMENT Film	**20** DIRECTLY RELATED INSTRUCTION
23 DIRECTLY RELATED INSTRUCTION	**24** LESSON 3: PERSONALITY DEVELOPMENT Special Speaker	**25** DIRECTLY RELATED INSTRUCTION	**26** LESSON 4: PERSONALITY DEVELOPMENT Special Student Reports	**27** DIRECTLY RELATED INSTRUCTION
30 DIRECTLY RELATED INSTRUCTION	**31** LESSON 5: PERSONALITY DEVELOPMENT Role Playing			

each part of the program for the purpose of coming to definite decisions about specific requirements and policies to be introduced. A good job here will assure smooth operation and a minimum number of problems throughout the year. No effort has been made to divide the content into lessons, thus requiring overall planning by the teacher–coordinator before attempting to use the unit. If it cannot be taught in the ten days allocated for orientation, it is recommended that more time be used.

Orientation—A Unit of Instruction

Purposes:
1. To bring about thorough understanding of what is expected of students in the classroom and on the job
2. To introduce certain areas of information of initial importance to beginning workers
3. To acquaint students with proper methods in the use of the study guide and other instruments used in connection with work and study
4. To explain fully how students and their work will be evaluated at school and at work

   I. Purpose and Nature of Cooperative Education
      A. The general plan
          1. To provide opportunity for real job experience in an occupation for which students have appropriate aptitudes, career interest, and personal and physical qualities
          2. To provide an opportunity for students to acquire general and technical knowledge which will enable them to make progress while in school and after graduation
          3. To explain that the agreement under which students are placed on jobs is between the *school* and *employers*
             a. The job, a part of the school work.
             b. Credit for school work and job experience (cannot fail one and pass the other).
             c. All problems arising in connection with the job immediately presented to the coordinator (examples).
      B. Values to students and employers (see Chapter Twelve)
      C. State and federal laws
          1. Federal Insurance Contributions Acts—Federal Income Tax
          2. Child Labor Law and Wage and Hour Law

3. Workmen's Compensation Law
4. Social Security and Medicare
   (*Note*: It is suggested that these laws be introduced at this time, keeping in mind that a full-fledged unit will follow. Simply point out what the student should know in the beginning.)

D. Job requirements
   1. Student time on the job required to equal or exceed the time in school
      a. Not less than 15 hours of school time during each week at the rate of three or more hours per day.
      b. Work on Saturday and at other times used to bring total work time to the required amount.
      c. Total time per week in school and on the job not to exceed 40 hours (Child Labor Law).
      d. Student is expected to be on the job every day, with any variation to be with full knowledge and approval of the employer and teacher–coordinator.
      e. Explaining the job absentee policy.

E. Initial employer expectations
   1. Promptness—getting to work on time and beginning work without delay
   2. Being sincere—exhibiting sincere interest in the job assignment
   3. Being willing and cooperative
   4. Being properly dressed and groomed
   5. Being friendly with employer and other workers
   6. Sticking to the assignment given by the employer
   7. Being sure you understand what you are expected to do
   8. Always being loyal to the school and to the employer
   9. Observing absentee policy

F. School requirements
   1. Student expected to meet all school requirements
      a. Class attendance.
      b. Quality of work in other classes.
      c. Not using work as an excuse for not meeting all requirements in other classes.
      d. School absentee policy.

G. Related instruction
   1. Directly related instruction
      a. Explaining the schedule for directly related instruction (program of work).
      b. Reviewing the purpose of directly related study.
      c. Stressing the individual responsibility the student must

199

assume (more than has been expected of students in the past).

d. Stressing the importance of technical information as it relates to job experience (correlation).

e. Explaining that here is an opportunity for students to use their own initiative and intelligence in finding, understanding, and using information for their own benefit.

f. Encouraging students to take advantage of this opportunity to the end that they might develop personal abilities of great value to them throughout their lives.

2. Generally related instruction

a. Explaining the schedule for generally related instruction (program of work).

b. Explaining the purpose of generally related instruction and how it differs from directly related instruction.

(1) To provide information of general interest to all students.

(2) Explaining that such information may not always be related to job experience but will contribute to the individual's ability to adjust to circumstances and conditions on and off the job.

(3) Mentioning areas of information which may be pursued and why.

(a) Personal development.

(b) Human relations (how to get along with people).

(c) Employer–employee relations.

(d) Money management.

(e) Business ethics.

(f) Business law.

(g) State and federal laws.

(h) Health.

(i) Citizenship.

c. Explaining what is expected of students.

(1) Attention.

(2) Participation.

(3) Good notes.

d. Explaining plan for evaluation.

(1) Tests at appropriate times.

(2) Examination.

II. Classroom Procedure in Directly Related Instruction (See Chapter Eight)

A. Conduct expected

1. Entering and leaving the room

      2. Seating arrangement
      3. Explaining nature of classroom procedures as compared with the conventional classroom
      4. More freedom—more responsibility
      5. Student expected to exhibit interest in his own field of work and conduct himself accordingly
      6. No study for other courses during directly related periods
      7. Degree to which talking and other means of communication with other students will be permitted, emphasizing that all activities must be carried on so as not to disturb other students

  B. How the coordinator will help students during their directly related study (see p. 162)
      1. Help in selecting assignments (each student must have an assignment each period)
      2. Check correlation with job experience
      3. Help find and interpret information
      4. Observe individually what each student is doing
      5. Check progress records
      6. Counsel individuals relative to their problems
        a. School problems.
        b. Job problems.
        c. Personal problems.
      7. Give individual *oral* tests on study guide assignments to test retention of technical information
      8. Require the student periodically to prove correctness of answers given to questions in completed assignments (authentication)

III. How To Use the Study Guide and Related Instruments
  A. Purpose of the study guide
      1. Study guide designed to aid the student in study of materials directly related to job experience
      2. Study guide as an aid to study and not a *workbook*
  B. Demonstrate the processes of:
      1. Marking the progress record
      2. Locating jobs in the analysis with attending assignments
      3. Fulfilling the assignment
  C. Correlation
      1. Directly related study as closely related to job experience as possible (give some examples)
      2. All daily assignments selected as nearly as possible according to experience on the job the previous day
      3. Where this correlation not possible, student asking coordinator to help him make an adjustment

D. The daily job report
1. Each report sheet covering a week's work
2. To be completed and handed in on Monday of each week
3. Encouraging accuracy in reporting job experience
4. Insisting that each job experience be written in one time only
5. Each student with a job-report sheet as it is explained (work out a hypothetical week of work)

IV. Student Club Work (See Chapter Ten)
A. Purpose and nature of club work
1. Leadership development
2. Development of sociability
3. Educational experiences
4. Group recognition
5. To mirror nature of part-time cooperative education
B. Type of activities
1. Educational
2. Social
C. Employer–employee banquet
D. State convention

V. Grading
A. Explaining fully how the student's grade will be determined (see Chapter Eleven)
1. Directly related study (review evaluative criteria for completed directly related assignments)
2. Generally related study (review evaluative criteria for generally related work)
3. The employer's evaluation
a. Passing out employer's report form.
b. Reviewing each point.
c. Explaining that blank spaces at bottom of card will be filled in by the employer and will represent special skills related to the individual job.
4. Club work—how evaluated
5. Explaining again how the grade will be determined
6. Introducing grading form (p. 238)

VI. Summarizing
A. Reviewing and emphasizing the following:
1. Those things to which the student should give his immediate attention
2. Introducing and discussing typical problems students may encounter in their first contacts with their jobs
3. Emphasizing that first impressions are lasting

202

    B. Characterizing the teacher–coordinator's relationships with students and employers
       1. Best interest of students as individuals prime concern of the school
       2. Students expected to cooperate in every respect
       3. Students expected to assume their responsibilities to the employer and to the school
       4. Teacher–coordinator working closely with all employers (visitation)
    C. Reemphasizing values of program to the student with attending responsibilities
    D. What the student can expect if he will do the following:
       1. Accept and discharge his responsibilities
       2. Assume the right attitude toward all concerned
       3. Be a willing, loyal worker and student
       4. Cooperate fully with all concerned
VII. Giving a test on what has been taught
    (*Note*: Ask students for direct answers to questions which will reveal whether or not they understand what is expected of them in school and on the job. Questions of modern types, such as true–false, multiple choice, and so on, should not be used on the orientation test, because the student should not be given an opportunity to guess what is expected in the classroom and on the job.)

Additional Units of Instruction

Additional generally related units of instruction should be selected in accordance with the greatest needs of the student group in question, with first consideration being given to employer–employee relations, personality development, human relations, health habits, work habits and attitudes, and psychological adjustment.

Other units may be developed in such subject-matter areas as:

1. Parliamentary procedure.
2. State and federal laws.
3. Money management.
4. Job application and interview.
5. Citizenship.

Typical Problems in Generally Related Instruction

Problem 1 Avoiding procrastination in preparing to teach units of generally related information

Most teacher–coordinators are not well enough versed to teach the informational areas normally included in the generally related instructional program, without specific research and preparation. This deficiency requires preparation before the teaching of each lesson. There are several factors which contribute to this rather common teacher–coordinator deficiency. Perhaps the greatest of these resides in teacher-education programs, which, for the most part, fail to emphasize preparation to teach generally related subjects and to provide ample and appropriate background courses. In addition, the employment policies of many schools do not consider ability in this areas as a prerequisite to employment.

The preparation of an annual "program of work" for both first- and second-year students has been recommended in order that essential preliminary arrangements may be made for the teaching of generally related subjects. Failure to take advantage of such a predetermined schedule of instructional units, lesson by lesson, in securing essential reference materials in the subject-matter areas to be taught, may eliminate the possibility of appropriate preparation to teach. The first requisite of preparation is the availability of appropriate reference materials.

Some teacher–coordinators find it difficult to adjust to the difference in the formality of the generally-related-subjects classroom and the relatively informal directly-related-subjects classroom. The latter requires very little specific preparation because the responsibility of acquiring the directly related knowledge rests with individual students. On the other hand, the responsibility of transmitting subject matter to students in generally related instruction rests primarily with the teacher–coordinator. In directly related instruction the application of a multiplicity of classroom techniques requires very little preparation after they are mastered, while generally related instruction requires specific day-by-day preparation and the application of conventional teaching methods.

In failing to properly adjust to the differences in these classroom environments the inexperienced teacher–coordinator usually tends to allow the informal routine of directly related instruction, which requires no preparation, to carry over into the conduct of generally-related-subjects classes. This tactical error is accompanied by the tendency to meet generally-related-subjects classes without being properly prepared to teach. This lack of preparation is basic to a number of classroom faults, such as simply reading the outline of the scheduled unit to the students and requiring them to record it in their notebooks. A variation of this would be reading from reference books and requiring that notes be taken. Another alternative to which the teacher–coordinator might resort is to instruct the students to "get your study guides and go to work." This is the classic dodge which is most often employed by the unprepared teacher–coordinator.

There is really no acceptable alternative to "preparation to teach" generally related information. This fact is emphasized at this point to alert the embryonic or inexperienced teacher–coordinator to the necessity of budgeting time for the preparation of each lesson. The tendency to procrastinate in this respect must be overcome.

Problem 2 *Employing teaching methods and techniques in sufficient variety to eliminate the probability of monotony and boredom in the generally-related-subjects classroom.*

The teacher–coordinator who finds classroom discipline difficult tends to be guilty of malfunction in the generally-related-subjects classroom. Such an individual is often inclined to continue, without variation, any practice which seems to solve classroom problems.

Although the lecture, or some variation of it, probably will prove to be the most popular method of transmitting information to students, it should not be employed to the total exclusion of other methods and techniques. The teaching process may be greatly enriched by combining the lecture, at opportune times and under appropriate circumstances, with techniques such as panel discussions, buzz groups, and conference sessions. Such combinations are useful in treating questions and problems tactically presented in the lecture. All of these techniques are dependent on optimum student participation, the most effective safeguard against monotony and boredom.

Problem 3 *Keeping the instruction germane to the circumstances with which students are personally involved*

This problem does not refer to the correlation requirement in directly related instruction. It does, however, point out the danger of presenting generally related instruction out of context with reality. This mistake suggests that failure to relate the subject matter to actual circumstances with which students are involved in their total environment will relegate it to the academic realm in which many other high school subjects are included. In other words, "what the employer expects from the employee" would have little value as a body of information without being considered in the light of student relation-ships with their employers. By the same token, a study of grooming and dress as an important element of personality would be ineffective as information isolated from its significance to the individual in the world of work and in other phases of the environment. Accordingly, a portion of all lesson plans, regardless of the method being employed, should be devoted to the application of the information presented to real circumstances. In many instances such applications may be accomplished through student response to questions in terms of circumstances with which they are familiar.

Problem 4   Preparing students to receive information which is to be presented to them (motivation)

The suggested lesson-planning procedure in Figure 19 includes "preparation of the learner" as the first step in the teaching process. Unfortunately, however, many teachers tend to overlook the importance of motivation as a factor in students' tendency to accept information presented to them. The students are not likely to learn that which they do not want to learn. It becomes the responsibility of the teacher to activate the motivation process through the provision of a variety of incentives designed to satisfy the basic drives and simple motives of the students in any given class. In the case of CE students properly selected and placed, motivation should not present a difficult problem. As a matter of fact, it should be reduced to an explanation of why the information to be presented should be a part of their knowledge and how it will be of value to them.

The teacher–coordinator cannot assume that student groups will recognize the values of the information which is to be presented to them without being prompted. It is necessary, therefore, to devote sufficient time to the motivation step to assure that students are ready to receive that which will be taught. It is useless to proceed to succeeding steps in the teaching process before such receptive attitudes are accomplished.

The embryonic teacher–coordinator would do well to become acquainted with the areas of psychology which involve basic drives, simple motives, and incentives. Understanding the basic principles in these psychological areas will be helpful in accomplishing the motivation step in the teaching process. For example, the teacher–coordinator should come to understand that all human beings are subconscious victims of the "need for attention," to a greater or lesser degree. Accordingly, anything that individuals, either consciously or subconsciously, interpret as being an acceptable avenue to the attraction of favorable attention to themselves is a successful incentive. It necessarily follows that the teacher–coordinator's responsibility is to suggest that possession of the information to be presented, as a part of the students' knowledge, would enable them to act and react in fashions which would place them in a favorable light in the eyes of those they would like to impress. If the teacher–coordinator can successfully develop this idea in the minds of the students, the desired action will follow.

In dealing with a class, the teacher–coordinator must recognize that a single incentive cannot be expected to satisfy the multiplicity of motives which will be present in a CE class. It becomes necessary, therefore, to weave into the preparation step a number of incentives collectively designed to trigger the stronger motives which can be expected to be distributed among the class membership. A listing of such motives should range from "fear of failure" to "will to power." Although the process of coming up with an appropriate selection of incentives to include in the preparation step will tax the ingenuity of the teacher–coordinator, it will be well worthwhile in terms of the results of the teaching effort. It is in this phase of the teaching process that the master teacher excells.

Problem 5 *Compensating for the lack of textbooks in generally related instruction*

A traditional characteristic of CE is that generally related instruction content is usually developed in a series of units keyed to a number of reference sources rather than to a single textbook. This procedure has been necessary primarily because the diversified nature of the content usually renders it unsuitable for commercial publication in a single volume.

First-year cooperative students may experience some difficulty in departing from the traditional routine in regular high school classes based on a specific textbook. Such a routine normally includes a daily assignment of a specific number of pages in the textbook, reciting in accord with teacher instructions, review as a preliminary to being tested on a given number of pages that assignments during a given period have covered, and finally the test.

Since the absence of a textbook eliminates the possibility of such a routine, it becomes necessary for the student to acquire the information at hand in a different manner. One way of compensating for the absence of a textbook is by becoming adept in listening to and recording notes from teacher–coordinator's lectures in order to preserve the information and keep it available for reference throughout the learning period. Such notes should serve as a medium of study and review in preparation for tests in lieu of the traditional textbook.

The recommendation that the instructional process in generally related subjects be enriched to the greatest possible extent through "student-centered activities" should bring to bear more of the senses in the learning process than are usually employed in a "teacher-centered" textbook approach. Such practices should enhance learning and increase retention efficiency.

High motivation can be expected to result from the influence of the discovery of needs related to problems of adjustment to the environment in which the student intends to live and work. This discovery should produce an eagerness to acquire appropriate information which does not accompany the academic approach involving the use of a textbook.

The teacher–coordinator is the architect, builder, and presenter of the generally related unit of instruction. Failure in any one of these responsibilities, or to compensate effectively for them, will seriously detract from the learning opportunity of the students. The traditional textbook approach may hold some advantage in that the more able students could acquire the information they want, in spite of the teacher, by simply reading the textbook. Here again, the importance of the basic qualifications and preparation of the teacher–coordinator comes into focus. Human frailty and subject-matter deficiency are the greatest hazards in generally related instruction. Such deficiencies, however, can be effectively countered through study and meticulous preparation for each lesson.

Suggested Activities

1. Using the suggested lesson-planning procedure (Figure 19) or a reasonable facsimile thereof as a point of departure, prepare as many lesson plans as are necessary to incorporate the total content of the orientation unit which begins on page 198. Keep in mind that these lesson plans will be the basis of the teacher–coordinator's initial teaching experience.
2. Prepare an examination to be given as the culminating phase of the orientation program. The test should be designed so as to constitute written evidence that students understand what is expected of them at school and on the job.

3. Using the excerpt from the sample program of work in Figure 21 as an example, develop a program of work for the nine months of the school term. Although some adjustments may be necessary to compensate for unanticipated local circumstances, this schedule of activities should serve as a reliable basis upon which to develop the classroom program for the year.

4. Develop a plan designed to encourage students to apply information received in generally related instruction to job problems and circumstances. The plan should provide for feedback through students and employers.

5. After sufficient research in such psychological areas as simple motives, basic drives, and incentives, explain fully how they may be applied to the motivation step in the teaching process.

chapter ten

Student Club Work

The value of extracurricular activities in the form of student clubs in the educational program is well established. Membership in such organizations is so popular that it has been necessary for some schools to limit the number with which each student can be affiliated.

Interest in student clubs in the various phases of vocational education brought about the development of occupationally oriented youth organizations. These clubs differ from the typical high school youth organization in that their programs tend to become an integral part of the instructional program. They may also be designed to play an important role in interpreting the program they represent to administration, faculty, parents, students, and the general public.

There follows a listing of the most prominent occupationally oriented national youth organizations developed to serve the needs of students enrolled in the various federally reimbursed programs of vocational education:

Future Farmers of America (FFA)
Future Homemakers of America (FHA)
Distributive Education Clubs of America (DECA)
Future Business Leaders of America (FBLA)
Vocational Industrial Clubs of America (VICA)

The remaining portions of this chapter deal with the fundamental aspects of youth organizations applicable to all vocational areas. This information should serve well as a guideline to development of clubs at the local level, which includes diversified CE.

Purposes and Values of Student Clubs

The first step in the establishment of a youth organization is a full understanding and appreciation of its purposes and values. The teacher–coordinator should examine these very carefully in order to generate enough initial enthusiasm, based on appropriate premises, to provide the necessary leadership in the establishment of such an organization. This responsibility is mentioned at this point to emphasize, in the beginning, the importance of teacher–coordinator leadership. Although there are many other factors of success, none can overcome the lack of this vital element.

To Compensate for the Loss of Extracurricular Opportunities

When high school students enroll in CE they automatically sacrifice the opportunity to participate in many extracurricular activities, because these are normally scheduled during the time that the students are at work. A club organized for a student group should therefore have as one of its objectives compensation for this loss. It necessarily follows that all activities should be arranged at times and under circumstances which will permit CE students to participate. The germaneness of the club program to the current occupational concern of the student should elicit interest and enthusiasm superior to that normally resulting from participation in regular high school extracurricular activities.

To Serve as a Medium of Communication

One of the most difficult problems encountered by students is explaining the purposes and values of CE to those with whom they are associated in the school and the community. The student club should be a suitable and efficient medium through which to interpret the nature of CE. Club projects and activities should serve as a mirror reflecting the program in action.

To Provide Opportunity for Leadership Development

One of the greatest values of youth organizations is the opportunity they provide for the emergence and development of individual aptitudes for leadership. The fact that most organizations require the election of officers inevitably sets the stage for individuals to offer themselves for election either voluntarily or at the insistence of their peers. Being elected to an office is a reflection of peer regard and an expression of willingness for the favored individual to occupy a position of leadership. After being elected, however, the officer is burdened with the responsibility of faithfully performing the functions of the office in a manner pleasing to the club membership. Failure to please will be prima facie evidence that basic leadership aptitudes are not present. The elected officer will have failed to successfully negotiate the first step into the realm of leadership to which the peer group has opened the door.

On the other hand, the successful fulfillment of the responsibilities of the office will lead into more responsible positions of leadership available in subsequent phases of the life of the individual. Each success will bolster leadership ability and serve as an incentive to the individual to aspire to each succeeding level of opportunity. A prime objective of all youth organizations should be to provide opportunity for the discovery, emergence, and development of leadership potential. The fact that everybody cannot occupy positions of leadership suggests that the ability to perform the functions of membership (followship) in an organization is also an important personal ability. Another important objective of all youth organizations, therefore, should be to champion the development of ability to function effectively as a member. Both leaders and followers are required to accomplish meaningful programs of work.

To Gain Favorable Recognition

A basic personal motive is to achieve recognition as an individual. Far too often individuals fail, by their own devices, to satisfy this subconscious urge, with resulting frustration. Such individuals may discover that satisfying recognition results from membership in a live youth organization and participation in its projects and activities. The collective impression of the membership of the organization, through appropriate projects and activities, should command favorable recognition, while the individual, by virtue of his own personal efforts, may go unnoticed.

An important value of youth organizations, therefore, is the opportunity they afford for their members to participate in projects and activities of sufficient quality and importance to win favorable recognition in the school and the community.

To Provide Opportunity for Civic Involvement

Being a good citizen is not always a natural attribute of many individuals. On the contrary, such an ability may develop gradually as a result of a series of successful and satisfying civic experiences encountered inadvertently or as the result of conscious planning. Opportunity to participate in such experiences is often limited because the environment provides limited opportunity. Under such circumstances, individuals may fail to discover their own aptitudes for civic enterprise, with a resulting dearth of interest and involvement.

Opportunities for participation in the projects and activities of a youth organization should be an effective proving ground for civic adventure. Such participation should develop consciousness of and respect for the responsibilities of citizenship through school and community projects.

To Provide Opportunity for Participation in State and National Activities

The affiliation of local clubs with state and national organizations presents opportunity to become acquainted with peer groups in other sections of the nation. The fact that local clubs often find that the caliber of their programs is comparable, if not superior, to those in other locales is a source of self-respect and confidence. Discoveries of this nature are normally made through participation in activities and contests which are a part of state and national convention programs. Being privileged to participate in such programs is a gratifying experience often envied by less fortunate students. Traveling and competing with students from other sections of the nation presents educational and social opportunities which cannot be achieved in any other way. The value of these experiences to student club representatives demands that the local club program include projects and activities through which attendance to state and national conferences can be achieved.

To Provide Opportunities To Develop Sociability

High school juniors and seniors are often more or less delinquent in the social skills because they may not have taken advantage of opportunities previously available to them. Consequently, they find themselves at a disadvantage in coping with the requirements of social events.

Inadequacies of all sorts may combine to fashion individual patterns of social ineptness.

An important function of youth organizations should be to provide recreational and social activities designed to provide opportunity for the development of appropriate social skills. It may even be advisable to meet the problem head on by providing formal instruction in areas where greatest deficiencies exist. For example, dancing lessons or perhaps lessons in bridge or other appropriate card games may be provided for those who are receptive to such instruction.

To Provide Educational and Professional Experiences

Cooperative education students who are placed in an occupational area in which they have career interest tend to be concerned about any personal development which is interpreted to be a contribution to their educational and professional stature. This tendency provides a fertile field in which to cultivate attributes which enhance leadership ability through the employment of such skills as:

1. Conducting a meeting according to Robert's Rules of Order.
2. Participation in a meeting through the making of motions and resolutions appropriate to the situation at hand.
3. Reacting to and discussing motions and resolutions presented by others.
4. Ability to prepare and deliver a public address.
5. The introduction of guests and speakers on formal occasions.
6. Organizing and directing the functions of an organization.
7. The discharge of responsibilities at all levels in carrying out club projects.

Characteristics of Successful Student Club Programs

A successfully organized and operated youth organization will invariably reflect certain identifiable characteristics. A recording of such characteristics should constitute acceptable guidelines in program development as well as criteria for evaluative purposes.

There follows a list of typical success factors, together with pertinent commentaries.

214

Attitude of the Teacher–Coordinator

The teacher–coordinator should recognize from the beginning that the success of a student club will depend to a great extent upon interest and willingness to devote time to it. The probability that the program of such an organization will involve many activities which occur outside of the usual work day suggests that the coordinator would need to be available during periods which may be in conflict with leisure time. Willingness to make this kind of sacrifice is a factor of success in the operation of a student club program.

Such an attitude will depend upon the intensity of the teacher–coordinator's concern for the welfare of students and respect for the values of club activities. Negative or indifferent attitudes will cause neglect of responsibility or will discourage club activities during leisure periods. In either event the possibility of recreational and social functions will be practically eliminated, thus failing by default to satisfy an important area of student needs.

Attitudes such as those suggested above will frequently account for inactive student clubs or may prompt their organization solely for the purpose of satisfying a school policy or perhaps the insistence of an outside agency to which the teacher–coordinator is responsible, such as a state department of vocational education. A student club organized to satisfy purposes of this kind can easily be relegated to superficial existence, functioning only at times when it is necessary or expedient to prove its existence.

Student Leadership

Students are prone to misinterpret the election of officers to be a popularity contest. Such an attitude would not ensure the emergence of capable leadership. On the contrary, it would tend to elevate individuals to office who were currently enjoying popularity for reasons not necessarily related to potential leadership ability. In addition to the suggestion that the need for strong leadership should be fully discussed with the student group before the election of officers, the teacher–coordinator may find it advisable to serve as an ex-officio member of the nominating committee.

From this vantage point the adviser can cause potential nominees to be considered from the standpoint of leadership potential rather than from popularity stemming from some other source. A student club that can effect and maintain a plan for the selection and election of its officers which will ensure the emergence of the strongest possible leadership from its ranks will have matured to the point of being capable of engineering its own destiny.

A Plan of Operation

The program of an on-going student club should reflect the results of capable and effective leadership through such characteristics as the following:

1. Meetings are regularly scheduled in sufficient number to facilitate an active program and to maintain meaningful continuity.
2. Meetings are conducted in accordance with an appropriate ritual and an established order of business which is desirable and attractive to students.
3. All business is transacted through the employment of Robert's Rules of Order or a reasonable facsimile thereof.
4. Dues are fixed and are paid regularly by the entire membership.
5. There is a program of work which includes worthwhile projects in social, educational, and civic areas.
6. Each member of the club is afforded meaningful involvement in the program of activities through the assignment of appropriate responsibility.
7. An annual budget is prepared at the beginning of the school year, together with a definite plan to finance the projects it includes.

Policies such as those described above will result only from persistent and capable leadership. Student clubs with plans of operation satisfying such criteria will be capable of harnessing the capability of entire memberships and of applying it to worthwhile projects and activities in the school and community. The net results of such a group accomplishment would be favorable recognition from the community and personal growth on the part of each club member.

The Club Project

The project has been characterized as an important medium through which many of the values of student clubs can be attained. It seems, therefore, that a suggested procedure would be in order.

216

Selecting the Club Project

The leadership and wisdom of the teacher–coordinator are most important in the consideration of club projects for the year. It should be his or her prerogative to suggest suitable projects in all areas in which the club program is to be developed. Consideration of the suggestions, however, is a matter of concern of the club as a whole. The entire club membership should participate in the selection of projects for in-depth consideration. Projects identified in this fashion should be considered by the group from the following standpoints:

1. Feasibility relative to the collective interest and ability of the student group.
2. Appropriateness with respect to the purposes of the club.
3. The cost in relationship with the financial ability of the club.

Another important teacher–coordinator function is to insist that an equitable balance be maintained among educational, social, and public service projects.

The following listing of suggested projects should be helpful:

Typical Educational Projects

1. Sponsoring a leadership training conference for newly elected club officers throughout the school.
2. Sponsoring special events, such as a back-to-school day or an alumni day.
3. Planning and presenting a program at a school assembly, a local civic club, or other suitable audience.
4. Planning and financing attendance to a state convention.
5. Preparing an open house program for faculty, administration, or parents.
6. Planning programs for a regular club meeting to include such educational activities as special speakers and films.
7. Planning, promoting, and conducting events such as an annual employer–employee banquet.

Typical Public Service Projects

1. Adopting a needy family at Thanksgiving time.
2. Adopting an orphan for Christmas.
3. Assisting in taking a school census.

217

4. Designing, locating, and erecting highway signs in accordance with public interest.
5. Joining other school clubs in a worthy public service project.
6. Joining a local civic club in a community project.

Typical Social Events

1. Dance.
2. Skating party.
3. Picnics.
4. Seasonal parties.
5. Receptions.
6. Luncheons.
7. Other currently popular social events.

Suggested Method of Attacking a Project

One of the most important lessons an embryonic leader can learn is how to get a project under way. Although this procedure may take a number of forms, its central core will involve the following parts.

Establish Project Purposes

Understanding and accepting the purposes of a given project on the part of the club membership is the first requisite of success. The president of the club, assisted by the teacher–coordinator, should lead the group in the establishment of purposes and in their interpretation in terms of expected outcomes. The enthusiasm reflected by the group can be taken as a reliable indication of the probable success of the project in question. A project that elicits little or no enthusiasm from the membership of the club probably should be reconsidered. Let it be assumed, for example, that an educational project such as an open house for the faculty were to be assigned an appropriate combination of the following purposes:

1. To develop a better understanding of CE on the part of the high school faculty.
2. To display evidences of student accomplishment in related instructional activities.

3. To demonstrate how related instruction is accomplished.
4. To give students an opportunity to assume and discharge host responsibilities and to gain experience in appropriate social behavior.
5. To fix attention on appropriate grooming and dress.
6. To afford opportunity for leadership development.

Preparing an Annual Budget

After the club membership, as a whole, has selected the projects and activities to be included in its program for the year, an annual budget should be prepared. This responsibility may be delegated to a special finance committee for initial consideration, to be followed by action of the club membership, as a committee of the whole.

Let it be assumed,for example, that a given club determines that the following projects and activities will be included in its annual program:

Educational Projects
1. Open house for faculty	$50.00
2. Sponsoring alumni day	$50.00
3. Planning programs for regular meetings to include special features and refreshments	$100.00
4. Employer–employee banquet	$300.00
5. Travel to state convention	$250.00

Public Service Projects
1. Adopting a needy family for Thanksgiving	$50.00
2. Adopting an orphan at Christmas	$50.00
3. Joining a local civic club in a worthy and appropriate public service project	$100.00

Social Events
1. Quarterly breakfast meetings	$180.00
2. Christmas party	$100.00
3. Fall and spring picnics	$100.00

General Operating Expenses
1. Miscellaneous	$100.00
Total	$1,430.00

The finance committee should assign the most accurate estimate it can make of the cost of each item included in the proposed program, as shown. In this instance $1,430 may be an acceptable estimate of the fiscal needs of the club for the year. The chairman of the finance committee should present the budget proposal in this amount to the club as a whole for consideration and approval.

Funding the Budget

The entire club membership should be included in the consideration of the various types of fund-raising projects appropriate and feasible. The club president, assisted by the teacher–coordinator, should lead this group consideration, which should culminate in the adoption of projects in sufficient scope and number to raise the estimated amount of money needed to finance the annual budget.

Perhaps the first source of revenue to occur to the student group will be the regular dues to be paid by each club member. This source may be acceptable to new students as an initial reaction to the very pleasant realization that they will be earning, perhaps for the first time, a regular monetary wage. Their attitude may be "Why not! I will have plenty of money." Wise leadership, however, should prevail in advising that willingness to participate in fund-raising projects should eliminate the necessity of the club membership to tax itself to the point of financing the entire budget. This alternative should cause the dues to be fixed at a level which would not constitute an unbearable burden and would inspire their payment throughout the year.

The following list of typical fund-raising projects should be supplemented by suggestions that will come from the group.

Sales Projects

1. Christmas cards.
2. Mops and brooms.
3. Sponges.
4. Packaged merchandise.
5. Magazines.
6. Candy.
7. Light bulbs.
8. Pennants, tee shirts, programs, etc., related to athletic activities.

Nonselling Fund-Raising Projects

1. Talent show.
2. Cake walk.
3. Concessions at athletic events.
4. Student directory.
5. Sponsoring dances and other currently popular events.
6. Sponsoring professional shows in the school auditorium.

These lists by no means exhaust project possibilities available to alert groups of young people. The club membership should be encouraged to select projects most compatible to the group as a whole in terms of its collective abilities and interests. Some segments of the club membership may be attracted to sales projects, while others may feel more comfortable with the responsibility of sponsoring a nonselling project such as a talent show. A wise selection of projects, therefore, should challenge the entire membership through requiring the application of abilities and interests which compare favorably with those possessed by the group as a whole. It would not be unusual for a club membership to divide itself into groups, with each selecting a project in accordance with its own collective interests and abilities. The wholesome competition that could result from multiple projects being carried on simultaneously could inspire enthusiasm and effort which could not otherwise be achieved.

Fund-raising projects should be scheduled in accordance with the need for funds. A well-organized and active club may have one or more such projects in operation at all times throughout the year.

The proposed budget, together with the club's plan for financing, should be submitted to appropriate administrative officials for approval before any commitments are made. Failure to gain approval may jeopardize administrative relationship and detract from official cooperation and help essential to the successful financing of the club program.

General Characteristics of Fund-Raising Projects

The point has been made before that an important characteristic of a successful organization is that every member is given and accepts a designated responsibility for some phase of the organization's program of work. In line with this principle, the fund-raising efforts of a club should be shared by its entire membership. It may be necessary for the club leadership to insist that hesitant members, or those who may tend to neglect their assignments, assume and discharge membership responsibility.

Failure to insist on participation by all members could result in a few members of the club doing all the work, while the entire membership enjoys the fruit of their efforts. An indefinite continuation of circumstances of this kind will inevitably have a negative effect on the morale of the club and detract from its ability to accomplish its objectives. A prime leadership responsibility, therefore, is to effect and maintain an equitable distribution of the effort required to keep the club active and viable.

Although the specific purpose of fund-raising projects is to finance the club program, their educational values should be a paramount concern. Projects that accomplish the acquisition of funds without attending educational values should not be included in the program of a youth organization.

Another distinct characteristics of all fund-raising projects should be that the financial returns are commensurate with the collective efforts of those who participate. Fund-raising projects should provide opportunity for club members to earn the money necessary to finance their program, rather than to present a means by which the needed funds will be forthcoming without the expenditure of individual and collective effort on the part of club members. Let it be assumed, for example, that an alert teacher–coordinator were able to secure a coin-operated bottled-drink dispensing machine, together with a highly desirable franchise location. Such an arrangement could conceivably finance the entire annual club program without effort on the part of the club membership. In effect, this would result in "getting something for nothing."

Under circumstances of this kind, the club membership can be expected to retreat from the principle of paying, through individual and collective efforts, for project benefits. The resulting influence on the moral development of those concerned is entirely out of character with the general purposes of youth organizations. The suggestion, therefore, is that all fund-raising projects be carefully screened from the standpoint of their requirement for contribution of efforts, on the part of the club membership, which are commensurate with the expected financial return.

The Employer–Employee Banquet

An expression of appreciation to employers for the opportunities they afford for students, through CE, enjoys traditional status as an important element of student club programs. Although such an event may take many forms, the most common is the annual employer–employee banquet. There follows a brief characterization of a typical event of this kind. It should be kept in mind that although the form of the program may vary in accordance with local circumstances, it should retain the following basic characteristics:

1. Its principal purpose should be to express appreciation to employers for their cooperation with the school in providing educational work experience for students.
2. It should be planned and financed by CE students as a paramount feature of their annual club program.
3. The program should be formal to the extent of reflecting student cognizance of good taste and propriety.
4. The guest list should include school board members, city officials, state legislators, advisory committee members, school administrators, representatives of the press, all employers, and others who bear significant relationships with the program.
5. All students should have definite parts on the program, ranging from introduction of their employers to major platform roles.

There follows a suggested step-by-step procedure which should be helpful in planning an employer–employee banquet program:

1. Establish the purposes and values of the banquet.
2. Establish the date.
3. Determine the program theme.
4. Determine the limits of the guest list.
5. Determine the nature of the banquet program.
6. Determine how the banquet will be financed.
7. Determine the general decor.
8. Decide how guests will be welcomed.
9. Determine the seating arrangement.
10. Consider appropriate subjects for the principal address.
11. Consider whom to invite as principal speaker.

12. Determine the type of entertainment to be included in the program.
13. Determine special awards to be made.
14. Develop a sample program.
15. Appoint committees and assign responsibilities.

Typical Problems Involved in the Operation of Student Clubs

Problem 1 Overcoming or compensating for factors which tend to retard the social activities of the club members

The provision of social events designed to afford opportunities for the development of social skills is an important function of clubs organized for cooperative education students. Teacher–coordinators often find that the basic character of student groups becomes more obvious in social functions than in classroom activities. This difference could be reflected through unwillingness of the girls to date the boys, or vice versa, or downright refusal of one segment of the group to meet another on a social basis. The fact that the cause and effect of such circumstances are unpredictable demands that each problem of this nature be dealt with on its own merits.

Club leadership may elect alternatives ranging from an all-out attempt to overcome the retarding factors, to complete abandonment of the social aspects of club activities. In the first instance failure may result, while in the second it is assured by default.

The basic cause of antisocial tendencies among club members may stem from family social and economic status, religious affiliation, ethnic lineage, or other dividers inherent in the social structure. The fact that enrollment requirements of CE involve none of these, but rather are based on individual need and desire for the experience and ability to profit from it, sets the stage for incompatible social dogma which can be depended upon to change in character and intensity as the student groups change from year to year. Teacher–coordinators may find this area of club work to be the most challenging of all and to provide opportunity for the application of their most creative efforts.

Problem 2 Adapting the club program to student schedules

The CE student spends a maximum of four hours in the classroom and an additional four hours on the job each school day. The fact that the time in school is restricted usually relegates study periods to the evening hours after work for the day is done. In addition, cooperative students may work on Saturdays and holidays.

The almost complete utilization of time in the discharge of the responsibilities imposed by CE causes the student to have less time for study, extracurricular, and leisure-time activities than regular high school students. It stands to reason, therefore, that it would be poor judgment on the part of club leadership to design a club program which would require the application of time by club members which is simply not available. The wisdom of the teacher–coordinator should prevail in the initial planning stages to the extent of preventing inexperienced students from "biting off more than they can chew."

The lack of time which can be applied to club activities on the part of students is often accepted as basic justification for the use of class time for club meetings. The time available should also be applied as a prime criterion in judging the appropriateness of projects to be included in the club program. The saturation of the student's daily schedule may preclude enough time being available to pursue fund-raising projects to the extent necessary to finance complicated and expensive educational, public service, or social projects. Consequently, the cost of projects in terms of money as well as time should be prime factors in their consideration.

The scarcity of time to apply to fund-raising projects frequently influences a club to confine its program to the fiscal ability which can be accomplished through the paying of dues and periodic assessments. This easy way out constitutes a compromise that will produce a minimum program tending to leave the group unchallenged and perhaps, in the end, reluctant to pay the bill. On the other hand, an inspired club membership will find the time to accomplish fund-raising activities in sufficient scope to finance a program which they believe will reflect credit to them as a student group.

Problem 3 *Assuring the emergence of the strongest possible student leadership from club membership*

Student groups with potential ability to accomplish worthwhile club projects are often relegated to inactive or ineffective status by virtue of weak student leadership. On the other hand, those officers possessing leadership potential can be developed rapidly through appropriate leadership trianing activities. It becomes obvious, therefore, that the teacher–coordinator should be primarily concerned with the methods by which student officers are selected by their peers, and the provision of a leadership development plan which will transform leadership aptitude into ability in the shortest possible time. Following a procedure of this kind will produce predominately successful results, while allowing nature to take its course will tend to produce predominately negative results.

Problem 4 *Inspiring interest in the valid values of club activities as opposed to primary concern for superficial purposes and fringe values*

Hedonistic interests may tend to dominate the thinking of high school students at the expense of sincere concern for accomplishments in more mature value areas. The interpretation of this tendency in terms of interest in club functions would suggest that high school students may be expected to recognize and rally to those activities which they interpret as leading to pleasant experiences more quickly than to those which promise other forms of reward. Although wise teacher–coordinators will not fail to capitalize on this basic characteristic of youth in building initial interest in the club and its program, they will not allow it to defeat its more mature purposes and values.

The club program should play an important role in the maturing process of CE students. It should also provide a medium through which many skills can be developed which are vitally important to individuals as citizens at work and in the community in which they will live.

Problem 5 *Planning the club program and working the plan*

Although the development of a program of work for a student club is a valuable experience, it is frequently ignored in favor of a meandering course of activities which seldom develop sufficient momentum to challenge the club membership. The teacher–coordinator must compensate for the inexperience of students in the initial stages of development through leadership which will give direction in program planning and provide prudent guidelines relative to its extent and character.

After the program of work is developed, the teacher–coordinator may find it necessary to develop ways and means of diplomatically insisting that it be carried out according to plan. It will also be necessary to compensate for weaknesses which show up in the ranks of student leadership as the program develops.

Suggested Activities

1. Prepare a statement requesting permission to organize a student club to be submitted to school officials for consideration and approval. The statement should include a complete description of club purposes and values to students as well as to the school and community.

2. Prepare a statement for presentation to CE students relative to student club programs. Include in the statement those program elements which should inspire student interest.

3. Devise a step-by-step procedure that could be followed in the introduction and initial organization of a student club.

4. Using the items listed under "A Plan of Operation" on page 216 as major divisions, develop a student club plan. Each division should be detailed to the extent necessary to satisfy the indicated requirement.

5. Using the fifteen items listed on pages 223–224 as an outline of procedure, develop an employer–employee banquet plan.

chapter eleven

Testing
and Grading

Evaluation of Directly Related Instruction

Each supervised and directed study assignment should include a comprehensive test on the technical information included in this study. These tests are designed to measure the comprehension of students. Their objective nature, together with the answer sheets, makes the determination of an accurate grade for each assignment possible without regard for the teacher–coordinator's level of competency in the occupational area in question. Grades derived from these tests should be a good indication of the student's comprehension and retention during the period immediately following the study of the technical information.

Although these scores may be accepted as sufficient evidence upon which to base a grade, they do not guarantee that the technical information involved has actually become a permanent part of the student's knowledge to apply to the solution of job-oriented problems. For this reason individual oral testing (see Chapter Eight) is advocated. A selection of questions, included in tests previously taken, should be presented to the student orally. If the student can correctly answer these questions orally after the lapse of at least two weeks' time, practical command of the subject matter may be assumed. Assurance in this respect may be encouraged by student and employer reports of on-the-job incidents which involve the application of technical information covered by the tests. The teacher–coordinator should make every effort to provide easily accessible avenues for feedback of this nature.

228

Written Term Tests and Examinations

Group tests and examinations as a part of supervised and directed study in directly related instruction are not practical by virtue of the individual nature of student assignments. Because the study in which each student has been involved is different from that of every other student's study, individual tests or examinations must be prepared for each student. Semester tests can be compiled, if they are necessary because of school policy, by the selection of a representative set of questions from tests in assignments completed by individual students during the period to be covered by the test. The time consumed in the preparation and grading of such tests, however, overbalances their value.

Notebooks

The teacher–coordinator may find it advisable to evaluate notebooks periodically in terms of the quality of the notes being kept and the degree to which instructions are being followed.

Written Work

Regardless of the method used in measuring achievement in directly related study, the following aspects of all written work should not be overlooked in the evaluative process.

Following Instructions

This evaluation should have to do with the instructions included in the supervised and directed study assignment as well as supplementary instructions given by the teacher–coordinator. Students who fail to follow instructions should be penalized.

Quality of Writing

Cooperative education students probably write as much as any other student group. Writing is the principal medium through which they can communicate the degree of excellence of their accomplishment in directly related study. This fact suggests that the mechanics of writing should be considered as an important area of learning in directly related instruction.

Students bring with them varying degrees of writing ability when they enter the program. In the pursuit of daily study guide assignments, they are required to take notes, write summaries, and take tests. This daily writing exercise may serve to improve and fix good writing habits. By the same token, poor writing habits may be intensified and more permanently fixed when they are left unchallenged. Consequently, the writing of all students should be carefully examined and evaluated to the end that good writing ability be preserved and improved, while poor writing ability will tend to be improved through persistent requirements on all written work.

Quality Versus Quantity of Work Required

The amount of work to be required from each student frequently constitutes one of the most difficult problems with which the teacher–coordinator has to deal. Students tend to expect uniform assignments and requirements, as a result of their experience in conventional courses. In combating this tendency, the teacher–coordinator should develop a system of evaluation which will accomplish the following:

1. Discourage the idea that a specified number of study guide assignments must be completed during any given period of time.
2. Develop a scoring system which will judge the student according to the quality of work done rather than the number of assignments completed or the time involved.

   A point system might be developed to value each assignment in accordance with the amount of research required. The number of such points accumulated during any given period should be a fairly accurate indication of the amount of work done by any given student. Standards should be established in the marking system which would tend to satisfy the student's desire to know approximately the amount and quality of work he or she will be expected to accomplish to earn a given grade.
3. Include incentives designed to cause students to proceed at their own best rate of speed, with emphasis on the value of each assignment to them personally rather than on the meeting of specified requirements or matching the accomplishment of other students.
4. Encourage the relating of each assignment as closely as possible with work experience and place a value on application of technical information gained in the classroom to job-oriented circumstances.

Evaluation of Generally Related Instruction

Each lesson plan used in the teaching of various generally related units, such as employer–employee relations, should include a test covering the subject matter included in the lesson. This test may be administered as the culminating step in the teaching of each lesson, or it may be combined with others to make up periodic or unit tests. In either event the test on subject matter presented by the teacher–coordinator should produce marks acceptable for use in determining the total grade. The evaluation of performance in other classroom activities, such as role playing and participation in conferences and small-group activities, will, for the most part, be accomplished subjectively by the teacher–coordinator. Each grading period should produce enough marks to appropriately represent generally related instruction in the determination of the total grade of each student.

Determining the Total Grade

The fact that students enrolled in CE are involved in at least four major efforts complicates the process of evaluation. It becomes advisable, therefore, to devise a plan which will take all effort areas into account according to their importance.

The complication arises from the necessity of finding ways and means not only to measure achievement in all effort areas, but also to blend the results in accordance with their comparable values in the overall grade. Although there may be several acceptable approaches to this problem, the following suggested step-by-step procedure should be helpful to inexperienced teacher–coordinators in setting up an initial plan for the determination of term and semester grades of students. The possibility that time and experience may prompt modification of this plan to satisfy changing personal concepts and local circumstances should not be allowed to alter its basic elements.

Establishing Areas of Judgment

Determining the areas in which students will be judged is essentially the first step in evaluation, for two very obvious reasons. In the first place, students should be told how they will be judged in advance of the application of their efforts in the discharge of the responsibilities imposed upon them by virtue of being enrolled in CE. In the second place, making these areas of judgment a matter of record will establish guidelines for use in the development of the evaluation process.

There follows a listing of the four areas in which major effort is required of CE students. It is determined, for the purposes of this example, that they shall constitute the basic areas of judgment.

1. Directly related instruction.
2. Generally related instruction.
3. Work experience.
4. Club work.

Weighting the Judgment Areas

It now becomes the responsibility of the teacher–coordinator to determine the value of each of these areas as they relate to the whole. The fact that a major portion of the class time normally is devoted to directly related instruction prompts the assignment to it of a value relatively greater than that assigned to generally related instruction. The tendency of most employers to grade too high may be compensated for through the assignment of a lower relative value to their evaluation of the student's work experience than to either of the instructional areas accomplished in the classroom. Club work usually draws the smallest relative value of the four areas because of its informal nature and the fact that it is usually evaluated by subjective judgment on the part of the teacher–coordinator. Assigning relatively low values to the employer's inflated subjective evaluation of work experience and the teacher–coordinator's subjective evaluation of participation in club work reduces their influence on the total grade but still takes them into significant account.

Having reasoned thus far in the process of determining the relative importance of the areas in which the student will be judged, let it now be assumed that the following weighting factors are established.

Judgment Area	Weighting Factor
1. Directly related instruction	40
2. Generally related instruction	30
3. Employer's rating	20
4. Club work	10

In effect, this means that the teacher–coordinator has determined that the judgment areas as they are listed above shall account for 40, 30, 20, and 10 percent of the student's total grade, respectively. It should be noted at this point that, aside from exercising good judgment, there is only one rule applicable to the process of assigning these relative values. Their sum must always equal 100.

Determining Numerical Grade Points for Directly Related Instruction

For the purpose of this evaluation process, grades in all areas should be recorded numerically as opposed to the common practice of recording letter grades. The following table will illustrate this principle:

Letter Grade	Numerical Grade
A	5
B	4
C	3
D	2
F	1

This simply means that a grade of A will be recorded on the grade form as 5, a grade of B as 4, and so on.

Determining Numerical Grade Points for Supervised and Directed Study

It was suggested earlier that grades in supervised and directed study should be determined primarily through tests on completed study guide assignments and periodic oral tests to measure the retention of technical information. There are other areas which could enter into the evaluation process, but for the purposes of this writing they shall be limited to the two mentioned above.

Let it be assumed, for example, that a student accomplishes the following marks on study guide assignments and attending oral tests in directly related instruction during a given six-week grading period (see Chapter Eight):

Test on assignment 93	C–3
Test on assignment 86	B–4

233

Test on assignment 91	C–3
Test on assignment 74	A–5
Test on assignment 77	C–3
Test on assignment 84	B–4
Oral test	C–3
Oral test	D–2

$$\text{Average } \frac{27}{8} = 3.37$$

A common average of these grades is 3.37. This figure should be recorded in the Numerical Grade column opposite Directly related instruction. (See Figure 22.) In this case the oral tests are assigned values equal to the study guide assignment tests to emphasize the importance of retention of technical information. Time and experience may cause the teacher–coordinator to change this relationship.

Determination of grades in directly related instruction in occupationally specialized CE programs such as distributive education which do not exclusively employ the supervised and directed study method will differ from the above in only one respect. The grades earned in technical units of instruction such as "Salesmanship" may replace an appropriate number of the study guide assignment and oral test grades. The rest of the testing and grading plan, which follows, is applicable to CE in all specialized occupational areas.

Determining Numerical Grade Points for Generally Related Instruction

The description of generally related instruction in Chapter Nine suggests that grades be determined largely from tests on generally related units of instruction, such as employer–employee relations and personality development, together with marks on participation in panels, conferences, role playing, buzz sessions, and other forms of instruction. For the sake of illustration, let it be assumed that the student compiles the following record during the six-week grading period in question:

Test on employer–employee relations	A–5
Test on personality development	C–3
Panel discussion	B–4
Special report	B–4

234

Conference participation   C–3
Buzz session participation   D–2
                                                                 _____

                                        Average $\dfrac{21}{6}$ = 3.5

A common average of these grades is 3.5, which may be recorded in the Numerical Grade column opposite Generally related instruction. Under actual circumstances, however, the teacher–coordinator should make a fair determination of the relative values of participation in classroom activities and unit tests.

It may be determined, for example, that an average of the grades assigned to classroom activities such as panel discussion, special report, conference, and buzz session will be assigned a combined weight equivalent to that of one test. If this should be the case, the calculation above would change as follows:

Test on employer–employee relations   A–5
Test on personality development   C–3
Classroom activities (average)   C–3
                                                                 _____

                                        Average $\dfrac{11}{3}$ = 3.67

In this case the average 3.67 should be recorded in the Numerical Grade column opposite Generally related instruction, in place of 3.5. (See Figure 22.)

Determining Employer Rating, Numerical Grade Points

The employer's evaluation of the student's work experiences may be accomplished through the implementation of the job-experience evaluation form. See the sample form in Figure 8 (pp. 88–89). Eighteen of the twenty-three items on this form relate to personality traits and five to skills peculiar to the individual job in question. To continue this example of the evaluation process, let it be assumed that the employer submits the following job-experience evaluation for the grading period under consideration. The letter grades assigned by the employer have been given numerical value as indicated:

235

1. Personal appearance and bearing		A–5
2. Courtesy		A–5
3. Willingness to work		A–5
4. Disposition		A–5
5. Physical vitality		A–5
6. Cooperativeness		A–5
7. Ability to take correction		A–5
8. Ability to follow instructions		A–5
9. Neatness in work		B–4
10. Thoroughness		B–4
11. Initiative		B–4
12. Dependability		B–4
13. Industry and effort		B–4
14. Enthusiasm		B–4
15. Judgment and common sense		A–5
16. Self-reliance		A–5
17. Attendance		A–5
18. Punctuality		A–5
19. Accuracy		B–4
20. Speed		A–5
21. Skill		B–4
22. Visualization		A–5
23. Technical knowledge		A–5

$$\text{Average} \quad \frac{107}{23} = 4.652$$

A simple average of the numerical values of marks awarded by the employer is 4.65, which may be recorded in the Numerical Grade column opposite Employer rating. (See Figure 22.)

This evaluation is typical of employer tendency to grade too high and accounts for the lower "weighting factor" assigned to it on the grade forms.

In the illustration above it will be noted that only 5/23 of the employer's evaluation is determined by job skills (items 19–23). Under normal circumstances this weighting would seem to overemphasize personal characteristics at the expense of the actual job skills involved in the student's daily work experience. It is suggested, therefore, that the teacher–coordinator again exercise judgment in establishing a fair value relationship between these two major elements of the work experience. For purposes of illustration, let it be assumed that job skills and personality traits are given equal values in the evaluation. The above calculation would change as follows:

Personality traits (average)	A–4.66
Job skills (average)	A–4.60

$$\text{Average}\quad \frac{9.26}{2} = 4.63$$

It will be noted that the overall grade was not changed because high marks were assigned to all items, thus producing a high average regardless of the method used in its determination. On the other hand, if and when the employer comes to more realistic and objective evaluative practices, the latter form of calculation should result in a more realistic characterization of work experience.

Determining Club Work, Numerical Grade Points

In order to continue the illustration of the evaluative process, let it be assumed that the teacher–coordinator evaluates club work according to the following criteria:

1. Overall grasp of club purposes	C–3
2. Contribution to club meetings	B–4
3. Assumption of responsibility	F–1
4. Ability to function (Robert's Rules of Order)	F–1
5. Team effort	C–3

$$\text{Average}\quad \frac{12}{5} = 2.40$$

The average of the marks awarded by the teacher–coordinator is 2.40, which should be recorded in the Numerical Grade column opposite Club work, on the grading form.

Using the Grading Form

The recording of the above individual student averages on the grading form in Figure 22 will continue the sample evaluation of the student in the four judgment areas. After the numerical grades are determined, they should be multiplied by their weighting factors. The results are shown in the Weighted Grade column. The sum of the weighted grades divided by 100 is 3.62, which is the total numerical

Figure 22   Sample Six-Week-Term Grading Form

Judgment Area	Weighting Factor		Numerical Grade	Weighted Grade	Total Grade
1. Directly related instruction	40	X	3.37	= 134.80	
2. Generally related instruction	30	X	3.67	= 110.10	
3. Employer rating	20	X	4.65	= 93.00	B
4. Club work	10	X	2.40	= 24.00	
			Total	$\dfrac{361.90}{100} =$	3.62

A = 5, B = 4, C = 3, D = 2, F = 1.

grade for the grading period. By a process of interpolation this numerical grade is found to be equivalent to a letter grade of B, as shown in the Total Grade column.

It is suggested that the grading form be duplicated in quantity in a size convenient for filing purposes. A complete grade file should be maintained for each student and should be available for viewing at appropriate times. It would be highly desirable for the student to be present when the grade is calculated, and that the entire process be understood.

Although the method suggested above is not entirely objective, neither is it totally subjective. As a matter of fact, it strikes a comfortable medium between the two extremes which should be acceptable to students. They tend to like the mathematical functions employed in the determination of grades, which suggests that the teacher–coordinator's opinion and judgment play an insignificant role in the total process.

If the preceding plan is employed in the determination of six-week term grades, semester grades may be determined by averaging the total numerical grades assigned to the three six-week terms. For example, suppose that the term grades awarded to a student for the three terms in the first semester of the junior year are 3.78, 4.32, and 3.43. The average of these three term grades is 3.84, the equivalent of a letter grade of B for the semester.

The above grade-determination process is offered for the purpose of illustration and should not be considered as a validated procedure.

238

Preparatory teacher–coordinators should terminate their study of this important phase of CE by developing their own plan, combining their own concepts with the principles set forth in this chapter.

The design of the grading plan is an important preliminary teacher–coordinator responsibility, and it should be completed before the opening of school in order that it may be fully explained to students during the orientation period. They should be fully advised of any adjustments in the plan which become necessary during the school year.

Typical Problems in Testing and Grading

Problem 1 *Evaluating assignments from study guides of nonuniform design*

It was mentioned earlier that securing study guides designed according to a uniform pattern for all occupations included in a given program was extremely difficult and probably not possible. The significance of this discrepancy is the difficulty of effecting a uniform evaluative process in directly related instruction. Since the occupational areas included in CE classes may be represented by a variety of study guide forms, it can be expected that some will depart from the design described in Chapter Eight. Such departure may be evidenced through variation in the type and number of assignments, the type of test questions, and the presence or absence of answers to test questions. Study guides which do not include answers to test questions tend to force the teacher–coordinator into subjective judgment of unfamiliar areas of technical information. In order to escape such intolerable circumstances, it may be necessary to resort to alternatives such as the following:

1. Dependence upon oral testing as a major basis of the evaluation of directly related instruction.
2. Evaluation of areas unrelated to technical information, such as:
   a. How well instructions have been followed.
   b. Quality of writing, including spelling, sentence structure, and writing style.
   c. General quality.
3. A feedback plan which will produce evidence of the successful application of technical information on the job.
4. A plan which would cause students to authenticate technical information included in completed assignments.

239

A plausible combination of these items could produce an acceptable plan of evaluation even though it may be highly subjective and time consuming. Entering the related-subjects classroom for the first time without a preconceived marking plan will render the teacher–coordinator vulnerable to the tragic necessity of awarding grades without plausible bases at the end of grading periods. Being unable to justify grades, when questioned by students, places the teacher–coordinator in an untenable position and will create a barrier to desirable relationships.

The determination of grades for students who are placed in occupational areas for which study guides are not available presents a different situation. It is generally understood that the availability of study guides and ample sources of reference should be important factors in the evaluation of occupations being considered for inclusion in CE. In spite of this warning, however, teacher–coordinators frequently place students in occupations with which they are unfamiliar without checking out the availability of instructional materials. The net result of such an error is the presence of students in directly related instruction without a study guide or ample and suitable reference materials. Such students are prone to become problems which require time and personal attention at the expense of other members of the class.

Problem 2 *Budgeting and managing classroom time so as to include essential classroom activities*

Some of the more important classroom activities which are inherent in supervised and directed study are as follows (see Chapter Eight):

1. Supervising students in the selection of study guide assignments in accordance with work experience (correlation).
2. Helping students find and interpret technical information.
3. Oral testing.
4. Counseling students.

The time required to discharge the responsibilities involved in items 1 and 2 will vary from day to day. The fact remains, however, that these two activities are vital phases of supervised and directed study and must receive the attention necessary to sustain instructional progress. The application of time and effort to those classroom responsibilities should by no means by allowed to eliminate oral testing and counseling.

On the contrary, it should cause the teacher–coordinator to be prepared to make the best use of the time available during each period, and to call on a given student for oral testing as soon as the responsibilities included in items 1 and 2 have been satisfied. This preparation should include the selection of questions in advance from tests included in study guide assignments which have been completed and turned in by the student being tested. In the case of counseling, areas appropriate for discussion should have been predetermined to eliminate delay in getting counseling sessions under way.

The advice that student counseling should be specifically structured simply means that some counseling areas should be predetermined, such as problems with employers, employer evaluations of work experiences, and circumstances having to do with in-school programs. This fore-thought should not eliminate or detract from nondirective counseling, which may stem from problems raised by students. Although it may be convenient to combine oral testing and counseling, better results will accrue from a complete separation of the two activities.

Individual differences should not affect the frequency of oral testing. The fact that good readers will turn in more completed study guide assignments than those in poorer-reading-ability brackets should not be considered in determining the frequency of oral tests. All students should be scheduled for the same number of oral tests per six-week period, with the content of the individual tests being determined by the content covered by the individual student.

If, for example, it is decided that each student shall be subjected to two oral tests per six-week term, it is quite possible that the slow reader may not have completed an assignment during the interim between tests. For the slow student, therefore, questions for the second oral test in a given six-week period may have to be selected from study guide tests from which questions may have previously been selected. By this means a poor reader would be given opportunity to excell in the retention of technical information which he has mastered and has found applicable to the solution of job-oriented problems.

On the other hand, the good reader may have completed one or more assignments during the interim between tests, and his oral test questions may be selected from the work covered in the newly completed assignments. In either case the results should be the same, because the purpose of the oral test is to measure student ability to retain technical information and its use in complementing work experience.

It becomes obvious that the teacher–coordinator should schedule oral tests for entire six-week periods to the extent that each student will be tested at least two times. Let it be assumed, for example, that a

241

CE class has an optimum enrollment of thirty students, scheduled in two sessions of fifteen each. If each student is to be tested orally twice during the six-week period, one student should be tested per day from each section. This plan would cause each student to appear twice on the testing roster during the thirty school days included in the six-week term.

Problem 3 *Compensating for individual differences in supervised and directed study*

One of the most difficult problems involved in the total process of evaluation in CE is finding ways and means of dealing effectively with individual differences with particular reference to reading ability. Selling the idea to students that the quality of work, depth of study, and retention ability will produce an appropriate grade in supervised and directed study without significant regard for the number of study guide assignments completed as compared with other students frequently presents difficulty.

As a general rule, the poor or slow reader will accept this concept more readily than the high achiever. It may be quite difficult, for example, to convice the good readers and the high achievers that they are being fairly treated when the poor readers and low achievers are awarded the same grade that they get for completing a smaller number of assignments. The high achievers can be expected to take exception to a grading system that would produce such results.

All students must come to understand that supervised and direct study is restricted to individual study, by each student, of information directly related to their own work experience. For this reason, individual accomplishment in the classroom is not comparable to that accomplished by any other student.

The success of the grading plan will depend upon the following:

1. The completed design of the plan prior to the beginning of school.
2. Successful presentation of the plan to the CE class during the orientation period.
3. Ability to explain and enthusiastically justify the plan in every detail.
4. Consistency and firmness in administering the plan.

The absence of any one of these success factors will jeopardize the success of any grading plan. For this reason embryonic teacher–coorinators should be impressed with the importance of being prepared to deal with grading problems in accordance with these success factors.

242

Problem 4 *Depending too heavily upon the employer's evaluation of the student's work experience in determining term grades*

Young teacher–coordinators frequently begin their work experiences without recognition of the importance of a preconceived plan for determining student marks. The fact that the employer's evaluation of the student's work experience probably will be the most tangible evidence to be found would produce a great temptation to use it as the basis of the term grade. It is quite possible that this practice would be temporarily acceptable by virtue of the novelty of the program and the lack of insight of those in position to judge. This acceptance could serve as an incentive to the inexperienced teacher–coordinator to continue the practice.

It is suggested, however, that the continued acceptance of such a practice would be short-lived because of its superficial nature and obvious failure to represent the total program. The fact that the employer's evaluation of the work experience of students has very little to do with classroom work, coupled with inconsistency between employers and the uniform tendency to grade too high, will eventually be recognized by school officials and students. Such recognition will tend to destroy respect for the in-school instructional program and to become the basis for justifiable criticism. Student reaction may be reflected through negative attitudes toward related instruction and classroom inefficiency.

Problem 5 *Making the testing process an educational experience*

The overemphasis of the value of the "grade" is probably modern education's greatest handicap. The necessity of maintaining sufficient grade levels to sustain peer ratings and the respect of the adult world tends to become so important to students that they lose sight of educational values. It may be more important to the student, for example, to get a high grade than to master technical information to the extent that it can be applied to work experience, or to identify and strengthen weak personal characteristics.

In order to combat this "educational ill" the teacher–coordinator must find ways and means to champion the educational values of CE at the expense of the usual emphasis on grades. Consequently, in supervised and directed study CE students must sincerely accept the principle that the technical information assigned for study has value only as a part of their knowledge which can be applied to the solution of job-oriented problems. The accumulation of this information in notebooks and the taking of tests are means to this end rather than ends within themselves. This understanding should mean to the student the mastery of technical information to the extent and degree that it becomes a useful tool.

When this principle is accepted, students will see in tests opportunity to measure their understanding of the technical information they have been studying. Failure to answer test questions correctly will signal areas of information which should be restudied. Oral tests will be recognized as a measure of ability to retain technical information long enough for it to become a fixture in the student's knowledge. The development of attitudes such as these will tend to deemphasize the importance of the test as a grading device and champion it as an avenue to desirable educational experiences.

The same attitude should prevail in generally related instruction and other measurable aspects of the related instructional program. Let it be assumed, for example, that students can be brought to consider instruction in "personality development" as an opportunity to identify personal traits which should be strengthened, or perhaps eliminated, and to initiate personal improvement programs designed to produce the desired improvement.

The above or similar attitudes should cause students to discount the importance of the grade in favor of the educational values which will accrue to them. The teacher should be alert to opportunities to encourage such attitudes and to appropriately reward all stages of their development.

Suggested Activities

1. Prepare a feedback plan which will produce evidence of the successful application of technical information acquired in the classroom to the solution of on-the-job problems and circumstances.
2. Devise a plan that will cause students to authenticate technical information they included in completed study guide assignments.
3. Accepting the allegation that employers tend to grade too high, make a listing of the steps a teacher–coordinator might take to improve the job-experience evaluation process.
4. Devise a plan that might be followed by the teacher–coordinator in scheduling and administering oral tests in directly related instruction.
5. Using the suggestions in this chapter as points of departure, design a plan for determining total term grades of CE students.

Part IV

Public Relations Essential to Cooperative Education

chapter twelve
Values of Cooperative Education

chapter thirteen
In-School Relationship Development

chapter fourteen
Community Relationship Development

Introduction to Part IV

One of the most vital responsibilities of the teacher–coordinator is the development and preservation of compatible relations with those publics which make important contributions to the environment in which CE must function.

Public relations is much more than publicity, although publicity is an important aspect of good public relations. Publicity may be defined as simply doing something worthwhile and advising the public accordingly. Public relations, on the other hand, refers to the total spectrum of relationship development, which includes the following:

1. The identification and recognition of all publics which make notable contributions to the environment in which the program functions.
2. Assessing and evaluating the attitudes of each public.
3. The deliberate development of educational programs designed to promote and preserve positive attitudes based on the understanding and acceptance of the purposes and values of CE.
4. Persistent planned pursuit of this program through all available media to the end that all publics will eventually come to reflect positive and permissive attitudes toward CE.

As implied above, public relations development insofar as the teacher–coordinator is concerned is a matter of developing attitudes positive in nature and conducive to the successful operation of CE in any given school and community. In this respect the term *attitude* may be defined as the spontaneous tendency of individuals to react positively or negatively to CE when it comes to their attention. How does the individual react, think, and comment when the program or the teacher–coordinator is mentioned in a defenseless setting? Is the involuntary reaction positive or negative, or is it one of indifference? Perhaps the most difficult of these attitudes to deal with is indifference, which indicates that individuals have no interest in the program or have failed to attach significant value to it.

As a general rule, negative attitudes result from a misunderstanding of purposes and values. Such misunderstanding should be dissipated through the presentation of appropriate information in the right manner, at the right place and time. This assumption is made on the premise that the purposes and values of CE cannot be justifiably rejected when they are properly understood.

The teacher–coordinator and CE become synonymous to the various publics with which the program is involved. It would be well, therefore, for teacher–coordinators to recognize that they cannot separate themselves from the program in the eyes of those with whom they work. High-quality personal ability, bearing, and stature will credit the program, while the absence of such characteristics may have negative effects. Teacher–coordinators who command respect through the quality of their service will also command respect for CE.

The fact that CE departs drastically from traditional educational programs normally found in the school frequently causes it to be viewed with concern by some publics. Various elements of the school and community may decide that its purposes and values are noneducational in nature and that it is designed to serve noneducational purposes. Such attitudes will persist in and out of the school until the educational purposes and values are presented, understood, and accepted by all publics.

For the sake of emphasis, let it be said at this point that CE will be successful in proportion to the degree that the publics controlling the environment in which it functions come to understand and accept its purposes and values. It necessarily follows that public relations based on program purposes and values must be given initial and continuous attention. It is also suggested that ignoring this principle will pave the way to failure.

The following statement of purpose will serve as a point of departure in the design and development of appropriate public relations activities. The purpose of CE is to provide opportunity for junior and senior high school students to acquire marketable skills and knowledge in occupational areas for which they have appropriate aptitudes, vocational interests, and personal qualities, to the end that they will be qualified to accept employment at beginning levels after graduation from high school in the occupations for which they have been prepared. These objectives are to be accomplished through organized part-time work experience in local business and industrial establishments selected by the school and through the study of related technical information in the school.

The outcomes of successful adherence to this purpose are elaborated in Chapter Twelve, in terms of values to principal program participants. These values constitute the framework of the public relations activities which follow.

The principal publics which bear importance to CE may be broadly classified within the two major areas of in-school publics and out-of-school publics. Chapters Thirteen and Fourteen deal, respectively, with these areas of public relations.

chapter twelve

Values of Cooperative Education

The valid purposes of CE should be the focal point of public relations activities. Under actual circumstances, however, a better response can be expected from a thorough explanation of program outcomes in terms of values expected than from a recital of noble purpose. Public relations activities directed at a specific public should be more effective, therefore, when they are related to the true values expected to accrue to that public.

The fact that many of the program values are potential in nature tends to make them less obvious and perhaps less attractive than the more obvious and immediate superficial fringe values. It may be easier, for example, for a potential employer to justify the employment of a student for the purpose of satisfying an immediate need for a part-time employee than it would be to consider it to be an opportunity to provide an educational work-experience program for a young person whom there will be an opportunity to employ as a full-time worker after graduation from high school.

In the first instance the employer would attach value to the immediate productive ability of the student, while in the second he would discount the value of immediate production in favor of the ultimate outcome in the form of a well-qualified full-time employee. The second attitude is essential to satisfactory relationships in CE. The acceptance of this philosophy does not eliminate the possibility of profiting from the productive ability of the student in the form of supplemental production.

The school should be concerned with the values which should

accrue to all program principals, but it should vigorously exert the effort necessary to keep the program student-centered. The best interest of the student should be held as the ruling factor in all matters of judgment.

Program Values to Employers

The employers or their designates have been cast in the role of on-the-job teachers and their places of business as school laboratories. The fact that CE is dependent upon this type of employer participation imposes the responsibility on the school of keeping them informed concerning the values to be expected and to organize and direct the program in a fashion that will guarantee them.

Better-Qualified Employees

The school should develop a student selection plan which will inspire confidence on the part of employers in the qualifications of students recommended to them as potential CE students. The employers should come to understand that such recommendations are based upon the results of the total effort and ability of the school to help its students to develop career plans in terms of their basic aptitudes and vocational interests. They should not doubt that students recommended have been determined to be basically qualified for success in the type of work in question. Employers should also understand that their responsibility in the selection process is to determine whether individual students are qualified to fit into their organizations from the standpoint of personal characteristics and qualities. The part the school plays in this process of student selection constitutes a valuable service to employers not otherwise available to them.

Dependable Source of Qualified Workers

Meaningful cooperative arrangements between the school and the employers in its service area should provide a dependable source of well-qualified employees for jobs economically important to the community. Such an arrangement should assure the availability of qualified workers in sufficient numbers to maintain the economic stability of the community and to provide qualified manpower to satisfy normal economic growth and expansion requirements.

Whenever a community, through its schools, fails to satisfy these basic requirements, its economy can be expected to falter as the first step in the process of economic degeneration. Decadence in this respect eventually renders a given community incapable of competing on equal terms with more progressive neighboring communities. This difficulty brings into focus a basic characteristic of CE in that those enrolled are predominately the future citizens of the community. For this reason the cost of their education becomes a direct investment in the economic stability of the community and guarantees its continued growth and development.

Determination of On-the-Job Educational Specifications by Employers

In addition to the opportunity of selecting students through the school, employers have the privilege of teaching them how to do the job as they want it done, in their own place of business. The pattern of training and its limits are initially established jointly by the school and the employer through the preparation of a schedule of work experiences as a preliminary to the placement of the student on the job. This schedule, derived from an analysis of the occupation in which the student is to be placed, constitutes the guidelines for on-the-job instruction and the coordinating efforts of the school through the teacher–coordinator.

During the course of training, the students should become fully adjusted to the total on-the-job environment in which they may subsequently work full-time. During the same period the employers will have ample opportunity to observe the compatibility of the students with coworkers and supervisory personnel, thus enabling them to judge the probability of future problems. In addition, the students' capacity for continued development should become increasingly obvious as the training period nears its end. If the students' scores in all areas are satisfactory, they should be more valuable as beginning full-time employees of the employers who taught them than would other available individuals. No other form of education currently fostered by the school provides local employer advantages equivalent to those mentioned above.

This consideration should by no means be allowed to imply that the employer is obligated to employ the student at the end of the training period, or that the student is obligated to accept full-time employment. A basic principle of CE requires the freedom of both parties in this

253

respect. There is, however, a joint responsibility on the part of the employer, the student, and the school to examine the possibility of full-time employment upon graduation from high school. Circumstances may become complicated by virtue of the tendency of some employers to become reluctant to pay their program graduate according to prevailing wage scales. Under such circumstances graduates from the program may be forced to change employers in order to attain the pay to which they are entitled.

Training Less Expensive to Employers

Four of the most vital elements of CE are student selection, directly related instruction, generally related instruction, and on-the-job training. The school provides two of these elements and plays an important role in the other two. It would be extremely costly to the employer to duplicate the program without the help and cooperation of the school. To do so would entail the provision of specifically qualified teachers and classroom facilities for the related instruction as well as professional service in the trainee selection process.

Thus it becomes obvious that the cost of an educational program of comparable quality and extent would be prohibitive to the individual employer. On the other hand, the cooperative arrangement with the school relieves the employer of all fiscal responsibility, with the exception of the monetary wage paid the student. Although the benefit which may accrue from student production is somewhat intangible, it definitely has a bearing on the cost of training.

Employee Turnover Reduced

Cooperative educational programs properly conceived and operated in accordance with accepted policies and standards ensure that students recommended to employers will have been subjected to a rigid selection process, which includes the following:

1. Original screening to establish basic qualifications for enrollment relative to need for and ability to profit from the training.
2. The identification of career interest in terms of basic aptitudes and vocational interest through psychological testing and other appropriate means.
3. A thorough examination of school records in an effort to identify academic strengths and weaknesses, attendance and discipline problems, prevailing peer relationships, and attitudes toward authority.

After careful examination of all the evidence which results from this investigation, the teacher–coordinator and the potential student should be able to jointly identify the occupational areas which provide the best chances for success.

Full-time employees who ultimately result from this process should not become the victims of employee dissatisfaction, which normally leads to a change in jobs. It has been said that new workers currently entering the labor force are destined to change jobs several times before becoming occupationally fixed. It seems that this turnover, with its attending cost to employees and employers, can be charged directly to the general failure of the school to pattern its educational program after the career needs of its students. Cooperative education will be successful in combating employee turnover in proportion to the degree that the occupational curiosity of the beginning worker is satisfied before entering full-time employment.

Employer Opportunity To Render a Public Service

Most successful businessmen are good citizens and they can be expected to welcome opportunities to render a service to the community in which their business is located. It stands to reason, therefore, that a good citizen would welcome an opportunity to enter into an arrangement with the school designed to produce a dependable supply of well-qualified workers for the community, to provide opportunity for the future citizens of the community to prepare themselves for the jobs which will be available to them after graduation from high school, and to utilize the employer as an on-the-job teacher in his own place of business as an educational laboratory.

In addition to being a source of personal pride to the employer, these elements of public service should accrue to the community at large in the form of socioeconomic improvement factors. Collectively, these factors should contribute heavily to the social and economic stability of the local community.

Program Values to Students

The prime concern of the school should be to build CE around the "best interest" of the students who enroll in the program. This concern is mentioned again at this point to emphasize the danger of allowing the program to lapse into an arrangement designed primarily to benefit program principals other than students. A circumstance of this kind would result when the prime concern of the school is, for example, restricted to satisfying the need of local employers for part-time workers without regard for the career needs of students. Such a program would be "employer-centered" in that the focus would be upon serving the immediate need of employers at the expense of students. Superficial fringe values accruing to students under an arrangement of this kind would not justify the cost in terms of the educational time and credit they are required to invest.

There follows a listing of valid student values together with brief commentaries.

Bridges the Gap Between School and Work

Properly selected and properly placed CE students are privileged to meet and solve many of the problems involved in making a satisfactory adjustment to the world of work while still in high school. As high school students, they have immediate and continuous access to all the forms of aid provided through modern educational systems. The advice and counsel of teacher–coordinators is probably the most valuable of these services, in that they constitute an immediate and sympathetic audience to which student problems may be presented. Difficulty encountered on the job on any given day can be discussed with the teacher–coordinator before returning to work the next day. In this fashion the student profits from the experiences and wisdom of the teacher–coordinator in determining the best course of action to follow in the solution of the problem at hand or in adjusting to the condition which caused the problem.

It seems obvious that graduates from CE would have many advantages over the conventional high school graduate. Perhaps the greatest of these is that adjustment to the world of work should have been achieved by the time of graduation from high school. On the other hand, there is no assurance that conventional high school graduates can or will cope successfully with the problems they will encounter in post–high school adjustments. At best they will be left to their own devices in attempting to solve such problems without having been properly prepared.

Makes Education More Meaningful

Another value that should accrue to students is the discovery of the importance of ability to communicate with all elements of the environment in which they work. Such a discovery may improve the attitude toward tool subjects in communications which are required as a part of the high school program. A typical student attitude, such as "What good will English do me?" may be changed to "I must learn how to read, write, and speak well enough to transmit my thoughts to those with whom I live and work, and to understand the thoughts they present to me."

Other characteristics or demands of the work environment should serve to emphasize the importance and value of other conventional high school subject-matter areas with sufficient force to convince the individual student of their worth. All this motivation should be instrumental in helping students to change their whole attitude toward school—from what may be total emphasis on making the highest possible grades with the least possible effort to earnest desire and effort to acquire knowledge which will be useful in successfully negotiating the next step they will take after graduation from high school.

Opportunity To Validate Occupational Choice

One of the most important functions of guidance in the school is working with students in the identification of their aptitudes and vocational interests and helping them to judge their occupational significance. Aptitudes and vocational interests coupled with personal characteristics should be the most dependable criteria for use in the identification of occupational areas in which individual students should have the best chances for success. The ultimate test of the authenticity of occupational objectives based on decisions reached through this process must, as a general rule, be accomplished through try-out periods in the pseudo-occupational environments which can be provided within the curricular confines of the school.

To say the least, pseudo-experiences leave much to be desired and fall short of providing an environment of sufficient authenticity to allow students to judge its receptiveness to their total being, including their aptitudes, vocational interests, and personal qualities. In other words, the experiences the school can provide in its classrooms and laboratories can never be a replica of the real work environment to the extent that they will serve as a dependable occupational proving ground. The opportunity to gain occupational experience on real jobs is an inherent part of CE. This experience constitutes the best possible proving ground for occupational interests in that it provides an infallible compatibility test.

Errors in occupational choice should be the exception rather than the rule when the decision is made in accordance with accepted CE practices. The fact that some mistakes are inevitable, however, lends prestige to the opportunity cooperative students have of testing their occupational choices on real jobs. The teacher–coordinator should be sensitive to early signs that students are uncomfortable in the environment in which they are working. When circumstances becomes acute enough to assure that occupational maladjustment is present, the students in question should be subjected to total reassessment of their basic aptitudes, vocational interests, and personal qualities as an initial step in the process of readjustment. The best interest of the students should be the prime basis for any change which becomes necessary.

Aids Student Maturation Process

Students who are subjected to a new environment which they find to be receptive to them tend almost immediately to reflect newly born self-confidence in their ability to cope successfully with immediate and future problems involved in entering and satisfactorily adjusting to the world of work. In other words, properly selected and properly placed students find themselves able to cope satisfactorily with important, often unstated, personal questions, such as these:

1. After high school, what?
2. Will I be able to earn a satisfactory standard of living?
3 Will I be able to hold my own with my peers?
4. Will I be able to establish and properly sustain a home and family?
5. Will I be able to attain a position in adult life which will satisfy the ambition my parents and teachers hold for me?

This newly accomplished personal insight should constitute a giant step in the maturing process in the form of improved attitudes and realistic concern for current responsibilities at home, school, and on the job. The tangible and intangible employer values previously described will tend to be amplified through the sincerity with which students come to regard their classroom and on-the-job experiences as avenues to the accomplishment of coveted personal goals.

Develops Marketable Skill and Knowledge

The fact that a majority of contemporary youth will not enter college, coupled with an educational program primarily focused on preparation for college entrance, constitutes a most alarming dilemma. In addition, it is a matter of fact that a relatively small percentage of the jobs which will be available in the future will require a baccalaureate degree. Many of those enrolled in the secondary school and those to follow, who enter college, will be forced to seek employment in occupational areas which require skill and knowledge that they do not have.

The opportunity afforded to high school students, through CE, is one avenue through which this traumatic experience can be avoided. Disillusioned college students who fail to find suitable employment in the area of their college preparation may eventually find themselves applying for work in organizations headed by former CE students of their own vintage. If this should happen, it would mean that the CE students will have advanced to responsible positions, in the occupation for which they have prepared as high school students, during the time required for the college graduates to earn their degree and to search for employment. All of these considerations place a high value on the opportunity to develop marketable skill and knowledge in appropriate occupational areas while in high school.

Earns While Learning

The fact that the student is paid a monetary wage, which should be comparable to that paid to other beginning workers, should not be allowed to become the most important value of CE to the student, the employer, the parents, or the school. At the time that the amount of money earned becomes the most important concern of the program, the less tangible educational values tend to diminish and eventually disappear.

On the other hand, the money-earning potential, when kept in proper perspective, holds a distinct student advantage and value. It often serves as a means of financing a high school education which given students could not otherwise afford.

Having an opportunity to earn a regular wage during the junior and senior high school years could well be the determining factor in holding potential dropouts in school, especially when the dropout tendency stems from financial need. Under such circumstances the interest in earning money need not detract from or destroy other program values, nor should it be construed as a sign of insincerity in avowed occupational intent. Students who feel that they have to work in order to aid their parents in financing their high school education could be the most strongly motivated of all CE students.

Program Values to the School

The fact that CE should be student-centered does not prevent some very important values from accruing to the school. Brief descriptions of some of the most important of these values follow.

Enriches the Curriculum

The establishment of CE enables the school to enrich its curriculum by offering specific educational experiences in all career potential areas included in the business and industrial structure of the community. This service becomes possible as the result of the cooperative arrangement between the school and local employers who make their places of business available as laboratories and members of their staff as on-the-job instructors. Such an arrangement expands school laboratory facilities to include the combined physical facilities of the community, together with an attending instructional staff qualified by virtue of ability to produce successfully under actual circumstances.

Considered collectively these elements of the cooperative arrangement between the school and local employers guarantee the environment in which cooperative students gain work experience to be a replica of that in which they will subsequently work. This authenticity is one of CE's greatest contributions to education. Pseudo-school-laboratory experiences under the direction of instructors often poorly qualified with respect to successful work experience are replaced with actual on-the-job experiences under the direction of well-qualified on-the-job instructors.

Specific enrichment factors are as follows:

1. The total educational program is expanded to include opportunity for specific educational experiences in all qualified occupational areas represented in the geographical service area of the school. This development expands the occupational breadth of vocational education from limited offerings in coventional instructional programs to include an indefinite number of occupations, depending upon the economic character of the community.
2. On-the-job instruction is provided under the direction of occupational artisans at no cost to the school.
3. The environment in which the experience takes place is an exact replica of the environment in which the student will ultimately work, as compared with pseudo-experiences which can be provided in school laboratories.

260

Projects the School into the Community

All CE students leave the school building at a given time to continue their school day in an appropriate number of local business or industrial establishments. By this means the educational program is extended into the community through the places of business annually selected as training agencies.

The very nature of the teacher–coordinators' work places them in daily contact with employers and workers in the places of business in which students are placed. Less frequent contact with other places of business will occur in the course of activities designed to keep the entire community aware of what is going on in vocational education. Thus it can be seen that the teacher–coordinator serves a vital purpose in the development of the school's sensitivity to community educational needs. In addition, the teacher–coordinator is normally given the responsibility of projecting the school into the community through the organization of continuing educational programs to meet the needs of employed workers.

Deters Dropout Tendency

Although the holding power of the school varies from community to community, the fact remains that the rate of dropout is inordinately high. In some states more than half of those students who enter the ninth grade will not graduate from high school. This rate represents a great loss in human resources which might be prevented by holding potential dropouts in school until they can profit from guidance and vocational education, with particular reference to CE.

It may be assumed that the dropout tendency stems largely from a lack of interest and challenge in the educational program. Concrete knowledge of the opportunities available in high school may be attractive enough to bridge the gap between the unchallenging areas of education and those of greater interest. This possibility lends great prestige to the career-centered educational plan which seeks to develop occupational awareness in the elementary school and provide occupational orientation in the junior high school. These student bodies are important publics for CE which merit the rapt attention of the teacher–coordinator and other appropriate officals. Every possible effort should be made to alert pupils at these early grade levels to the opportunity which will be available to them, beginning at the eleventh-grade level, to develop career interest which may be identified in the junior high school occupational orientation program.

Relieves the School of High Facility Costs

The fiscal ability of any given community limits the educational program which can be fostered by the school. The cost of vocational education in sufficient scope and variety to satisfy the employment needs of the community and the needs of students enrolled in the school often becomes prohibitive. This cost may cause local school officials to seek an educational plan to provide the occupational breadth that is essential to well-rounded vocational education programs at a cost which can be afforded.

Through CE the school is relieved of the prohibitive cost of providing laboratories in sufficient number and variety to satisfy the diversified employment needs of the community and the attending educational needs of those students destined to compose the future work force. By using local business and industrial establishments in lieu of publicly financed laboratories for each legitimate occupational area represented in the community, the school immediately becomes capable of meeting these diversified student and community needs.

Program Values to Parents

The responsibility of parents to help their sons and daughters to chart a dependable course through the trying high school period is frequently more than they can handle without help. The school offers many services designed to be helpful in this respect. One of the most prominent of these aids is the maturing effect of arousing career interest in an appropriate occupational area and the pursuit of its development through CE.

There follows a brief discussion of the principal benefits of CE to the parents of cooperative students.

Helps Relieve Teenage Tension

The uncertainty which haunts many teenagers relative to the unknown which awaits them after graduation from high school is often relieved through satisfactory guidance and counseling experiences. This relief is especially evident when such experiences culminate in the identification of career interest in an occupational area, together with an educational plan designed for its accomplishment. An experience of this kind should establish a point of departure for more meaningful parental relationships than have previously been possible. The strength of purpose which may be generated by the student is often a source of parental relief from the strain of uncertainty which has previously dominated their relationship.

Perhaps it should be mentioned that the exact opposite of the situation above may occur in the case of parents who do not believe that the best interest of their son or daughter is being served by participation in CE. If there is no real interest beyond fringe values such as the monetary wage or perhaps getting away from school for half of the school day, it seems that parental concern is justified. On the other hand, if the student is sincerely concerned with the valid values of CE, parental counseling is in order.

Requires Constructive Use of Leisure Time

Leisure time is frequently a source of parental concern. It is seldom possible for them to plan activities which will satisfactorily involve nonschool time. On the other hand, teenagers left to make their own decisions will seldom use leisure time in a fashion entirely constructive and pleasing to parents. For this reason a dependable arrangement, such as CE, which usurps a major portion of the leisure time is often a welcome relief to the parent as well as the student.

Teaches Fiscal Responsibility

It can be assumed that those students who are sincerely concerned with the pursuit of occupational competence will also be sincerely concerned with the proper utilization of the financial resources which accrue to them as CE students. The most prominent expenditures should be for clothing, school supplies, recreation, and other areas of need normally satisfied by parents. Escaping such costs should be a welcome relief to the family budget.

The possibility of an irresponsible response to newly acquired financial ability should be mentioned. Students who enter CE primarily to acquire financial ability to make purchases which their parents refuse to make for them would tend to increase rather than decrease family tension and anxiety. This possibility should bolster student selection plans which ensure that only qualified students become enrolled in CE.

Certain aspects of generally related instruction should be helpful to students in effectively managing their income. Instruction in money management is especially appropriate because cooperative students, for the most part, are experiencing their first employment, with attending income management responsibility. Becoming familiar with basic elements of budgeting, saving, and investment plans should be helpful in developing desirable and dependable fiscal responsibility.

Suggested Activities

1. An important covenant in the school's relationship with employers is described in the following statement: "Employers should understand that recommendations of potential CE students by the school are made in terms of the student's aptitudes and vocational interests as they compare with the success requirements of the occupation in question." Describe a plan the school might follow in satisfying this condition.
2. Prepare a statement describing the advantages of CE graduates over conventional high school graduates in post–high school adjustment in the world of work or as college students.
3. Devise a plan which involves the guidance system in validating the avowed vocational intent of CE students.
4. Prepare a statement developing the idea that CE is an effective means of expanding the occupational breadth of comprehensive vocational education programs.
5. Explain in a written statement how CE satisfies the following basic principle of vocational education: "Vocational education will be successful to the degree that the environment in which it takes place compares favorably with that in which the student will eventually find employment."

chapter thirteen

In-School Relationship Development

The most important in-school publics are school administration, faculty and other professionals, students, and various supporting personnel. The success of CE will depend upon the degree to which these publics understand and accept its valid educational purposes and values. It necessarily follows, therefore, that the teacher–coordinator should devote initial and continuous attention to the development of appropriate relationships with these publics.

The prime purpose of relationship-development activities should be to develop positive attitudes toward CE. It will be necessary for teacher–coordinators to find ways and means of effectively presenting appropriate information in the right manner and at the right places and times. They should become adept in the use of all media available in all acceptable ways. The following list of media and attending methods should be helpful in determining which should be utilized in given public relations efforts.

Media and Methods for School and Community Relationships

Medium	Method
1. Newspapers and house organs	a. Feature articles, illustrated with photographs and short copy
	b. Human-interest stories with photographs and attending captions

Medium	Method
	c. Editorials (timely and seasonal)
	d. Periodic articles depicting program purposes and values
	e. Paid advertisements for student recruitment, or announcing school events
2. Radio and television	a. Spot announcements
	b. News items
	c. Symposium, panel, demonstration
	d. Addresses
	e. Role playing, skits, etc.
	f. Films
3. Organizations	a. Participating relationships with such organizations as PTA, service, industrial, civic, labor, education (local and state), church, and youth
	b. Participation in the programs of these organizations
4. Former students	a. Alumni association
	b. Follow-up of former students
	c. Placement service
	d. Invitation to return to the school for a visit
	e. Asking those who are available to participate in radio and television programs
	f. Using photographs in local newspaper with short stories or captions
5. Bulletin board	a. Periodic displays developed around appropriate and timely themes
6. School publications	a. Feature stories prepared by student reporters and photographers
	b. Periodic announcements and articles by student reporters

Medium	Method
7. Open house for faculty, administrators, and other professional personnel	a. Demonstration of instructional techniques and results
	b. Showing relationship between related instruction and work experience
	c. Role playing and skits by students
	d. Exhibition of student projects
8. Exhibits	a. Show windows, and exhibit areas of public buildings
	b. Traveling exhibits
	c. County fairs
9. Advisory committees	a. Serving as envoy in company and civic affairs
	b. Periodic representation through company advertising media
	c. Keeping the organizations represented by the membership informed relative to cooperative education
	d. Representing cooperative education wherever representation is needed
10. Cooperative students	a. Living examples of youth who are educationally fulfilled
	b. Enthusiastic recommenders of cooperative education to other students
11. Student club	a. Inspiring active participation in intraschool affairs
	b. Encouraging the celebration of special events such as Thanksgiving and Christmas to involve in-school and out-of-school publics
12. Adult classes	a. Employed adults properly served through adult classes expressing graditude through support of the school

Medium	Method
	b. Fostering and promoting classes for employed adults to the greatest feasible extent
13. Contests	a. Encouraging the student club to organize and conduct timely and appropriate contests in the school and community

Calendar of Suggested Relationship-Development Activities

The pressure under which the teacher–coordinators work may tend to influence the channeling of their efforts to areas of responsibility other than relationships development. For this reason it is suggested that an appropriate amount of time and effort be guaranteed through the preparation of a calendar of suggested activities for the entire year. (See Figure 23.) Care should be exercised in balancing these activities between the various in-school and out-of-school publics and the methods used. Supplemental efforts should be planned and directed at problem areas found to be prevalent in any given public. Carefully and persistently following an activities plan which involves a feasible combination of calendar items should guarantee the application of an appropriate amount of time and effort, equitably distributed among vital publics.

Figure 23 Calendar of Suggested Relationship-Development Activities

August   *Date*
1. Prepare and present calendar of activities for administrative approval.   _____
2. Hold initial advisory committee meeting to consider training stations for the year.   _____
3. Prepare material for publication via television and newspaper designed to alert employers to the imminent placement of new enrollees in the cooperative program.   _____
4. Accept invitation to speak to one or more civic clubs about program goals for the year.   _____

Date

5. Seek opportunity to speak to the faculty during pre-school workshops. Distribute brochure which depicts faculty role in cooperative education. _____

September
1. Prepare a report on student placement suitable for presentation to faculty, school administrators, and other appropriate publics. _____
2. Prepare a bulletin-board display depicting the need for students in unusual occupational areas. (See sample in Figure 4, page 55.) _____
3. Invite administrators and school board members to attend the second advisory committee meeting for the purpose of considering the program of work for the year. _____
4. Prepare materials for publication concerning program growth and development. _____
5. Accept invitations to speak to civic organizations concerning program values to the community. _____
6. Organize the student club and publicize its purpose and function as a part of the CE program. _____

October
1. Invite the school administrators to visit the classroom. (See page 279.) _____
2. Prepare an exhibit or demonstration for the county fair. Pass out brochures. _____
3. Seek invitation to present student symposium to PTA and civic organizations. _____
4. Prepare a student group to present an assembly program relative to the student values of CE. _____
5. Publicize the student club program of work for the year. _____
6. Ask the student club to sponsor, promote, and conduct an open house for the high school faculty and administration. (See page 289.) _____

November
1. Prepare a float or other appropriate representation for the homecoming parade. _____
2. Visit the homes of CE students upon invitation. (See page 295.) _____

Date

3. Ask the student club to sponsor, promote, and conduct an open house for parents and relatives of students. _____

4. Invite the local daily newspaper to assign reporters and supporting staff to the preparation of a feature story concerning CE and its contribution to the economic development of the community. _____

5. Prepare a portable display for showing at appropriate locations in the community. The theme of the display should have to do with an important aspect of CE. _____

December

1. Publicize public service projects of the student club, such as the adoption of a needy family for Christmas. _____

2. Invite school administrators to visit training agencies where students are placed. _____

3. Prepare appropriate representation in the Christmas parade. _____

4. Plan an assembly program to feature statements to the student body by graduates from cooperative education. _____

5. Prepare a news article featuring one or more program graduates. Use photographs. _____

6. Secure a cooperative education film suitable for presentation to in-school and community groups. _____

January

1. Invite administrative officials to attend an advisory committee meeting. _____

2. Invite student reporters and photographers from the school paper to prepare a feature story on cooperative education. _____

3. Invite local and state officials to visit the class. Have students prepared to explain how related instruction is accomplished. _____

4. Join a local civic club in designing, locating, and erecting appropriate road signs in accordance with the public interest. _____

5. Prepare a news article in the form of a report to the community on the accomplishment of cooperative education since its inception. _____

270

February   *Date*

1. Leadership training conference for all officers of student organizations throughout the school.   _____

2. Initiate and publicize a club planning committee for the annual employer–employee banquet.   _____

3. Accept invitations to address local civic club, featuring students to the greatest extent feasible.   _____

4. Prepare a news release in the form of a report on continuing education for employed adults.   _____

5. Prepare a news article describing the student club budget and fund-raising projects to finance it.   _____

March

1. Prepare an assembly program designed primarily to initiate enrollment process for next year.   _____

2. Prepare presentation for home rooms or activity periods involving sophomores and juniors.   _____

3. Prepare and present short presentations via television designed to alert employers and students that their interest in participating in the program should be made known to proper authorities.   _____

4. Prepare a news article concerning club plans to attend the state convention.   _____

5. Prepare special bulletin-board display which lists occupational opportunities for new enrollees. (See Figure 4.) _____

6. Announce through a news article the specific travel plans of those who will attend the state convention.   _____

April

1. Announce the mass meeting of potential cooperative students through all feasible in-school channels.   _____

2. Consider the advisability of mailing a letter or other form of information to eligible students and their parents. _____

3. Announce enrollment deadlines to coincide with the school calendar, culminating with spring registration.   _____

4. Arrange for television interviews with those students who will attend the state convention on the eve of departure. _____

5. Prepare news article on the employer–employee banquet program featuring the individual who will deliver the principal address.   _____

Date

6. Arrange for radio or television presentation featuring the "Community as a Laboratory" for cooperative education.   _____

7. Invite the press to attend the employer–employee banquet.   _____

8. Change the bulletin-board display.   _____

May

1. Schedule an advisory committee meeting for the purpose of presenting a report on student selection and the need for qualified training agencies.   _____

2. Prepare final publicity releases relative to employer–employee banquet.   _____

3. Prepare a news article relative to those who are graduating from the program and their plans for the future.   _____

June

1. Prepare and submit an annual report to appropriate administrative officials. (See Figure 24.)   _____

2. Prepare a news article featuring those parts of the annual report suitable for public consumption.   _____

3. Write an open letter to all cooperating employers expressing appreciation for their cooperation.   _____

4. Become involved in an appropriate professional improvement activity with appropriate announcements through regular channels.   _____

5. Seek opportunity to discuss program accomplishments and problems with appropriate administrative officials.   _____

July

1. Announce office hours during the month of July.   _____

2. Pursue summer conference or other professional-improvement activity.   _____

3. Take a vacation.   _____

Relationships with School Administration

Although the entire administrative staff has special significance to CE, the high school principal normally has the most vital relationship with the program. Policies originating in the principal's office will vitally affect environmental factors such as the following:

1. The student selection and referral plan.
2. The delegation of responsibility to the teacher–coordinator to finally determine who shall be enrolled with attending authority to return and recall students to and from the regular program during the enrollment period.
3. Administrative representation of CE to all in-school and out-of-school publics as an important educational program.
4. Fiscal support in sufficient scope to finance vital program needs.
5. Assuring the availability of essential elements of the school to assist in the proper conduct of the program.

It becomes quite obvious that administrative policy relative to the above environmental factors will be based primarily on basic administrative attitude toward CE. The fact that such attitudes will be based on what the administrators know about the program, from all sources, and what they believe its purposes and values to be suggests that the first step in an administrative relationship development program should be to become aware of the prevailing administrative attitude pattern.

Assess Administrative Attitude

Assessing the basic attitudes of the high school principal and other administrative officials should not be a difficult task. As a matter of fact, day-by-day relationships should be sufficiently revealing in terms of responses to problem situations which arise in the process of getting the program under way.

For various reasons, however, it is not always possible to judge the administrative attitude demonstrated during the employment process. True administrative attitude may not be revealed until after the employment process is completed. An example may be administrative refusal to allow the teacher–coordinator to have anything to do with the determination of the enrollment of the class. Such refusal may be based on the premise that other teachers do not have such a privilege. Under circumstances of this kind, the administrator is mandating that the teacher–coordinator's responsibility is to find jobs for the students who are assigned without regard for their vocational interests. If the principal insists on assigning students to CE according to the same policies which regulate student assignments to other courses, there is very little chance that the enrollment will consist of qualified students.

In the final analysis it may be determined that uninformed administrators tend to be burdened with various combinations of the following typical beliefs concerning CE:

1. It is a place to put those students who fail to produce satisfactorily in other areas of the educational program.
2. It is a suitable plan for misfits and disciplinary problems.
3. The enrollment should be limited to those who are not going to college.
4. Students of low intellectual ability should be given preference in the enrollment process.
5. The program is designed primarily for those who need financial assistance to stay in school.
6. It is designed to serve noneducational purposes.

These beliefs may be bolstered by mental fixtures concerning teacher–coordinators, such as:

1. They do not have enough to do in terms of class hours and total student contact.
2. The salary is out of line with the salaries of other teachers.
3. Too much unscheduled time is unaccounted for.
4. They are employed for twelve months but have no summer responsibilities.

It should be kept in mind that this sample listing of administrative and faculty beliefs includes those which commonly result when uninformed individuals are left to their own devices in assigning purposes and values. Although the resulting attitude toward CE may not be grossly negative, it could not be expected to foster a tendency to provide essential environmental factors which differ from those required for other high school courses.

The fact that the preceding listing of typical beliefs may fail properly to characterize a given administrator does not discount its authenticity as a general hypothesis upon which to base initial relationship development efforts. If the belief pattern of given administrators reflects a positive and permissive attitude toward the teacher–coordinator and CE, the suggested relationship development activities should serve to bolster this attitude and guard against any degenerate tendency. The suggestion is that a definite, deliberate, and continuous relationship development and maintenance program is vital to the establishment and maintenance of appropriate administrative relationships.

The assumption that the most constructive administrative relationships will be based upon understanding and appreciation of true program purposes and values demands that the teacher–coordinator be initially and continuously concerned with the task of bringing them to the administrator's attention in a fashion which will create a favorable impression and which will tend to counteract the typical beliefs listed above. Much of the success of such efforts will depend upon the basic qualities of the program from which the given relationship development efforts stem.

There would be little value, for example, in preaching "purpose and value" to an administrator when the program in question does not honestly reflect some resemblance of these qualities. On the other hand, producing a program which will basically inspire the desired administrative interest and concern may be quite difficult when the initial administrative belief pattern spawns an enrollment policy which causes students to be admitted who are not basically qualified. In a case of this kind, the administrator must be brought to understand that the first requisite of successful operation of the program is an enrollment policy designed to admit students who want, need, and are qualified to profit from the instruction. The enrollment policy should be settled before the beginning of school in order to prevent the loss of an entire year in program development and the unjustified dissipation of the educational opportunity of those students who are improperly enrolled.

The manner in which the development of administrative relationships is attempted is extremely important. High school principals, for example, are destined to be preoccupied and heavily involved in the discharge of their responsibilities. For this reason they cannot be expected to be willing recipients of lectures on the merits of CE from the teacher–coordinator.

As a matter of fact, they can be expected to resent and resist persistent efforts of this kind. It necessarily follows, therefore, that the tactics employed must be less direct and more diplomatic to be successful. Very little can be done to immediately change or correct errors inherently related to the school calendar, such as the student enrollment. For this reason major relationship efforts should be designed to correct such errors by the time the next school year begins.

The following suggested relationship-development activities may be helpful to inexperienced teacher–coordinators and should encourage the spawning of others from personal ingenuity.

It is most important that the administrator be impressed with the professional preparation and bearing of the teacher–coordinator, reflected through normal activities in the following ways:

1. Ability to talk intelligently and enthusiastically about CE.
2. Apparent knowledge of what should be done and ability to do it.
3. Concern for the problems of the total school as opposed to a narrow concern for CE at the expense of other elements.
4. Membership in and concern for the programs of local, state, and national professional organizations.
5. Complete awareness of the purpose that CE should accomplish as an integral part of the total educational program of the school.
6. Keeping friendship with administrators on a professional basis. (*Note*: It will be more effective and will last longer this way than on a "buddy–buddy" basis.)

Demonstrate Loyalty

Teacher–coordinators, in the course of discharging normal duties and responsibilities, come in contact with out-of-school publics much more often and on a more intimate basis than do high school principals and most other administrative officials. This association places them in very sensitive positions with respect to the opportunity to support the school and its staff, or failure to do so, when they find themselves involved in controversial circumstances relative to school policy or perhaps administrative or faculty action to which various elements of the community may have taken exception.

School administrators cannot be expected to be entirely confident until they are convinced that the teacher–coordinator is absolutely loyal to them and to the school. It seems advisable, therefore, to seek ways and means of relieving administrative concern in this respect. (See page 14 for a listing of typical circumstances which provide opportunity for the teacher–coordinator to demonstrate loyalty.)

Be Responsible

Willingness to accept responsibility and diligence in discharging it is a valuable characteristic which will greatly enhance desirable administrative relationships. Individuals who will accept the responsibilities delegated to them and who can be depended upon to discharge them without fail and in accord with the highest standards rapidly gain the confidence of those to whom they are responsible.

R. M. Frye

In this respect, however, teacher–coordinators may have to defend themselves against excessive assignments unrelated to CE. This overload could occur as a result of administrative belief that they do not have enough to do during unscheduled school time. The best defense against such an attitude is a program of activities so dynamic that the feedback from the community will promote its replacement with a sense of appreciation for effective representation of the school and recognition of the extent and the nature of teacher–coordinator responsibilities.

Being responsible also relates to requests that the teacher–coordinator finds necessary to present to administrative superiors. For example, a lack of confidence may cause the administrator to doubt that requests for financial support for the program are responsibly based on need and to suspect that they are unrealistically designed.

An illustration would be a teacher–coordinator's request for reference books. This approach to the principal may be in the form of a casual suggestion that reference books are needed in order to make authentic directly related instruction possible. Such a request is almost sure to leave the principal cold because it is not convincing and fails to inspire the necessary concern. The net result of this form of request would probably be no response, with attending teacher–coordinator disappointment and perhaps a feeling of being mistreated.

On the other hand, teacher–coordinators who research their need and prepare written requests listing the volumes needed, where they can be purchased, and the accompanying item and total cost, can expect a concerned reaction. In all probability such a request will be approved if, and when, the school becomes fiscally capable of making the purchase.

Another example could be the teacher–coordinator's request to be given the responsibility of determining who finally becomes enrolled in CE. The administrator may sincerely question whether this is a responsible request based on the best interest of the students involved and may discount it as a reflection of the teacher–coordinator's personal desire to have the opportunity to select the best students, measured by academic standards, at the expense of other teachers.

The administrator's response to requests of this kind, which depart from those normally coming from faculty members representing conventional phases of the school, will probably be based upon the teacher–coordinator's demonstrated tendency to respond and react responsibly to personal and professional challenges.

The teacher–coordinator should not fail to take advantage of every opportunity to meet and talk with administrative superiors or to supply appropriate literature, but should not depend upon such efforts to result in full understanding and acceptance of program purposes and values. As a matter of fact, a much more subtle and diplomatic approach must be developed to assure the administrator's undivided attention. At least one approach of this nature would be to capitalize on the administrator's concern for the image which the school projects to its in-school and out-of-school publics. For example, the attention which a high school principal accords to a teacher–coordinator discourse on the purposes of CE may be interrupted and divided by pressures stemming from other responsibilities, and the conference may be resolved into a head-nodding session without any significant communication taking place. For the same reason, literature presented to the principal may remain unmolested for an indefinite period of time.

On the other hand, high school principals can be expected to consider very carefully any written material, designed for distribution to any important public, presented for their approval. When viewed in this light it can be assumed that attention would be sharply focused by a request for approval to mail the letters to potential cooperative students and their parents. (See Figure 5, pages 57–58.) The assumption is that the principal would, in effect, base approval of these letters on the understanding and acceptance of their content. By the same token, an equal attention focus can be expected to be accorded to publicity releases, faculty and student brochures, television and radio program formats, and other public relations devices proposed for public consumption.

Questions on, or refusal to approve, any promotional material would set the stage for a meaningful and constructive confrontation which would guarantee the undivided attention of the administrator. If, under such circumstances, the teacher–coordinator fails to communicate effectively, there is little chance of developing the type of administrative relationship essential to the proper operation of CE programs.

Invite the Principal To Visit the Classroom

The high school principal should be given specific invitations to visit the related-subjects classroom at specific times, as opposed to casual suggestions that a visit would be welcomed. Having a student committee to extend the classroom visitation invitation would make it more impressive. Such visits should be timed to coincide with classroom activities which most vividly portray an important phase of CE. An example could be to invite the principal to visit directly related instruction at a time when the correlation of technically related information with work experience can be best illustrated. Having a student committee to explain and illustrate this process will impress the principal more forcefully than if the explanation is given by the teacher–coordinator.

A full understanding of the supervised and directed study method of teaching will help the principal to explain to the faculty how the teacher–coordinator can simultaneously teach technical information, on an individual basis, which is directly related to daily work experience in each of the occupations in which students are placed. The demonstration should be complete to the extent of including an explanation of how a study guide assignment is determined by the student and how it is accomplished in accordance with its instruction. (See the sample assignment in Figure 15, page 152.) The method employed in assigning a grade to the completed assignment test should also be fully explained. (See the sample test in Figure 17, pages 154–155, and the test answers in Figure 18, page 157.)

More than one classroom visit under the auspices of the student committee may be necessary to complete the principal's lesson on directly related instruction. If satisfactorily accomplished, however, the results will be much more effective than if the explanation had been made by the teacher–coordinator in an academic setting outside the classroom.

Invitations may also be extended to the principal to visit the classroom at times when generally related instruction is in progress. Here again a definite effort should be made to demonstrate an important aspect of CE. Suppose, for example, that the point had been reached in the unit on employer–employee relations where a conference or perhaps a panel discussion has been scheduled on "What the Employer Expects of Beginning Employees." If such activities are well planned and properly staged, they should very clearly reveal basic purposes and values of generally related instruction. In a case of this kind, the teacher–coordinator would be capitalizing on the administrator's basic concern for what is actually happening in the classroom, with the net result of getting undivided attention to basic purposes and values of CE.

Invite the Principal To Visit Training Stations

In accordance with an earlier suggestion, the principal should be encouraged to consider all training agencies in which students are currently placed to be extensions of the high school educational program. This feeling of responsibility, coupled with a natural desire to become acquainted with cooperating employers, should guarantee acceptance of the invitation to accompany the teacher–coordinator on training-agency visits. Such visits will be more effective if they are timed to follow the principal's visit to the directly-related-subjects classroom. The students who were the most prominent participators in the explanation and illustration of the supervised and directed study method of teaching should be the ones to be visited at their training stations.

It would lend authenticity to directly related instruction if these students could be prepared to demonstrate the application of the technical knowledge they have acquired in the classroom to the solution of on-the-job problems, or in the performance of job responsibilities. It may be feasible to alert the employers to be visited with the suggestion that they be prepared to talk with the principal concerning their concept of CE. The administrator's visits should involve students, training agencies, and cooperating employers which properly connote valid aspects of CE. Visits involving less qualified students, training agencies, and cooperating employers should follow for the purpose of contrasting proper and improper circumstances and practices.

Teacher–coordinators should not lose sight of the opportunities that visiting training stations with their principals present. The following will be illustrative:

1. They have the undivided attention of the principal.
2. They have unexcelled opportunity to demonstrate valid relationships of classroom instruction with work experiences.
3. They have a chance to promote the concept that CE is an educational program.
4. They can dramatize CE as a valid projection of the public achool into the community.
5. They have opportunity to answer questions inspired by contact with reality.

Keep Administrators Informed

The school administrator, with specific reference to the high school principal, is often not well enough informed concerning the teacher–coordinator's responsibilities and activities during unscheduled portions of the school day and after-school hours. The principal may have some doubt relative to what should be going on during these periods as well as to how the time is actually spent. For this reason the teacher–coordinator should lose no time in informing the principal about activities during the unscheduled portion of the school day as well as during the time which extends beyond the school day. (See the list of suggested activities below.)

It should be made clear that this listing of suggested activities does not constitute a verbatim schedule, but rather is representative of the nature of typical unscheduled activities normally arranged in accordance with the teacher–coordinator's best judgment.

As a general rule, the high school principal will accept this characterization of the teacher–coordinator's unscheduled responsibility if the feedback from the community reflects enough evidence to support this confidence. Being forced into circumstances which require admission that the teacher–coordinator's whereabouts is unknown may be extremely embarrassing and could precipitate disastrous relationships.

In order to prevent the development of circumstances of this kind, the teacher–coordinator should make every effort to keep the principal informed to the greatest possible extent relative to off-campus activities during the school day. Periodic reports concerning after-school activities such as the following should also be helpful:

1. Advisory committee meetings.
2. Addresses to civic clubs.
3. Television and radio programs.
4. Adult classes organized.
5. News articles published.
6. Other special activities.

The fact that an important part of CE is carried on in the classroom as an integral phase of the educational program does not guarantee that the high school principal and coadministrators are well-enough informed about program accomplishments. It is suggested, therefore, that an annual report be prepared which will succinctly present major program accomplishments during the period covered by the report. A sample of such a report appears in Figure 24.

In addition to the reports suggested above, the principal and other administrative officials should be supplied with an official list of the occupations and training stations finally approved by the advisory committee for the placement of students. The process by which this approved listing is developed is fully treated in Chapter Two.

Perhaps the most revealing and meaningful report to the principal is one which lists the students who are placed, together with their occupational objectives and training sponsors. The alert and sensitive teacher–

Figure 24   Cooperative Education Annual Report

_____ High School

Covering the School Year 19____–19____

I. Number of Applicants and Placements

There were _____ applications for enrollment in cooperative education this year. _____ were submitted by boys and _____ by girls.
_____ of the boys and _____ of the girls were placed in qualified
training stations and enrolled in the program in September. _____
boys and _____ girls were added to the enrollment at midterm, making a total enrollment for the year of _____ .

II. Student Names, Occupational Objectives, and Training Agencies

A listing of students together with their occupational objectives and
training agencies is attached.

III. Dropouts, Graduates, and Carry Over

During the year there were _____ dropouts, _____ transferred to
other schools, _____ entered military service, and _____ are unaccounted for. There were _____ seniors who completed training with
the class of 19____ . _____ juniors will be carried over into next
year's program. Of the graduating seniors, _____ were honor students.

IV. Total Pupil Hours and Earnings

There were _____ class meetings, taught by the teacher–coordinator,
and _____ on-the-job work hours under his auspices—making a total
student-hour load of _____ . The total earning of all students during
the nine-month school term was $ _____ .

V. Follow-up of Last Year's Graduates

A follow-up study of the _____ students enrolled in the program last
year reveals that _____ juniors were carried over to this year. Of the
_____ who completed the training, _____ are employed in the occupation for which they were trained, _____ are employed in closely
related occupations, _____ are working in occupational areas unre-

Figure 24 *(continued)*

lated to their training as cooperative students, _____ are unemployed, _____ are continuing their education, _____ are in military service, and _____ are unaccounted for.

VI. Comments on Notable Aspects of the Program

(Note: Record in this space information concerning any aspect of the program deemed to be of interest to the principal and other administrative officials.)

VII. Recommendations

(Note: Place in this space carefully phrased recommendations which are designed to strengthen the program and to eliminate barriers to progress.)

Respectfully submitted,

_____
Teacher–Coordinator

coordinator will, no doubt, find other areas of interest upon which to submit administrative reports. Here again, however, caution is suggested in the design of the total reporting program, because reporting at random and without judgment could have little or no meaning to the recipient. The teacher–coordinator should design the reporting program to keep administrative officials properly informed without exceeding the bounds of good judgment.

Faculty Relationships

The inexperienced teacher–coordinator may tend to discount the importance of personal and professional relationships with the faculty and other professional staff members and their attitude toward CE. It must be kept in mind that each member of the faculty influences a segment of the student body, large or small, depending upon the strength of leadership. Potential cooperative students will, in all probability, confer with their favorite teacher concerning the advisability of enrolling in the program. The advice of the teacher will surely stem from basic understanding of the purposes and values of the program and the type of student it is designed to serve.

If, for example, the English teacher determines that the prime purpose of CE is to make it possible for those who need financial aid to work part-time while going to school, he or she will recommend that only those who need financial aid apply for enrollment. As this illustration is carried a bit further, it becomes evident that under circumstances where the faculty as a whole shares the attitude of the English teacher, only those students who are in need of financial assistance will be advised to seek enrollment. The net result would be the restriction of the cooperative student population to those who have financial problems.

Other faculty understandings and beliefs based on superficial program purposes and values can be expected to produce similar results in restricting enrollment to given types of students without regard or concern for the values the program holds for other qualified students. All these misconceptions compound the importance of correcting inaccurate or spurious information which feeds normal faculty curiosity from a variety of unofficial sources.

Relationships with guidance staff members is of utmost importance because normal procedure may place them in the role of referring students for enrollment. This responsibility places a high premium on their understanding and acceptance of enrollment qualifications. The following suggestions should be helpful to inexperienced teacher–coordinators in initiating and promoting desirable relationships with professional coworkers.

Assess Faculty Attitudes

Basic faculty understanding and the degree of acceptance of program purposes and values will be less obvious than are those of the administration primarily because of the greater numbers involved and the less tangible contacts available to the teacher–coordinator. It can be assumed, however, that a given faculty will tend to share the sets of administrative beliefs suggested on page 274, with special importance attached to those having to do with the teacher–coordinator. Faculty members may be more concerned about the teacher–coordinator as an individual and his responsibilities as they compare with their own than with the purposes and values of the program. Faculty attitude toward the teacher–coordinator will, therefore, strongly influence its attitudes toward CE. This probability lends prestige to the personal and professional image the teacher–coordinator is able to project to the faculty.

Project Professional Image

The tendency of individual faculty members to take exception to teacher–coordinator responsibilities, qualifications, and compensation as compared with their own requires action designed to counter the resulting attitude toward CE. Formal efforts to promote faculty understanding and acceptance of program purposes and values should not be abandoned, but rather special efforts should be exerted in the projection of a sound professional image by the teacher–coordinator. Program propaganda will not be acceptable to the faculty until the teacher–coordinator is generally accepted as a qualified professional person.

In other words, the first job of teacher–coordinators in the development of faculty relationships is selling themselves. The high school faculty can be expected to judge them in accordance with criteria similar to that employed by the administration and suggested on page 276.

There follow, however, some suggested activities which should be helpful in gaining faculty recognition and confidence.

Be Friendly and Cooperative

The teacher–coordinator's advent as a faculty member will normally be greeted by friendly and curious attention on the part of all elements of the school. Such attitudes on the part of the faculty should be cultivated and encouraged by equally affable reactions on the part of the teacher–coordinator. This empathy can be accomplished, at least in part, through successful accomplishments of the following:

1. Responding warmly and sincerely to friendly gestures extended by faculty members in chance meetings and in other informal circumstances.
2. Showing interest and concern for the problems of other teachers.
3. Being enthusiastic about the total school.
4. Showing willingness to be cooperative in the accomplishment of faculty goals.
5. Assuming a fair share of extracurricular activities.
6. Reflecting sincerity and enthusiasm about CE and its contribution to the total educational program.

Under no circumstances should the teacher–coordinator allow personal reactions to a cordial faculty welcome to be steeped in familiarity to the extent of jeopardizing the ultimate development of genuine professional relationships. The suggestion that caution of this nature be exercised in initial faculty contacts should not eliminate the possibility of the ultimate development of warm personal relationships with faculty members. Continuous effort should be devoted to the merging of CE into the total educational program, with the least possible friction, as opposed to the tendency to characterize it as being something different which requires extensive concessions at the expense of other program elements.

Supply Information to the Faculty

Aside from the importance of the personal image which the faculty holds of the teacher–coordinator, the fact remains that permanent faculty attitude will be based on what it ultimately accepts as the basic values of CE, and the contribution it is designed to make to the total educational program. Thus it can be assumed that it is possible to temper or change initial faculty reactions which do not contribute to favorable program climate, through appropriate relationship-development activities. Such activities should be well planned and timed to occur at the most opportune periods of the school year.

One of the most essential areas of understanding on the part of the faculty is that it shares in the responsibility for the success or failure of cooperative students. A normal outgrowth of such an understanding should be recognition that students accepted for enrollment, upon faculty recommendation, are representative of the total educational

Figure 25 Sample Brochure for Teachers Relative to Cooperative Education

1. *Definition*
Perhaps the best definition of cooperative education is: a school and community laboratory through which high school students find expression in real job situations for that which they have learned in subject-matter courses. The program simply brings together the student, his educational background, and occupational opportunity. Do not confuse cooperative education with part-time job-experience programs. Cooperative education is an *educational program*, which is designed for those students who want, need, and are qualified to profit from the instruc-

tion. Part-time job-experience programs simply provide opportunity for students to work part-time without regard for career intent.

2. Cooperative Education Represents the Total School

Technical instruction in cooperative education is given through the media of language, mathematics, and other high school subjects. Hence every student placed through the program is an exhibit not only of the teacher–coordinator's efforts but of the total teaching results of _____ high school.

3. The Selection of Cooperative Students Is Important

Cooperative education resembles to some degree other school activities, such as football and band, which are dependent upon public support and are subject to its appraisal. For this reason, cooperative students should be carefully selected in order that a wholesome program prestige might be developed and maintained through the success of the students placed in the various training stations. Every one has an obligation to problem students, but cooperative education is not the place for all of these people, although it should assume a fair share of the responsibility for this student group. But under no circumstances should the business and industry in the community be expected to pay for the experience of being the victims of problem students. Their doing so would not contribute to a desirable reputation of the school.

Students accepted in cooperative education should have desirable character traits, such as dependability, integrity, courtesy, cooperativeness, and sincerity—characteristics not determined by scholarship. For this reason the selection of students does not depend upon grades alone. As a matter of fact, C students can be successful. In many cases D students are acceptable. This statement does not discount the desirability of A and B students but simply emphasizes that student selection should not be based on grades alone.

The cooperation of all teachers is requested in helping to identify students who are qualified to profit from this program. Its success will depend upon your help and cooperation.

4. Application for Cooperative Education

The student who decides to enter cooperative education must apply for enrollment by filling out and submitting an official application form to the teacher–coordinator prior to spring registration. This form must carry the signature of a parent. Will you please refer those students whom you believe to be qualified for enrollment to the teacher–coordinator? All students you recommend will be carefully considered for enrollment. Please contact the teacher–coordinator for any additional information you may need.

efforts of the school. In this light, student success or failure on the job reflects, respectively, credit or discredit to all teaching results.

Reference is made to the sample brochure for teachers, which is shown as Figure 25, as an instrument around which faculty relationship efforts during enrollment periods might be planned. A suggested procedure in the use of this instrument follows:

1. Prepare the brochure for distribution to administration and faculty members.
2. Request permission to speak briefly to the faculty during the pre-school workshop or other appropriate faculty meeting.
3. Build a short presentation (not more than 20 minutes) around the brochure.
4. Distribute the brochure after the presentation.
5. Express the desire to discuss the brochure contents at a later time with those who may be interested.
6. Design the program to emphasize the need for faculty cooperation.

Utilization of the brochure as suggested above should not terminate efforts to supply the faculty with information relative to the nature of CE. As a matter of fact, ultimate success will depend upon diplomatic persistence in this respect. It is extremely important, however, that faculty-relationship-development activities be confined within the bounds of good taste and propriety. Good judgment as to where, when, what, and how specific efforts should be applied is the key to success.

Additional devices through which appropriate information may be channeled to the faculty are suggested as follows:

1. An open letter to the faculty which describes the investment the student who enrolls in CE is required to make in terms of educational opportunity (*Note*: This letter could be developed around any other appropriate topical area.)
2. Articles in the daily newspaper which reflect credit to the role of the faculty in the student selection process.
3. Articles published in the official organs of professional organizations to which teachers belong.
4. Periodic reports to the faculty on the success or failure of currently enrolled students and graduates from the program.
5. The design and distribution of bulletins and brochures which appropriately reflect program purposes and values.

Hearing or reading complimentary statements regarding the contribution that teachers are making may well serve as the cue that prompts the attention and concern which normally precedes the desired action.

Hold Open House for Faculty and Administration

Teachers are prone to satisfy their curiosity and form opinions of the nature and quality of any phase of the educational program with which they are not familiar or do not understand, from any source which offers plausible answers to their questions. The probability that knowledge concerning related instruction acquired in this fashion will be valid is so remote that the provision of authentic information becomes essential to desirable faculty relationships. Although there may be many ways in which this information can be presented, one logical medium through which teachers may see for themselves what is going on in the related-subjects classroom is the open house.

Such a program should be designed to illustrate the methods employed in the teaching of directly and generally related subjects. Students should play a prominent role in this program similar to that suggested for planned administrative visits to the classroom discussed earlier. (See page 278.) Such a program should be held at a time when students and teachers can be available without conflict with their work. The open-house technique implies that the number of teachers present at any given time can be controlled so as to coincide with the number of students who are available to serve as hosts and guides for the tour of classroom activities.

The teacher–coordinator should design the program to feature the strongest available assets. If, for example, the student group is reasonably capable and is enthusiastically concerned about letting teachers know about their work as cooperative students, the type of open-house program suggested above should be effective. If the students are not enthusiastic, however, good judgment may dictate that a program be designed to terminate in a general group presentation. Such a presentation should involve the most capable students in a prepared presentation such as a panel discussion or symposium. In the final analysis, however, the presentation may have to be made by the teacher–coordinator if the class does not include appropriate student ability. A program of this nature should not be attempted if the presentation cannot be anticipated to be of sufficient quality to make the desired impression. Under no circumstances should such a program be allowed to advertise shortcomings and weaknesses in support of frantic efforts to attract favorable attention.

Poor performance on the part of the teacher–coordinator or students would almost surely serve to spawn negative attitudes where they have not previously existed and confirm adverse opinions which the program was conceived to dispel. Ability to capitalize on the strongest human and physical resources at hand is a most important success factor for a teacher–coordinator.

Confer with Teachers About Individual Students

It was emphasized earlier that the tool subjects, such as English and mathematics, should take on new significance to CE students as a result of their contact with reality through work experiences. The fact remains, however, that this significance may have to be emphasized by the teacher–coordinator in an effort to compensate for student failure to do so. In this respect the school may adopt the policy that satisfactory performance and accomplishment in the total educational program is just as important as the work experience.

If, for example, it becomes evident that spending approximately one-half of the school day on the job is affecting the student's ability to do satisfactory work in tool subjects such as English, it may be determined that the work experience should be curtailed to the extent necessary to inspire satisfactory work in the classroom. The impossibility of anticipating the policy of any given school in this respect negates the advisability of attempting to render judgment of such policies. The fact remains, however, that the teacher–coordinator should be vitally concerned with the progress of CE students in regular high school classes.

This concern often becomes an important factor in relationships with faculty members in that it inspires circumstances which champion mutual interests in given students. The teacher–coordinator should acquire copies of the grade reports of CE students at the end of each grading period. After a study of these reports, an appointment should be sought with each teacher involved with cooperative students, for the purpose of discussing the progress of each student. First attention should be given to those students who are failing.

The overall results of conferences of this nature range from a general opportunity to improve the teacher's concept of CE to the opportunity of making specific suggestions designed to serve the best interest of the student in question. Let it be assumed, for example, that the auto-mechanic student, who was mentioned earlier, is failing in English, primarily because of failure to produce themes in sufficient quality and quantity to satisfy the established requirements of the course. An appropriate suggestion on the part of the teacher–coordinator could be that the English teacher be supplied with a listing of topics from which the student might select or be assigned subjects for themes. Such a listing may include topics such as the following:

1. The function of the condenser in the automotive ignition system.
2. The ignition coil and its function in the automotive ignition system.
3. The five carburetor circuits.
4. The four-stroke cycle and its relationship to timing.
5. Differential action in the automotive power train.
6. Electronic ignition systems.

This listing could be made to include topics in sufficient number and variety to provide the breadth of choice necessary to permit the correlation of theme writing with current areas of study in the related-subjects classroom. The assumption is that the cooperative automotive student could be expected to display greater interest in researching and writing about "The Function of the Condenser in the Automotive Ignition System" than in a topic holding little interest or relevance, such as "The Pyramids of Egypt." The English teacher should be able to accomplish his or her goals in either case, in that the quality of writing could be judged in either area. When the proper correlation exists, the writing of themes to satisfy an English requirement will strengthen directly related instruction in the related subjects classroom and vice versa.

The same type of arrangement can be worked out in all occupational areas in which students are placed. The fact that correlative possibilities with English are the most numerous and obvious should not obsure such opportunities in other subject-matter areas. Sincere and persistent efforts in this realm of faculty relationships should reap excellent results in the form of increased teacher understanding and respect for CE.

Relationships with Cooperative Education Students

The potential success of CE in any school system depends heavily upon the image the student body holds of the program and of the teacher–coordinator. Although those students enrolled at any given time should always be considered as an integral part of the student body, they should be treated separately in relationship-development efforts. The necessity for this stems from the tendency of student bodies and faculties to base opinions and attitudes on what is seen in and heard from this student group. It necessarily follows, therefore, that the teacher–coordinator should be initially concerned with the development of understanding and appreciation of the purposes and values of CE on the part of CE students. There would be little chance of selling a student body or any other public on program merits when currently enrolled students were emitting potent negative attitudes and exhibiting a lack of understanding of and respect for the program. What, for example, will cooperative students be prone to say in answer to questions such as these from curious students:

1. What do you do in the related-subjects classroom?
2. Why did you enroll in cooperative education?
3. What good is cooperative education to you?
4. What kind of a person is the teacher–coordinator?

When the answers to these questions, and countless others which curious students can be expected to pose, are positive in nature and indicate understanding and sincere concern and respect for true program purposes and values, the effect on student-body attitude should be positive and constructive. On the other hand, negative and indifferent responses will have the opposite effect.

The following suggestions should be helpful to inexperienced teacher–coordinators in attempts to provide an appropriate foundation for the image that CE students will reflect on and off the campus.

Teach Program Purposes, Values, and Outcomes

The teacher–coordinator should leave nothing to chance relative to the understanding and appreciation CE students have of the program and what it should mean to them. The fact that this understanding should have been treated thoroughly during the enrollment process does not eliminate the need for continued emphasis in the initial phases of the teaching program and periodic reference thereafter. The formal teaching of program purposes and values, expected outcomes, and the cost to students in terms of educational opportunity should be concentrated in, but not limited to, the orientation period. Teacher–coordinator neglect in this respect could result in the projection of a damaging image on the part of qualified students as well as those who are improperly enrolled.

Represent the Cooperative Education Student Group

Teacher–coordinators should be ready and able to represent their student groups wherever and whenever the opportunity to do so occurs. The character of such representation and the manner in which it is accomplished should inspire student pride, confidence, and respect. Group awareness of the fact that it can depend upon a quality of representation, in all matters at all times, which will reflect credit to it and the program, should inspire respect for and confidence in the teacher–coordinator. Loyalty to students and persistent efforts to represent them appropriately at all times and under all circumstances should prompt a feeling of pride in affiliation with CE.

Set a Good Example

Many of the teaching and student relationship-development efforts in CE have to do with methods and techniques of effectively coping with actual circumstances as opposed to pseudo-classroom teaching. This concern places the teacher–coordinator in an ideal position to demonstrate by personal example rather than to simply tell students how such circumstances should be met. It can be expected, therefore, that the establishment of high standards of performance through personal examples should enhance the teacher–coordinator's image in the eyes of CE students. Such examples should challenge them to aspire to high standards of excellence in their own performance.

Establish and Maintain Reasonable Standards

Reasonable standards of accomplishment and conduct in the classroom and on the job should be established and persistently maintained. Such standards should serve as a firm foundation for meaningful teacher–student relationships. Perhaps the most important concern in developing this relationship is the necessity that cooperative students understand and accept what is expected of them in the entire realm of CE. This need coincides with an earlier suggestion that students who understand what is expected of them are prone to conform with such expectations to the extent of their ability. Important factors in teacher–student relationships relative to standards of conduct and achievement include the following:

1. They are reasonably acceptable to students because they challenge rather than discourage.
2. They have been approved by appropriate administrative officials.
3. They apply to general conduct at school, in the related-subjects classroom, en route to the job, and on the job.
4. They refer to the quantity and quality of production in the related-subjects classroom.
5. They have to do with the maintenance of an acceptable quality of work in regular high school courses.
6. They do not depart drastically from standards and requirements in other elements of the school.
7. They are thoroughly understood by all cooperative students.
8. They are subject to teacher–coordinator judgment in accordance with circumstances.

It should be emphasized that standards should be designed to challenge cooperative students to achieve on the highest possible levels rather than to serve as instruments of regimentation. They should also serve as avenues through which the teacher–coordinator can constantly express personal concern for the welfare of all students and assure them that their best interests are being served at all times.

Be Fair, Firm, and Friendly

The teacher–coordinator who is able to apply the three F's— *fairness, firmness, and friendliness*—in all areas of student relationships will find the results to be most gratifying and conducive to maximum accomplishment. There must be no doubt in the mind of students relative to the fairness of the teacher–coordinator in dealing with them as individuals. All students must be convinced that they will be judged by the same standards and with the same degree of severity as are all other students under the same circumstances. They must know that any variation in this respect is not vacillating permissiveness based on favoritism, but rather is justice based on sympathetic understanding of circumstances which justify mitigation of the judgment.

The students will accept no compromise in the area of fairness in their relationship with the teacher–coordinator, but they may come to understand that fairness can be consistent without being uniform. Each student presents a different set of circumstances which must be taken into consideration in rendering fair judgment in all performance areas.

Teacher–coordinators should develop the ability to radiate firmness in working with students and should leave no doubt that they mean what they say. They should be equally firm in establishing standards of conduct, production in the classroom and on the job, and in general decorum on and off the campus.

If the three F's are to be completely mastered, fairness and firmness must be tempered with friendliness to the extent that teacher–coordinators can smile while they are saying what they mean. Students will respect consistency in the teacher–coordinator's disposition in that they can depend upon it being about the same from day to day. They will respect efforts to let them know what is expected and the certainty of correction when they fail to measure up.

The teacher–coordinator should avoid at all cost any tendency to reign with permissiveness punctuated with temper tantrums designed to correct the intolerable conditions sure to develop. Teacher–coordinators should not have to periodically "blow their top" in order to develop enough momentum to challenge students pursuing courses of conduct inappropriate and out of character. They should condition themselves to the point that relationships with students can be structured on a stable framework of fairness, firmness, and friendliness, to the end that students will regard them as friends who will deal with them fairly and firmly at all times.

Visit Homes of Cooperative Students

The more the teacher–coordinators know about the students enrolled in CE, the more able they should be to work effectively with them. Familiarity with home conditions should be helpful in dealing with personal problems which develop under in-school and out-of-school circumstances. Coming from broken homes, for example, may account for student attitudes which militate against proper adjustment to the environments to which cooperative students are subjected.

Visiting the homes of students should contribute to the teacher–coordinator's image of each student in his total environment. For the most part, such visits should be welcomed and appreciated as a gesture of personal interest in students and their families. The teacher–coordinator is cautioned, however, that some students may be the victims of embarrassing home conditions and would prefer that outsiders not know about them. Under such circumstances an uninvited visit could worsen rather than improve the attitude of the student. The suggestion is, therefore, that the teacher–coordinator visit the homes of students only upon invitation. It should be made known to the entire student group that such invitations would be welcomed, and that visits will not occur without them.

Relationships with the Student Body

The achievement of appropriate relationships with CE students will serve as a firm foundation upon which to develop relationships with other publics with particular reference to the student body as a whole. The teacher–coordinator can proceed with additional relationship-development activities with confidence that the image of the CE student group will support rather than defeat them. The following suggestions should be helpful to inexperienced teacher–coordinators in relationship-development efforts with the student body as a whole.

Develop Appropriate Image in the Eyes of the Student Body

Perhaps the most constructive approach to the development of effective relationships with the student body, or any other public, would be to consider the question: What should my personal image and that of the program be in the eyes of the student body? Let it be assumed that the answers to this question would be as follows:

1. The teacher–coordinator is a professionally competent person who represents the school and all of its parts on the highest possible plane.
2. The teacher–coordinator is well groomed and properly dressed at all times.
3. The teacher–coordinator is sincerely interested in students and can be depended upon to be helpful when needed.
4. The teacher–coordinator is a good citizen and makes appropriate contributions to the life of the community.
5. The teacher–coordinator represents a program of vocational education which presents unexcelled opportunity for those students who want, need, and are qualified to profit from the instruction

Seek Early Introduction to the Student Group

The teacher–coordinator should diplomatically seek the earliest feasible introduction to the student body through the most appropriate channels. This exposure could be accomplished through being introduced by the principal of the high school, at a general assembly or other appropriate program which involves senior high school students. At the time of such an introduction the teacher–coordinator should be prepared to make a short statement designed to inspire student interest and curiosity in CE. The principal may need to be convinced that the function of the teacher–coordinator involves the total student body to an extent which exceeds that of other teachers by an amount which justifies the granting of this special privilege. Persuasion of this kind may serve to focus the principal's attention on important program characteristics which might otherwise fail to be noticed.

Accept Responsibilities with Student Groups

Teacher–coordinators should be ready, willing, and able to accept and discharge periodic responsibilities with student groups which may be assigned to them. The provision of faculty supervision and sponsorship for extracurricular student activities is often a difficult problem for high school principals. For this reason, they, as well as affected student groups, can be expected to appreciate willingness to accept such responsibilities on the part of the teacher–coordinator. As a general rule the administrator will not permit individual faculty members to be overloaded with extracurricular responsibilities. In the case of exceptions to this rule, however, the teacher–coordinator should guard against assignments which will cause neglect of CE activities.

In addition to periodic assignments, there are other types of responsibilities involving continuous service, to which faculty members are elected by student groups. Responsibilities of this nature could include offices such as class sponsors and advisors to any permanently constituted student group within the extracurricular activity program. Although being selected by a student group may be regarded as an accomplishment, teacher–coordinators must keep in mind that their first responsibility is providing supervision and leadership for their own student groups. Under no circumstances should this responsibility be neglected in favor of other student groups.

Develop Sincere Interest in Students and Their Problems

In the final analysis the acceptance and discharge of the responsibilities which the teacher–coordinator accepts should reflect sincere interest in students and their problems. Although this concern is a basic characteristic of the successful teacher, it often suffers when applied to extracurricular responsibilities which usurp free time. It would be far better to refuse to accept such responsibilities than to accept and then neglect them. Neglect of this kind will not only sap the vitality of the affected student organization but will also constitute a flagrant display of insincerity and irresponsibility which could have a disastrous effect on the general attitude of the student body.

Be Properly Dressed and Groomed at All Times

Professionalism has been emphasized as an important factor in relationships with all important publics. Appropriate dress and grooming habits are important ingredients of professionalism and are among the most obvious features of the personality. The general appearance of the teacher–coordinator, therefore, has a great deal to do with first impressions of all in-school publics. Embryonic teacher–coordinators should develop dressing and grooming habits which will cause them to reflect the image of professional persons. It is suggested that personal traits of this nature be characterized by adherence to the dictates of good taste and propriety as judged by local standards. Consistency in this respect will contribute to the teacher–coordinator's image in the eyes of the student body and reflect credit to CE.

The diversity of the teacher–coordinator's responsibilities, which includes continuous contact with off-campus publics, should be sufficient justification for dressing and grooming practices which may be more formal than those of other faculty members. It should be pointed out, however, that the quality of dressing and grooming habits cannot overcome failure to display appropriate bearing and posture in the teaching process or in addressing student groups in other capacities.

Be a Good Citizen

The image of teacher–coordinators in the eyes of student bodies will encompass their total activity spectrum in and out of the school. The teacher–coordinator's scope of activities should be broadened to

298

feasible limits rather than to give the impression that the CE program should be considered as something different and apart from other educational aspects of the school. Being a good citizen on and off the campus, therefore, would consist primarily of being willing to commit time and effort in concert with other citizens, to the solution of community problems and the preservation of its best interests.

The application of this principle should place the teacher–coordinator in positions of responsibility in community affairs in and out of the school. High-caliber performance in such positions of vantage should command the approval and respect of the faculty and student body. Failure to measure up, however, could be expected to have the opposite effect.

Provide Appropriate Program Information

The preceding suggested relationship-development activities should serve to arouse student-body interest and curiosity concerning CE. The degree of acceptance of information concerning the program will depend to a great extent upon the respect and regard students hold for the teacher–coordinator. The following techniques of presenting information to student groups are among the most appropriate:

1. Oral presentation of information on appropriate occasions.
2. Bulletin-board displays depicting various program characteristics.
3. Feature stories in the school paper prepared by student reporters.
4. Brochures prepared for student consumption.
5. Films depicting important features of CE.
6. Presenting panels composed of cooperative students. (*Note*: Let them tell their peers about the values of the program to them.)
7. Presenting employer panels depicting CE from their point of view.

The list of techniques of transmitting appropriate program information to student groups does not exhaust the possibilities, but it is suggestive. Good judgment in selecting the proper method of presenting information on a given occasion, coupled with quality in all other respects, should produce the desired student attitude.

Relationships with Supporting Personnel

The significance of the influence of supporting personnel who perform vital services in the modern school is often overlooked. Perhaps the most potent elements of this group are workers in administrative offices, such as secretaries, receptionists, and clerks, who handle routine administrative affairs. The importance of this group, with particular reference to secretaries, stems from the fact that they frequently enjoy administrator confidence and influence their opinions. The secretary in the principal's office, for example, may be extremely helpful or vice versa, depending upon personal attitudes toward the teacher–coordinator and CE.

It should also be kept in mind that secretaries are frequently the source of much of the information which emanates from the principal's office. This may be in the form of answers to inquiries from visitors to the office or from curious faculty members, or in supplying information by telephone in response to off-campus requests. When secretaries are left to their own devices in supplying such information, there is a good chance that it will be tempered by their personal attitude toward the teacher–coordinator and CE.

The supporting elements of the staff in most modern schools would include other workers, such as food and maintenance personnel. Although the relationships with these groups may be less important than those with workers in administrative offices, they should be made aware of the teacher–coordinator's affiliation with the high school faculty.

Typical In-School Relationship-Development Problems

Problem 1 *Tendency to neglect in-school relationship development*
Inexperienced teacher–coordinators are often prone to take their relationships with in-school publics for granted. This assumption could result from deficiencies in preemployment education, as well as a personal tendency of the inexperienced to presuppose knowledge and understanding on the part of those with whom they work. Let it be assumed, for example, that a newly employed and inexperienced teacher–coordinator finds that only low-producing and, for the most part, educationally retarded students are referred for enrollment.

Rather than recognize this as a reflection of the image of CE held by in-school publics, the inexperienced teacher–coordinator may take it as an effort by administrators and coworkers to sabotage the program. In the first instance, the alert teacher–coordinator should recognize the necessity of an organized relationship development effort designed to correct or adjust the faulty program concept. Viewing the circumstances as an effort to defeat the program or relegate it to inferior status, on the other hand, could lead to a defeatist attitude which could be a prelude to failure.

The development of the teacher–coordinator's awareness of potential public relations difficulties together with suggested safeguards as an important part of preservice education constitutes the best solution to this problem. It must be emphasized, however, that preparation in its best form will not necessarily overcome human frailty and ineptness in coping with human relationship problems. Neither will it overcome poor organizational and management ability as a basis of failure to apply time and effort in accordance with appropriate priorities.

Problem 2 *Failure to premise public relations efforts on demonstrable program qualities*

Let it be emphasized again that the teacher–coordinator's first responsibility is to produce the greatest possible quality in all of the vital aspects of CE as the first relationship-development effort. Featuring directly related instruction in public relation activities, without demonstrable accomplishment in the classroom, for example, would constitute misrepresentation of the fact and would eventually detract from rather than contribute to the in-school relationship pattern. Overstatement would be a mistake in circumstances involving other program elements and values which were not, to some degree, observable in the operational pattern of the program.

A prime principle of public relations, therefore, is to be sure that the product is good before trying to sell it.

Problem 3 *Planning and organizing public relations activities*

The timing and appropriateness of public relation activities is as important as the content and quality of the presentation. Recognition of this principle should be convincing proof to the teacher–coordinator that an overall plan should be developed in a convenient form, such as a relationship activities calendar. (See page 269.) A plan of this kind prepared prior to the opening of school should render all prescheduled activities vulnerable to the following considerations:

1. Ample preparation, planning, and organizational time.
2. Orderly involvement of special events and holidays included in the

school calendar as well as other events which occur in the community.

3. Enlistment of the aid of others when and where it is needed.
4. Scheduling of items such as special films.
5. Arranging for television or radio presentations.
6. Selection of media and methods.

Perhaps the greatest value of a relationship activities calendar is the contribution it makes to persistence in relationship-development efforts. It serves as a constant reminder of what should occur at given times as well as an accurate record of what has been accomplished. The converse of this would be a total lack of an overall plan, with relationship-development activities being limited to spasmodic and disorganized efforts prompted by necessity.

Problem 4 *Identification and exploitation of the teacher–coordinator's strongest personal assets*

It is quite obvious that teacher–coordinators should be endowed with personal assets and abilities in sufficient scope and quality to make acceptable performance possible under diverse circumstances. They should be able to render a good account of themselves in almost any type of circumstance in which they become involved. Ideally, this should include the ability to speak effectively to large or small audiences concerning CE, write effectively for publication, plan and present exhibits and displays, and effect meaningful personal relationships on a one-to-one basis. Not all teacher–coordinators will measure up in all categories. Hopefully, however, each one will have at least one strength which can be employed effectively in public relation activities. Accordingly, they must become adept at placing their best foot forward and in circumventing circumstances which would exploit weaknesses. If, for example, the teacher–coordinator writes well but is a poor public speaker, writing should be emphasized in personal public relations activities and help sought in filling public speaking engagements. These invitations often present opportunities to use student and employer panels and symposiums, as suggested on page 185. The principal or other administrative official or perhaps a member of the advisory committee may be willing to pinch-hit for the teacher–coordinator when the need is felt to call on them.

The expressions "speak effectively" and "write effectively" do not imply that teacher–coordinators must be orators or accomplished journalists. However, they should be able to communicate orally and in writing through the proper and effective use of the English language.

302

The general degree of excellence in this respect should equal or exceed that normally expected of a well-qualified professional person. Deficiency in writing or speaking will dramatize poor quality and destroy the effectiveness of the message.

Problem 5 *Establishing and maintaining standards that will command the respect of all in-school publics*

Almost without exception, the initial enrollment in CE will be composed of students who do not measure up to minimum enrollment standards. This fact is usually the result of preconceived notions of the administration and faculty relative to the purpose CE is designed to serve as a part of the educational program. A given school administrator, for example, may seek to establish CE in order to have a place for that inevitable student group which fails to produce effectively in any phase of the existing educational program. This basic administrative intent may not be revealed before the initial student group is referred for enrollment.

Under such circumstances, teacher–coordinators will probably have no alternative but to accept such student groups as gracefully as possible and do the best possible job with them. In so doing, however, administrative officials should be diplomatically advised of their misinterpretation of the purpose of the program. Teacher–coordinators should also guard against any inclination to compromise basic philosophy and principles relative to program purposes and values simply because administrators have ideas of their own as to the purposes CE should serve. A third tendency to be resisted is the establishment of standards of student accomplishment low enough to permit low-producing students to achieve high grades.

Inability to stand firmly in these areas will constitute a step toward failure because change in administrative attitude cannot be expected in succeeding years. Surrendering to such circumstances would tend to compromise the teacher–coordinator's philosophy and strength of purpose to the extent of destroying the reason for resisting. The program probably would then become earmarked for low-producing and problem students, and performance requirements would be established low enough to allow such students to qualify for high grades without commensurate effort.

On the other hand, the teacher–coordinator's dedication to appropriate standards should trigger relationship-development activities designed to replace administrative misinterpretation with clear-cut appreciation and acceptance of legitimate purposes and values. Rather than allow an unqualified and inept student group to defeat the program, therefore, a wise teacher–coordinator will use it as a point of departure in demonstrating, by contrast, the type of student needs the program is designed to serve.

Inexperienced teacher–coordinators are cautioned not to underestimate their administrators. In the first place, they are educators who have successfully demonstrated educational leadership of sufficient quality and scope to win the high position they occupy. This success could not have occurred in the absence of a sound philosophy relative to the purpose of education. Within the realm of this philosophy will almost surely be found an overwhelming desire to serve the student's best interest at all times.

Inasmuch as this must also be a central theme in the philosophy of the vocational educator, the only possible point of controversy would be in the definition of the student's best interest. It necessarily follows that the theme of relationship-development activities should be directed at clarification and alignment of understanding in this respect. The administrator and other professional staff members can be expected to adjust their concepts in the light of irrefutable proof that those previously held are in error.

It should not be difficult, for example, to demonstrate the impossibility of accomplishing the educational purposes of CE with students who have no real vocational interest or intent in the occupational areas in which qualified training stations are available. The dissipation of one-fourth of the educational opportunity through two years of enrollment in CE could hardly be construed to be proper stewardship of the student's best interest.

Suggested Activities

1. After a study of the calendar of suggested relationship-development activities (Figure 23), develop an alternative calendar for a school year composed of items compatible with personal capabilities and anticipated local circumstances. Although some adjustments may be necessary, this calendar should serve as an acceptable guide for relationship development for the new teacher–coordinator.
2. Prepare a detailed relationship-development plan involving school administration, faculty, and students. List a number of activities under each of these headings designed to inspire the desired attitudes. All activities listed should be in line with the personal capabil-

ities of the teacher–coordinator and anticipated local circumstances.

3. Prepare a 20- to 25-minute talk for presentation to the faculty during a preschool workshop or other appropriate preschool meeting. Build the talk around the brochure in Figure 25, with emphasis on the need for cooperation.

4. Write an open letter to the faculty describing the investment the CE student is required to make in terms of educational opportunity. Emphasize the importance of enrolling only those students who want, need, and are qualified to profit from the instruction.

5. Plan an open-house program for faculty and administration, designed to illustrate and explain the methods used in teaching directly related information.

6. Design an instrument suitable for use in keeping the principal informed of off-campus activities during the school day. Explain fully how this form could be used.

chapter fourteen

Community Relationship Development

The emphasis on in-school relationships in Chapter Thirteen should in no way detract from the importance of similar emphasis on the development of appropriate relationships with those out-of-school publics upon which CE is dependent for support. As a matter of fact, neglect in this area of public relations could be fatal. It is not difficult to envision, for example, the chaos which could result from the placement of properly selected students springing from enlightened in-school publics with employers who were intent upon securing student labor at less than normal cost, without concern for educational values. It stands to reason, therefore, that there is no acceptable alternative to an organized program of relationship-development activities designed to develop understanding and acceptance of the purposes and values of CE on the part of vital out-of-school publics.

Here again, it is suggested that the best assurance of the application of appropriate and consistent effort is a carefully prepared relationship activity program which involves an equitable distribution of time and effort between vital publics in and out of school. (See the sample calendar in Chapter Thirteen.)

Local circumstances will determine to some extent which community publics are most vital to CE. To illustrate, let it be assumed that organized labor is an important factor in community A, while community B is unaffected. In the first instance, hostile or indifferent attitudes toward CE could deny the placement of students in the occupational areas over which jurisdiction is exercised. This barrier would, in effect, eliminate these occupations from the occupational spread of the school's vocational education program. It stands to reason, therefore, that organized labor is a vital public and that nothing should be left undone by the school in its relationship development efforts with this segment of the community. On the other hand, the school in community B, unaffected by organized labor, would not be concerned with such relationship-development efforts.

Typical publics about which the teacher–coordinator should be concerned are treated in the remaining portions of this chapter. Under no circumstances, however, should the publics included in this treatment be considered as all-inclusive, but rather to be illustrative of those likely to be present in any community.

Relationships with Employers

The fact that CE could not exist without cooperating employers crystallizes the importance of initiating and maintaining appropriate individual and collective relationships with them. There follows a series of suggested activities which should be helpful in the establishment and maintenance of appropriate employer relationships.

Assess Employer Attitudes

Assessment of attitudes should not present too many problems to the teacher–coordinator in that their revelation should be a prominent part of the potential employer's response to the request to employ a CE student. If basic attitudes are not revealed at this stage of the game, they can be expected to emerge at succeeding junctures which involve efforts of the school to evaluate the quality of students' experiences or to question circumstances surrounding the work experiences. In the final analysis, therefore, the alert teacher–coordinator should be aware of the basic attitudes of the employers as a by-product of normal contacts inherent in getting them involved in the program.

It seems advisable to consider typical attitudes normally assumed by employers who are left to their own devices in assigning purposes and values to CE and in determining their roles as cooperating employers. Although there may' be exceptions, such employers can be expected to exhibit a reaction pattern which would reflect varying combinations of attitudes, such as the following:

1. It is an opportunity to secure student labor to solve seasonal labor problems.

2. It is an opportunity to help needy students to finance their high school education.
3. It is an opportunity to secure student labor at less than normal cost.
4. It is feared that the employment of students will affect relationships with organized labor.
5. It is feared that involvement with students will inspire adverse customer relations.
6. It is feared that the employment of students will affect insurance rates and extent of coverage.

Such attitudes and others of similar nature are indicative of an employer's evaluation of CE solely in terms of an estimation of its advantages and disadvantages without regard for career needs of students and the educational responsibility and purpose of the school. The employer should not be condemned for having such attitudes for the simple reason that they are normal in the absence of an understanding of program purposes and values.

The school holds major responsibility in this respect because it is the sponsoring agency and the guardian of the student's best interest at all times. It stands to reason, therefore, that an initial and continuing responsibility of the school is to provide employers with authentic information in appropriate form and to cultivate their understanding and acceptance of it as a basis of cooperation with the school.

The following criteria are descriptive of appropriate employer attitudes toward CE and could well serve as objectives of relationship-development efforts:

1. A general reflection of understanding and acceptance of program purposes and values.
2. An acceptance of the mantle of on-the-job teacher and faculty membership with sincere concern.
3. An acknowledgement and an appreciation of the service of the school in the selection of students and the provision of occupationally related instruction.
4. A consideration of the place of business as a laboratory.
5. A regard for the time spent at work as an educational experience for the student rather than as a contribution to profits.
6. A general regard for CE as a dependable source of qualified workers.
7. A recognition of participation in the program as an opportunity to render a public service.

Develop Appropriate Teacher–Coordinator Image

The teacher–coordinator is an agent of the school and as such is primarily responsible for the direct contact with employers inherent in CE. What the teacher–coordinator is in the eyes of employers will strongly affect the latter's attitude concerning the program and their willingness to cooperate with the school. There follows a list of statements designed to characterize a desirable teacher–coordinator's image in the eyes of cooperating employers:

1. Warm and sincere response to friendly gestures extended by cooperating employers and other members of the firms in which students are placed.
2. Knowledge about education in general and mastery of theory and practice in CE.
3. Enthusiasm about CE and its values.
4. Firmness in the discharge of responsibilities incumbent upon an agent of the school.
5. Intelligent concern for training-agency problems and willingness to cooperate in their solution.
6. Insistence that program standards be maintained.
7. Championing of the best interest of students at all times.
8. Consistent loyalty to the school and all its parts.
9. Stature and bearing which results from proper dress and grooming, quality performance, good usage, and mastery of appropriate methods and techniques.

Although the above characterizing statements may seem to be a description of a superior individual, they are designed to describe a well-qualified professional teacher with special preparation and interest in CE.

Show Concern for Employer Problems

As suggested above, teacher–coordinators should consistently champion the student's best interest at all times. They should also defend the employer's best interest with vigor and concern at every opportunity. Employers should come to regard the teacher–coordinator as their representative of the public schools, through whom its services can be made available to them.

In effect, teacher–coordinators should eventually come to provide a service to small employers in the community which is the equivalent of that performed by personnel managers and educational directors of large self-contained organizations. In this capacity they would be depended upon, to an appropriate degree, to apply the facilities and abilities of the school in satisfying local needs for beginning employees, and in providing essential continuing educational opportunity for employed workers.

The essence of these services involves finding and placing the right students on the right jobs through CE, and the identification and satisfaction of educational needs of employed workers, through the resulting relationship with employers. In this fashion the facilities and abilities of the school become directly involved in the channeling of local human resources into the local business and industrial work force and in the provision of continuing educational opportunity designed to keep employed workers abreast of needs and requirements in the occupational areas in which they are employed.

Illustrative circumstances with which employers may become involved in their efforts to cooperate with the school are listed below. The teacher–coordinator should be alert to such problems and appropriately aggressive in contributing to their solution.

1. A student presents an irreconcilable problem for whatever reason or cause.

Employers must be assured from the beginning that the cooperative arrangement with the school does not require them to continue the employment of students who obviously are misfits and whose continued presence as employees is harmful to both parties. The teacher–coordinator should remove such students without delay when it is recognized that there is no chance for reconciliation or adjustment. When employers, individually and collectively, become confident that the school will relieve them of unanticipated compromising circumstances which result from their efforts to cooperate, they will not hesitate to become involved with students who are recommended to them.

The type of circumstances referred to above are those which would place the student in a compromising position equivalent to that of the employer. Failure to act in such cases, on the part of the teacher–coordinator, would produce an impasse removable only by the employer through discharging the student, or through the resignation of the student. Obviously, the best interest of either party would not be served by either action.

2. Unanticipated fiscal difficulties render the student an unbearable overhead expense.

As a general rule, the possibility of the development of this kind of circumstance can be identified in the training-station evaluation process prior to the placement of students. If, on the other hand, unanticipated financial reverses eliminate the employer's ability to continue the employment of the student as a nonproductive learner, the best interest of all concerned would be served by the removal of the student from the job and making the best possible adjustment. There would certainly be no merit in ignoring the situation or in attempting to hold to the original memorandum of training agreement which the employer is no longer financially able to honor. Failure to recognize circumstances of this kind and to act promptly can only serve to defeat the educational purposes of CE.

3. Problems arise with insurance carriers relative to liability and premium rates.

Insurance carriers sometimes present problems having to do with the employment of students less than eighteen years of age. In the eyes of the law, the student is the equivalent of any other employee and merits the same insurance coverage and protection. The problem usually stems from the increased safety hazard which attends a youth who is less than eighteen years of age. The reaction of insurance carriers may not be standardized, thus giving rise to the possibility of a divergence of policy between training agencies when more than one carrier is involved.

The employer who finds the increased cost of insurance too high a price to pay for the privilege of cooperating with the school through CE should be relieved at the earliest possible time. Problems of this nature should crystallize during the placement process, thus initially eliminating questionable training agencies before student placements are made. If, by chance, the problem does not surface until the school year is under way, the teacher–coordinator should make the best possible adjustment without delay. If such adjustment involves the removal of the student, it frequently can be delayed until the end of a semester in order that the high school credit will not be jeopardized. If, on the other hand, appropriate placement can be effected with another training agency, it should be done without delay.

4. Unanticipated problems arise with parents and relatives of students.

It was suggested earlier that parents of students should be included in the student selection process. One of the prime purposes of such initial contacts should be to alert them to the fact that CE is a cooperative arrangement between the school and local employers and that all complaints and problems should be presented to and adjusted by the teacher-coordinator as the official agent of the school. In spite of this effort, however, parents frequently do not understand that they should not, under any circumstances, confront the employer with problems surrounding the employment of their son or daughter as a student. When such confrontations do occur, employers can be expected to take serious exception to them. As a matter of fact, they may be moved to reconsider the advisability of continuing to serve as cooperating employers. The seriousness of this situation becomes apparent when viewed in the light of the possible effects on a retail business establishment when the employer in question is subjected to the wrath of parents who feel that their son or daughter has been mistreated. Not only would the relationship of the parents with the business be affected, but also the relationship with all of the student's relatives and friends. No sensible employer will continue a hazard of this kind for the privilege of cooperating with the school.

The best solution to this problem resides in proper relationships with the parents of students. Parents who understand and accept the functional principles of CE will present their real or fancied problems to the teacher-coordinator rather than to confront the employer with them. When this cooperation fails, however, the teacher-coordinator must be prepared to quickly rise to the occasion in effecting the best possible solution without delay.

Identify with Local Employer or Civic Organizations

The teacher-coordinator should seek avenues through which to communicate with employers as a group. Such a relationship is an essential supplement to the individual and personal relationships which result from the functional aspects of the program. Perhaps the most appropriate avenue to this accomplishment would be through industrial management or other organizations designed to cater primarily to the needs of employers. In the absence of such organizations in a given community, the next most appropriate type of organization would probably be the local chamber of commerce, followed closely by the civic clubs normally to be found in all communities of sufficient size to accommodate CE.

The term *identify* as used in the title of this section does not imply that teacher–coordinators must become active members of the organizations mentioned above. They may accomplish satisfactory results by becoming acquainted with individuals in each organization who are chairmen of committees with responsibilities germane to vocational education. Such individuals can be expected to be interested in CE and to offer the teacher–coordinator opportunity to speak to the club on topics such as "Cooperative Education and the Part It Is Designed to Play in the Economic Welfare of the Community."

Most communities have business and industrial development organizations charged with the responsibility of inspiring and steering business and industrial growth. Teacher–coordinators should identify strongly with such groups and become involved in their programs to the greatest feasible extent. Accordingly, they must arm themselves with factual information in sufficient quantity and depth to satisfy the needs of industries which may be considering location in the community. Such information should be designed to project the image of the school and the contribution it can make to an industrial climate.

Teacher–coordinators will find that successful participation in the civic affairs of their communities will provide exceptional opportunity to project their personal images as agents of the school to local employer groups.

Avoid Interruption of Work Experience

A common tendency in school–employer relationships is to allow the work schedule to suffer in favor of school activities and personal problems of students. Ironically, many employers will accept such neglect on the theory that the student is just a boy (girl) and as such should not be judged by the standards normally applied in judging adult workers. A double standard of this nature may have a negative impact on the student's attitude toward job responsibility.

From the beginning, the school should champion the importance of dependability on the part of CE students and encourage the employer to judge them sternly in this respect. Failure to hold job dependability as a prime objective of the work experience would be to condone an

313

undesirable juvenile tendency and to encourage a permissive attitude on the part of the employer, both of which would tend to defeat the development of the kind of job responsibility that the employer will subsequently demand. In this light it seems that the school has no alternative but to reduce interruptions of the work schedule to the lowest possible point and to insist that the employer judge the student by the same standards applied to regular employees.

Involve the Employer in the Student's Total Educational Program

Employers should be made to feel that they, or their designates, are on-the-job teachers and by virtue of this responsibility are bona-fide members of the faculty. The program should involve the employer beyond the point of simply supervising the work experience. Perhaps the best approach would be through encouragement of the employer to become concerned with the student in his total educational environment. The assumption of this kind of interest should promote concern for the quality of work-at-school equivalent to that for on-the-job work experience.

Employer interest in the work done at school, in the beginning, probably should be centered primarily in the directly related instruction and its relationship with the work experience. The plan for action suggested above, therefore, should keep the employer intimately informed concerning the student's areas of directly related instruction and on the quality of the work being done. The plan should provide opportunity for the teacher–coordinator to suggest ways and means through which technical knowledge, gained through directly related instruction, may be applied to the solution of on-the-job problems.

A method of keeping the employer advised concerning student progress in directly related instruction should be designed. There should also be provision for the employer to report instances which have successfully involved the application of technically related information. The teacher–coordinator should be expediently solicitant and as helpful as possible in bringing the employer to a desirable level of performance in this process of two-way correlation.

Under normal circumstances the student should be considered by the employer to be a potential full-time employee. It should not be difficult, therefore, to broaden this interest to include the student's total educational opportunity. Competence in language arts, mathematics, and science may come to occupy a level of importance in the employer's estimation equivalent to that of job skills and related technical information. Competence in both areas would enhance the student's value as a potential full-time employee.

The teacher–coordinator will find that some employers will welcome the involvement suggested above, while others will be reluctant. Accordingly, employers in a given CE program should be dealt with as individuals, with each of them being encouraged to participate to the greatest possible extent. Those employers who continue to participate in the program should become more fully concerned with the total educational opportunity of their students each succeeding year.

Show Appreciation

Being assured that their participation is appreciated is an effective condiment in employer relationships which can be expected to inspire the best possible employer cooperation.

The suggestion that the on-the-job instructor be considered as a bona-fide faculty member must be accepted by appropriate administrative officials, including the high school principal, if it is to make a positive impact on employer relationships. There follows a listing of actions relating to on-the-job instructors which could result from administrative acceptance of this principle:

1. They are placed on the faculty mailing list and scheduled to receive appropriate releases from administrative offices.
2. They are included in all faculty listings.
3. They are invited to attend and participate in faculty meetings.
4. They are recognized through public statements of the teacher–coordinator and administrative officials.
5. Training stations are visited periodically by appropriate administrative officials.

Administrative recognition of on-the-job instructors through these and other avenues locally conceived should be convincing evidence that on-the-job instructors are recognized and appreciated as important members of the faculty.

An annual letter of appreciation should be mailed to each cooperating employer. Such a letter should include appropriate elements of the annual accomplishments of CE that will contribute to a program image through which individual employers can identify their own contribution. The signature over which this letter should be dispatched is optional. It could be signed by the teacher–coordinator, but it probably would be more effective when signed by the superintendent of schools or perhaps the president of the school board.

Regardless of who signs the letter, it should be personalized to the greatest possible extent. Under no circumstances should it be a circular letter without personal salutation and signature. The content of the letter should be confined to pertinent factual information concerning program accomplishments and a profound expression of appreciation. The most effective time for mailing should be the period immediately following the closing of the regular school term.

Another way to express appreciation to employers is to invite them to school affairs such as Parent–Teachers Association meetings, special assembly programs, open-house programs, social affairs sponsored by the student club, and the employer–employee banquet. Special recognition should be accorded to employers who are present at any of these occasions. The employer–employee banquet affords an unexcelled opportunity to recognize and express appreciation to employers as a group. This recognition should be diplomatically accomplished by students, the teacher–coordinator, and a school administrator, preferably the superintendent of schools. Here again the emphasis should be on the values of employer participation as opposed to shallow flattery.

The teacher–coordinator should consistently express appreciation to employers as an integral part of the visitation technique. This should take the form of thoughtful acknowledgment of the employer's role in the program coupled with sincere effort to cause them to feel that their part is important and appreciated.

The teacher–coordinator should express a philosophy consistent with that of public education as a whole. The general public, with particular reference to employers, should not be led into believing that vocational education, with special reference to CE, is something separate and apart from the educational program in the school, but rather should be encouraged to understand that it is an integral part of it.

This philosophy should champion the idea that the most successful vocational education must be based on a strong general education background with special reference to competence in the areas of communications and computation. By the same token, general education has little practical value other than to serve as a means of complementing occupational skill and technical knowledge to the greatest possible extent. The teacher–coordinator's philosophy should clearly enunciate the principle that general education and vocational education are complements of each other and that neither of them can be completely fulfilled without the other.

Relationships with Parents

Parental relationships should be based upon the idea that the student's welfare is a prime responsibility and concern of the parents. Exceptions to this rule should be recognized and dealt with in accordance with the circumstances involved in each case.

As a general rule, therefore, parental relationship-development activities should be based on the accomplishment of such objectives as the following:

1. To clearly enunciate the effect participation in CE may have on meeting college entrance requirements.
2. To fully characterize the investment required of the student in terms of educational opportunity.
3. To fully explain the parental role in CE.
4. To provide information which will enable parents to intelligently counsel their son or daughter about the student values of the program.

Clarify College Entrance Potential

Parents should understand that CE is a vocational program designed to prepare individuals for employment at beginning levels, in chosen occupations, after graduation from high school. This definition does not eliminate the possibility of applying credit earned as a CE student in satisfying college entrance requirements. It does demand, however, that the instructional program be entirely devoted to the development of occupational competence in terms of skill and related technical knowledge, without regard for college transfer value.

Many colleges and universities will accept four vocational credits as a part of their entrance requirements. Variation among degree programs, however, eliminates the advisability of generalization in this respect. In other words, the parent should understand, in the beginning, that the applicability of vocational credit in satisfying college entrance requirements depends upon the area of interest and the institutions involved.

Unfortunately, the attitude of parents toward college attendance for their son or daughter cannot be depended upon to remain unchanged. As a matter of fact, parents who at the time their son or daughter enters CE do not plan college attendance for whatever reason may well change their minds by the time of high school graduation. Such parents can be depended upon to be very unhappy if and when difficulty is experienced in meeting entrance requirements of given degree programs by virtue of the portion of the high school program which was devoted to CE.

Under such circumstances the parents can be expected to vent their frustration through criticism of the school with particular reference to CE and the teacher–coordinator. Such criticism may be justified if the parents were not made fully aware, in the beginning, of the potential value of this high school credit in satisfying college entrance requirements. Such awareness should include the understanding that the CE student's high school program may be planned to satisfy entrance requirements if the institution and area of degree interest are known in the beginning.

In all fairness it should be noted at this point that many areas of study in colleges and universities allow as many as ten electives in their entrance requirements. Although this allowance may be true in a school of education or business, it may not be true in the school of engineering in the same institution. In the first case no difficulty should be experienced in meeting entrance requirements, while in the second, entrance may be denied pending the acquisition of the educational credit needed to satisfy the requirements. In the light of this rationale, there seems to be no justifiable alternative to the necessity of fully informing parents and students concerning the advisability of considering the possibility of a change of attitude toward college attendance.

Parents who are advised in advance of all potentialities will have no justifiable complaint against the school or CE relative to meeting college entrance requirements. The teacher–coordinator is cautioned, however, that it is quite difficult for many parents to eliminate the possibility of college, even though little or no potential exists. As a matter of fact, an unchallenged rumor that CE eliminates college will curtail enrollment possibilities.

Explain the Student's Investment in Terms of Educational Opportunity

Parents should be made fully aware of the investment the CE student is required to make in terms of time and credit. Students and parents are prone to overlook this important aspect of CE in favor of major concern for fringe values, such as credit for work experience, monetary returns, and relief from classroom confinement for one-half of the school day. If, for example, a high school student enters CE as a junior, four of the sixteen Carnegie units (two per year) required to satisfy high school graduation requirements will be devoted to this program. An equivalent amount of credit could be earned through conventional courses by the expenditure of approximately one-third of the time required in CE.

Many of the extracurricular activities included in the regular school program, together with after-school leisure-time activities, will have to be sacrificed because they are normally scheduled during the time the cooperative student is working.

When properly counseled, the parents should recognize that such an investment is entirely justifiable as a bona-fide part of career educational plans, which may or may not include college-level preparation, and is prompted by sincere vocational intent in the occupational area in which placement is sought. However, the parent will recognize that one-fourth of the high school educational opportunity, with attending time requirements and the sacrifice of extracurricular and leisure-time activities, is too great a price to pay for the monetary wage and other fringe benefits of questionable value.

In the first case CE becomes an unexcelled educational opportunity. In the second it could serve as a camouflage for the educational frustration of students and parents which results from failure to understand or to face up to educational reality. In either event the school must not be guilty of allowing parents to make faulty judgments based on misunderstanding or a lack of authentic information.

Explain the Parental Role

It is extremely important that the parents of students understand that CE is a cooperative arrangement between the school and local employers. They should be encouraged to accept the concept that the on-the-job work experience is the laboratory phase of the course much the same as the physics laboratory is a part of the physics course. In the light of this analogy it should become obvious that the school, through its agents, bears the same type of responsibility for CE that it does for physics or any other bona-fide high school course. Parents who accept this concept will understand that any attempt on their part to effect a direct relationship with the employer of their son or daughter would be entirely out of order. They will accept the principle that all problems and complaints should be presented to and adjusted by the teacher–coordinator.

The parents of students should encourage them to develop and maintain proper perspective relative to CE and its purposes and values. It should be regarded as an important part of their career educational plan rather than just a means of securing a part-time job. They should be encouraged to appreciate the opportunity to meet and solve many of the problems involved in adjusting to the world of work while they still have the benefit of the counsel and advice of their teachers and counselors.

Cooperative education provides an unexcelled opportunity to try out their aptitudes, vocational interests, and personal qualities under real job circumstances. If it should be found that these qualities do not mesh with job characteristics and requirements, an occupational adjustment can be made without significant loss to the student. The parents should discount the fiscal aspects of the program in favor of its educational values.

Students who come from broken homes or other undesirable home conditions and parental influence may present problems entirely different from those who come from well-adjusted homes. The teacher–coordinator and other appropriate agents of the school should devise ways and means of compensating for the home influences lost in circumstances of this kind.

In the final analysis, enlightened parents of CE students can be expected to give intelligent answers to questions raised during conversations with their peers, and to defend the program when and if it should come under fire in their presence.

Provide Parents with Authentic Information

Taking for granted that the parents of cooperative students are adequately informed about the purposes and values of CE in all probability would be an erroneous assumption. What they hear, read, or are told by potential cooperative students cannot be depended upon to make the desired impression. It would be more accurate to assume that they will see what they want to see in the program. If, for example, they are hard pressed financially, CE may seem to be the answer. If the son or daughter is experiencing difficulty in meeting the requirements of conventional course work, the two credits which can be earned annually may seem to be a legitimate and acceptable way to relieve the pressure of graduation requirements. The above and many more reasons may be accepted by parents as justification for entering the program without even becoming aware of its authentic purposes and values.

It is quite likely that the parents' initial knowledge of the program will result from the letter introduced earlier. Although this letter states the basic purposes and values of the program, it should not be depended upon to completely satisfy the need for information.

The previously suggested step-by-step plan for enrollment requires that one or both parents accompany the potential student in at least one interview with the teacher–coordinator before the enrollment process is completed (see p. 63). During this interview the letter should be followed up by a full explanation of its basic message.

The teacher–coordinator may elect to prepare a brochure for parents, which clearly outlines the previously explained purposes and values together with specific suggestions relative to the best form of cooperation with the school as parents of CE students. Such a brochure should not fail succinctly and diplomatically to describe the type of parental cooperation that will be expected by the school.

The probability that the most effective parental contacts will be personal in nature does not eliminate the advisability that some provision be made for the development of total program perspective. Perhaps one of the best approaches in this respect would be through an open-house program similar to that suggested for the faculty and administration (see p. 289) but designed primarily for parents of students who are enrolled. Special effort should be made to demonstrate the nature of the work done in the directly-related-subjects classroom and its relationship to the work experience.

Special programs prepared for Parent–Teacher Association meetings should be helpful in presenting appropriate information to parents as a group. Such programs, however, cannot be depended upon to get the information to the parents of all students for the simple reason that some of them may not be active members of the association.

In addition, teacher–coordinators should make themselves available to parents for the purpose of answering questions and cultivating understanding and appreciation of CE as an unexcelled educational program for those students qualified for enrollment. One way of accomplishing this availability would be to maintain an open office policy and encourage parents to call for appointments at their convenience. There may be times when a home visit would be the most appropriate action. The teacher–coordinator is cautioned, however, that such visits should be made only upon invitation.

Good results can be expected in parental relationship-development efforts through a wise combination of the actions suggested above. It may not be necessary to employ all of them, but it would be poor judgment to ignore the need for contact with parents on the assumption that publicity designed for the general public will satisfy their need for information.

Relationships with Employee Organizations

The possibility of anticipating the specific nature of problems in the realm of employee organizations is extremely remote. The fact remains, however, that the teacher–coordinator should be alert and prepared to deal intelligently with them if and when they occur. Perhaps the greatest hazard resides in the skilled trade areas over which organized labor has jurisdiction. Union locals occasionally misunderstand the purpose of CE to be in conflict with their own apprenticeship program. Circumstances could become untenable for students as well as the employers with whom they are placed, if a local union should take a determined stand against the program. Such a dilemma could result from failure of the school to initiate and maintain appropriate relationships with the important segment of the community, in the beginning.

Determined effort on the part of the teacher–coordinator should eliminate the problem through correction of the misunderstanding and in casting vocational education, with particular reference to CE, in the role of an effective feeder to the apprentice program. During this process the school should protect the best interest of the student and the employer.

Let it be emphasized that organized labor will be a staunch and dependable ally of vocational education when its purposes and values are understood and accepted. The fact that the membership of the local advisory committee includes equitable representation from employee organizations should be helpful in the solution of problems of this nature.

The following suggested actions should be helpful to inexperienced teacher–coordinators in the establishment and maintenance of satisfactory relationships with organized labor and other organizations which exercise jurisdiction over specific worker groups.

Take the Initiative in Relationship Development

The school, through the teacher–coordinator, should seek out and befriend local labor leaders as the first step in bringing about a relationship compatible with the best interests of both organizations. Nothing should be left to chance in developing the concept that the school is interested in cooperating with them in dealing with the educational problems of workers in occupational areas over which they have jurisdiction. An immediate and friendly response may be surprising to the inexperienced teacher–coordinator, who may not be aware of the relationship which has existed between organized labor and education on national levels since the enactment of initial federal legislative support of vocational education, early in the twentieth century.

As a matter of fact, organized labor on the national level has supported federal aid to vocational education at every opportunity since its inception. Labor leaders at all levels, including local union officials, are usually well informed concerning this long-standing national relationship, but they may not have interpreted it in terms of cooperative acts with schools on local levels. Accordingly, the stage should be set for the local teacher–coordinator to cast the school and local organized labor in cooperative roles in satisfying the educational and training needs of workers at all levels.

The first concrete evidence of the school's relationship development efforts might be the activation of organized labor's representation on the general advisory committee and the appointment of appropriate craft committees to serve the school in an advisory capacity concerning specific vocational courses.

Offer Services of the School

There are three basic services that the school, through its vocational program, can render to organized labor. One of the most important of these services is to recommend the apprenticeship program as one avenue into the world of work for the graduates of vocational courses. In effect, this places vocational education, including CE, in the educational structure as a feeder program for apprentice training. Such a relationship between the school and organized labor is mutually beneficial in that the school gains an additional entrée into the world of work for its graduates. Organized labor gains better-qualified apprentices than it is normally able to recruit.

The apprenticeship indenture normally includes the requirement

323

that the apprentice attend at least 144 hours of prescribed related instruction per year. Traditionally, the most convenient and legitimate source of this instruction has been the school, through its department of vocational education. This arrangement has been the substance of an unwritten agreement between education and organized labor on the national level since the passage of the Smith–Hughes Act of 1917. Here again, however, local labor leaders may not have interpreted this understanding on the national level in terms of local opportunity.

It stands to reason, therefore, that appropriate and timely suggestions by the local teacher–coordinator would have a good chance of being the answer to the need for help in providing related instruction for local apprentices. Instruction of this nature can usually be provided by the local school in the form of part-time or evening classes. State and/or federal funds are normally available for a major portion of the cost. In addition, employee organizations at local levels can frequently be depended upon for the remaining part of the cost.

The third basic service that the school can provide for employees organizations is the provision of instruction for employed workers beyond the apprentice level (journeyman). Such classes are designed to provide skill and information supplemental to daily employment. They provide an avenue through which employed workers at all levels may keep abreast of technological development in their respective fields of occupational interest.

It seems that having the above services to offer to local employee organizations should be effective in initiating and maintaining harmonious relationships. Success in this respect should eliminate all traces of competition with and duplication of the training prerogatives of the employee organizations in question.

Develop Appropriate Teacher–Coordinator Image

Teacher–coordinators should cultivate their personal ability to communicate intelligently with organized labor in terms of its own history, purposes, and values. Ability to relate and harmonize these philosophical elements with comparable elements of educational philosophy should serve to project the teacher–coordinator's image in the most effective light and inspire the most desirable response. Employee organizations and their members should come to regard the teacher–coordinator as their representative of the school, through whom its services can be made available to them. Such a relationship is invaluable to vocational education and will pave the way to harmonious development of the program to the greatest possible potential in any given community.

Involve Officials of Employee Organizations in the School Program

Involvement should work both ways. In addition to the teacher–coordinator's involvement in the educational programs fostered by local employee organizations, every effort should be made to get officials and leaders of these organizations involved in vocational education in the local schools.

The career educational plan requires a thorough exposure to the realities of the world of work. This exposure should include appropriate attention to organized labor and other employee organizations which exercise jurisdiction over given occupational areas. Local representatives of these organizations should be given ample opportunity to participate in the occupational orientation process to the end that students enrolled in elementary and junior high school grades will be made aware of the opportunities in and requirements of the world of work as seen by authentic representatives of the work force.

Students are seldom informed relative to the purpose and values of the apprenticeship program, how it may be entered, and the opportunities it affords for qualified individuals. They do not know, for example, that high school graduates who elect to enter the apprenticeship program can qualify themselves for positions at salary levels comparable to those available to college graduates, in a period of time equivalent to that required to earn a degree. Being fully aware of this possibility early enough in the educational program to permit intelligent career planning should be a valuable service to contemporary youth. The greater the involvement of representatives of local employee organizations, the greater the authenticity of the occupational orientation effort.

Relationships with the General Public

The relationship development activities discussed thus far have had to do with specific publics in and out of the school which contribute directly to the environment in which CE must function. The purposes of these efforts are to develop an understanding and an appreciation of the purposes and values of CE and to encourage each public to accept the role it is expected to play.

The media through which the general public may be contacted should include the local newspaper, radio and television, and public meetings. Each of these will be discussed briefly in the following pages of this chapter for the purposes of illustration. Teacher–coordinators should not limit their efforts to these media, but rather should capitalize upon the use of all available media.

The Local Newspaper

The local newspaper is potentially the most effective medium through which the general public can be kept informed about CE. The degree of cooperation expected will depend upon the degree of understanding and acceptance of program purposes and values on the part of key members of the newspaper staff with special reference to the editor and chief reporters. Newspaper editors can normally be depended upon to be public-spirited citizens keenly alert to vital community concerns. They should respond warmly to CE and its potential economic value to their circulation area.

Accordingly, the teacher–coordinator should consider the local newspaper as a most important medium and its staff a vital out-of-school public. What the editor knows and understands about CE should not be left to chance. On the contrary, special effort should be exerted to cultivate the best possible image to the end that program insight will be developed in terms of its purposes and values as they relate to the total community, including the school, business, and industrial interests, and the youth who are destined to be future employees and citizens. Success will be achieved when the editor feels moved to devote editorial effort and space to CE.

Although this editorializing would be highly desirable, it does not constitute the most important value of a "right" relationship. The most coveted relationship would include acceptance to the extent that the local paper would become a dependable medium through which the school can communicate with the public in general concerning CE. Under such circumstances the reporting and editorial staffs would be willingly available to help in the preparation of materials for publication.

Information concerning CE would be preferred material for publication, and would be given prominent location in the section in which it appears. Reporters would be made available to attend and report special events and to prepare feature stories. Materials submitted by the teacher–coordinator would be appropriately received and considered for publication.

Radio and Television

Radio and television stations devote a portion of their broadcast time each day to public service. This practice renders these media subject to the public relation needs of the school and makes them frequently the most available of all media.

The availability of television as a medium through which the general public may be kept informed places the responsibility for its effective use on the school and its agents. In this respect the teacher–coordinator should learn to capitalize upon the expertise of the professional staff of radio and television stations just as was suggested relative to the newspaper and its reporters and writers. The following suggested techniques are applicable to radio and television presentations.

Interviews with School Officials

There are times when a well-planned interview with a school official may be the most applicable technique for radio or television presentations, especially during the period when CE is being introduced to the school and community. Perhaps the first of these should involve the superintendent of schools or the principal of the school in which the program is scheduled to operate. The program should be built around predetermined questions and answers which deal with the general purposes and values of CE to students, community, and the school. The announcer for the station should moderate the program and should pose the questions to be answered by school officials.

The general purpose of a program of this nature should be to project a favorable image of CE to the community in general and to pave the way for the transmission of more specific information at later and more opportune times. If such a program becomes advisable before the teacher–coordinator is employed, school officials should call on appropriate representatives from the state department of vocational education to help prepare the questions and answers and possibly to appear with them on the program.

The same general format should be applicable to an interview program with the teacher–coordinator, with the exception that the content of the program should be designed to transmit more specific program information to given segments of the community. It is quite likely that the most effective interview program would involve a combination of the teacher–coordinator, currently enrolled students, program graduates, and possibly cooperating employers. When a program of this kind is well done, it should be impressive to broad segments of the community and of interest to the community as a whole.

Discussion Techniques Applicable to Radio and Television

The panel discussion can be a very effective technique on radio or television. The secret to successful use of this technique is the availability of knowledgeable people, in the topical areas to be discussed, who have the ability to express themselves succinctly and accurately, and an individual who is skilled in the art of chairmanship.

The panel discussion will serve equally well at public meetings, large or small. As a matter of fact, it has added value in this medium in that the discussion can be followed by a question-and-answer period involving the audience. In this case the chairman should explain, in the beginning, how and when the audience might participate.

The panel discussion should not be confused with the symposium, which is often employed under similar circumstances and with similar objectives. This program form serves well for use by the teacher–coordinator in presenting programs utilizing students or alumni, or an appropriate mixture thereof, as symposium members. These young people can be expected to deal more skillfully with prepared statements than with the extemporaneous reactions to questions required of them as panel members. The teacher–coordinator will find the symposium composed of currently enrolled students to be especially useful in presenting programs at civic club luncheons and other public meetings. Such programs should be carefully planned and thoroughly rehearsed in order to ensure the desired content and manner of presentation.

Spot Announcements

The spot announcement on radio or television is a very useful technique in keeping the general public aware of current activities in the local program of vocational education. Spot announcements may herald significant events such as the beginning of an extension course designed for adult workers or other occasions of interest to the general public. Spot announcements are usually programmed to be read periodically during the specified period of time. As a general rule, the teacher–coordinator supplies the content of the announcement to the station, subject to treatment by the professional staff. The following sample spot announcement is suitable for use on radio and television programs.

Attention All Tradesmen:

An extension course in blueprint reading is scheduled to begin on _____ in Room 112 of the _____ High School. The course is open to individuals employed in the building trades who have need to develop or improve their ability to work from blueprints. The class will meet on Tuesday and Thursday from 7:00 to 9:30 P.M. through _____ . Those interested in enrolling should call Mr. _____ at telephone number _____ .

It is quite obvious that spot announcements such as this can be adapted to a wide range of newsworthy items of interest to identifiable segments of the general public.

News Announcements

The news announcement is similar to the spot announcement in its conciseness, but differs in that it is usually designed to be included in regularly scheduled news programs. Its range of application may be broader than that of the spot announcement because it can be employed in advising the general public of any newsworthy event or activity. The following sample news release is illustrative of the types of announcements that can be made.

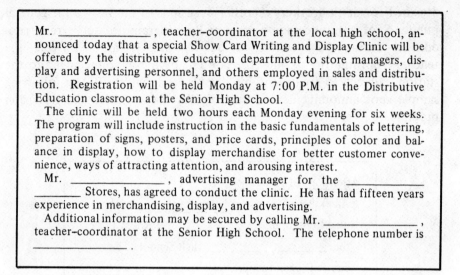

Mr. _____ , teacher–coordinator at the local high school, announced today that a special Show Card Writing and Display Clinic will be offered by the distributive education department to store managers, display and advertising personnel, and others employed in sales and distribution.   Registration will be held Monday at 7:00 P.M. in the Distributive Education classroom at the Senior High School.

The clinic will be held two hours each Monday evening for six weeks. The program will include instruction in the basic fundamentals of lettering, preparation of signs, posters, and price cards, principles of color and balance in display, how to display merchandise for better customer convenience, ways of attracting attention, and arousing interest.

Mr. _____ , advertising manager for the _____ _____ Stores, has agreed to conduct the clinic. He has had fifteen years experience in merchandising, display, and advertising.

Additional information may be secured by calling Mr. _____ , teacher–coordinator at the Senior High School. The telephone number is _____ .

Public Meetings

The teacher–coordinator is in a unique position to receive invitations to address various groups in the service area of the school. This constitutes an excellent opportunity to educate the general public as well as those special publics which make vital contributions to the environment in which the program functions. The new teacher–coordinator will be in great demand until ineptness as a public speaker is demonstrated. On the other hand, if first appearances are well received, the invitations can be expected to continue. Qualified teacher–coordinators have a message for the community in which they are working, but the probability of delivering it successfully may lie shrouded and veiled in the shadows of their command of the English language and ability to express themselves. Reasonable adeptness in these areas is not too much to expect from a university graduate, and willingness to devote the necessary time to preparation may be the key to the entire situation.

In this light it seems to be mandatory that the teacher–coordinator should spend the time that is necessary to write a number of basic talks, each of which can be readily adapted to a number of different, but similar, speaking assignments. It is not suggested that these speeches be read, but rather that the teacher–coordinator become so familiar with their content that he can speak with acceptable fluency from notes.

The public speaker who reads from a prepared script does so at the risk of losing his audience as quickly as it becomes apparent that the message is canned and is devoid of personal connotations germane to the occasion.

It would be well to remember that an audience, under normal circumstances, will accept the message of the speaker to the degree that it is relevant to its current concerns. In other words, a typical non-captive audience can be expected to give rapt attention to that which it wants to hear and to reject information in all other categories. The teacher–coordinator, therefore, should learn to include in talks the type of information that audiences will appreciate.

"Tell them what they want to hear" with the full knowledge that very little of what is said will be remembered, but that a favorable impression will linger in the minds of those who have listened. The net result of this kind of an impression comes to the surface upon subsequent contacts with individuals who may not remember what was said at the meeting but will remember that they were favorably impressed at the time. The resulting favorable attitude of employers and others with whom the teacher–coordinator works will contribute to an environment receptive and conducive to the development of CE.

On the other hand, if the teacher–coordinator should perform poorly in initial public appearances, the resulting impression upon the audiences will be so strongly retained that what is subsequently said will not be heard. The lingering impression would be negative, thus militating against the effectiveness of subsequent relationships with those who were in attendance. Here again, CE can be expected to assume the image the teacher–coordinator creates for it.

For the purpose of illustration, let it be assumed that a teacher–coordinator is invited to speak at a local service club luncheon with a membership composed largely of civic-minded retail merchants. It can be safely assumed that prime current concerns of such a group would include the availability of qualified sales and service personnel, the need for upgrading of current employees, and the economic growth of the community. The alert teacher–coordinator will build the talk around these areas of interest or others of current concern, casting CE in the role of a dependable source of qualified workers, an avenue to appropriate educational experiences for employed workers, and an important factor in the economic development of the community.

Remarks in these areas will be acceptable to the extent that they are germane to the local scene. The teacher–coordinator should research all areas to the extent that glib references can be made to occupational facts such as the number of employees, the annual turnover, the number of unfilled jobs, and other information related to the economic status of the community. A local audience can be expected to be interested in this type of information when it is properly documented, but to register little concern about similar information extracted from state or federal statistical records, or based on wild assumptions.

Typical Problems in Community Relationship Development

Problem 1   *The tendency to take relationships with vital publics for granted*

The point has already been made that one of the teacher–coordinator's most difficult problems is the equitable distribution and management of time and effort, especially in the realm of relationship-development activities. Inexperienced teacher–coordinators frequently find themselves so heavily involved in details that little or no time seems to be available for public relations activities. Under such circumstances the tendency may be simply to assume that publics vital to the program are properly informed about its purposes, values, and needs. To resort to such an assumption could render the program vulnerable to a disastrous imbalance of opinion between vital publics. Ignoring or taking for granted the basic attitudes of any vital public stands a good chance of upsetting the delicate attitude balance essential to the successful operation of CE.

Problem 2   *Maintaining training-station quality*

Keeping the stronger places of business involved as training agencies is of vital importance to the teacher–coordinator. The program cannot continue to serve its purposes if the quality and strength of the training stations in which students are placed are not maintained at acceptable levels. The permanent loss of one or more good training stations per year, for whatever reason, cannot be afforded. The probability that satisfactory replacements may be available for a few years does not remove the inevitable result that the quality of the educational opportunity will eventually suffer if annual training-station losses continue.

A basic program characteristic is that the occupations required to satisfy student needs will vary from year to year. There may be years when strong training stations are not needed because no students currently enrolled have need for work experiences in the occupational areas they represent. Under such circumstances the training station is simply recessed and should not be considered lost.

The establishment and maintenance of good and appropriate employer relationships is probably the most effective insurance against damaging training-agency losses. This rapport tends to improve those training stations that remain in the program year after year, to the ultimate end that they truly become a part of the school and the on-the-job instructor a member of its faculty.

The teacher–coordinator is cautioned that the consistent loss of desirable training agencies is symptomatic of an insidious disease which may develop so gradually that it may be at an advanced stage before becoming apparent. It is suggested, therefore, that training-station turnover should be examined through periodic study designed to reveal symptoms of decadence in early stages, together with indications of the cause of training-station instability. Such findings should serve well as bases for a revised approach to employer relationships.

The inexperienced teacher–coordinator is cautioned that such studies will be hampered by the absence of reasonably complete records of training-station turnover. It is suggested, therefore, that a method be designed to facilitate the annual recording of dropout training agencies with attending descriptions of the circumstances which prompted the employer's decision to permanently withdraw from the program.

Problem 3 *Harnessing the power of cooperative effort of all publics in the interest of CE*

The efficiency of the teacher–coordinator who functions without the benefit of effective and appropriate relationships with all of the publics vital to the environment in which CE functions is similar to that of an engine with nonworking cylinders. The power is simply not available in sufficient quantity and character to totally accomplish program purposes and values. Small difficulties which should be taken in stride tend to produce insurmountable problems. The program has little resistance to pressures to which it is routinely subjected in the school and community. Program activities tend to be influenced by selfish motives of the publics involved as opposed to primary concern for the best interest of students.

Problem 4 *The determination of the medium and method most adaptable for use in a given relationship-development activity*

Making the most effective use of available media is dependent upon considerations such as the following:

1. Which medium is most compatible with the public concerned?
2. Is the talent available which is essential to quality production?
3. Does the nature and purpose of the message to be transmitted impose special requirements on the medium and methods to be used?

The compatibility of the media used in public relations activities with given publics is vitally important. If, for example, the message to be transmitted is of primary interest and concern to parents of students, it may be a mistake to present it in the form of a speech to a local civic club. Far more desirable results may be expected when a medium more compatible to parents is employed, such as the Parent–Teacher Association. Depending upon the nature of the message, it may be more effectively presented and received in a letter addressed to the parents who are concerned.

The same reasoning may be applied to information of primary interest to current employers. This vital public could not be expected to respond satisfactorily to a message delivered in a speech to the local Parent–Teacher Association. More effective response could be expected if it was presented to local service clubs or other organizations primarily concerned with employer interests. Here again, however, a specially designed letter addressed to concerned employers may produce the best results. There may be other circumstances where the best results would accrue from personal contacts as a setting for well-planned conversations with individuals within the concerned publics.

It is not necessary to identify all the varying circumstances involved in selecting the medium to be used in a given attempt to reach a given public with a given message, to illustrate the importance of the decision. Perhaps it is enough to say that poor judgment in selecting the medium and the method to be used may cancel the probability of success, although all other aspects of the activity are properly conceived and well planned.

Another important consideration is the availability of the talent essential to quality presentation through the media available. The speaking ability of the teacher–coordinator, for example, becomes an important factor. If the quality of his speaking ability is inconsistent with that normally expected of a professional person, the media requiring presentations of this kind should be eliminated. An exception might be the enlistment of other appropriate school officials to make the presentation, or the use of appropriate panels or symposia.

An arrangement of this kind, however, may not be acceptable, depending upon the circumstances at hand. As a general rule, it seems that better judgment would rule out the consistent use of substitutes in favor of emphasis on the use of media and methods through which the teacher–coordinator can function satisfactorily. It may be, for example, that the underpar public speaker can function well as chairman of panels and symposia or has good writing ability or is especially adept at personal contacts. For poor speakers, far more desirable results will accrue from the use of methods through which their stronger talents can be applied.

Suggested Activities

1. Write a 20- to 25-minute talk for a local civic club describing the contribution CE is designed to make to the local economy.
2. Design a brochure describing the responsibilities of the school and local employers in successful CE programs.
3. Write a letter of appreciation to employers of CE students to be mailed after the closing of school. Emphasize program accomplishments and employer contributions.
4. Prepare a brochure for parents of CE students elaborating on the four objectives listed on page 317.
5. Design a form for the recording of annual training-station losses. Provision should be made for the recording of all vital data, including dates, individuals involved, actions taken, reasons for the loss, and appropriate anecdotes.

Part V

Teacher-Coordinator Administrative and Supervisory Responsibilities

chapter fifteen
Continuing Educational Opportunities

chapter sixteen
Miscellaneous Administrative and
Supervisory Responsibilities

chapter seventeen
Program Evaluation

Introduction to Part V

Preceding chapters have characterized the responsibilities of the teacher–coordinator in the areas of coordination, teaching, and public relations. Part V is devoted to the treatment of those areas of responsibility that are administrative and supervisory in nature.

Chapter Fifteen deals specifically with continuing educational opportunities as an integral phase of vocational education and as an important responsibility of the teacher–coordinator.

The opportunity for employed adults to receive the instruction they need to keep abreast of technological development in the occupations in which they are employed should be made available through the local school. This principle is based on the theory that graduation from high school is not enough and that a continuing educational opportunity must be made available to assure the well-being of local workers and the business and industry in which they are employed.

Chapter Sixteen treats additional administrative responsibilities, including the areas of community occupational study, program evaluation, student follow-up study, legal responsibilities, records, and reports. There are other phases of the teacher–coordinator's overall responsibility which may be classed as administrative or supervisory. For the most part, however, those named above are of principal concern. They represent responsibility areas which, if neglected, would seriously detract from the efficiency of the program and militate against its complete success. Chapter Seventeen suggests a plan for the evaluation of cooperative education.

chapter fifteen

Continuing Educational Opportunities

The provision of opportunity for employed adults to obtain the information and the skill they need to keep abreast of technological development and to make progress in the occupations in which they are employed is normally considered to be a responsibility of the general public and, as such, should be made available through the public schools.

The local school, therefore, should be responsible for the establishment and supervision of classes for employed adults in accordance with local needs. The teacher–coordinator should be qualified to discharge this responsibility and should be expected to do so. Help should be provided, however, when and if the responsibility becomes heavy enough to cause neglect of CE. A special coordinator for continuing education should be employed when it is justified by the demands of the program.

A well-planned program of part-time and evening classes for employed adults will be a great asset to the business and industrial development of the community. School officials, with special reference to the teacher–coordinator, should not underestimate the need for this type of education and the unexcelled community entrée it provides. Employed adults who are satisfactorily served through such a program will become enthusiastic friends and supporters of the school. Citizens who have been befriended by the school through classes arranged to meet their needs become an important factor in school bond elections and other local political matters which affect the school.

Determining the Need for Continuing Education

All continuing education should be established on the basis of needs recognized and understood by those who will be expected to attend courses in question. Potential enrollees cannot be expected to attend a course based on needs they are not aware of. A basic characteristic of successful educational activities of this nature, therefore, is their unveiled appeal to potential participants as avenues to the acquisition of skill and knowledge which they need to hold their jobs or to increase their position or income.

Motivation of less potency is usually not enough to compete successfully with the established way of life, which would be in conflict with attending a course. Employed adults should not be expected to give up leisure-time activities, which they enjoy, to attend a course of study which does not reveal to them the possibility of acquiring values such as those suggested above.

The teacher–coordinator is cautioned that a vital factor in the successful establishment and operation of courses of study for employed adults is accurate identification and interpretation of the needs they are aware of and want to satisfy. In this respect, needs obvious to school officials may not be recognized by those for whom a given course is established. This fact lends prestige to promotional activities designed to develop awareness of personal needs and the desire to satisfy them.

The key point here is that those attending adult courses are not captive audiences. They attend for the purpose of getting something that they want and need. If at any time it should become obvious to them that they are not getting what they came after, they will simply not return. The responsibility of the school for continuing educational opportunity is to determine need, establish and finance classes, employ qualified teachers, and promote and supervise the program.

The following suggested procedures should be helpful in determining authentic educational needs of employed adults and employers and the establishment of courses especially designed to satisfy them.

Establishing Incentives for Continuing Education

Much of the motivation of those employed adults who successfully participate in a course of study designed for them is inspired by the employer. Fear of losing a job or hope for promotion is usually directly or indirectly inspired by employers or circumstances which they create. In the beginning, therefore, the teacher–coordinator should be concerned about the attitude and interest of employers and their willingness to cooperate. Such interest and desire may inspire the provision of special incentives for employees, such as payment of costs of the course, time off to attend the class, or possibly a wage increase or a bonus as a reward for successful participation. Incentives provided by concerned employers may include, but certainly should not be limited to, those suggested above. Employer ingenuity will produce successful incentives if the concern is sincere and of sufficient intensity.

The mercenary tendencies of employers may be exploited by the teacher–coordinator in gaining their cooperation. If they can be convinced, for example, that successful participation of their employees in a given course of study will result in returns of monetary value, the desired action can be expected to follow. This incentive is an effective key to the acquisition of employer interest and may be diplomatically used as a focus of promotional activities.

The fact that the teacher–coordinators are in daily contact with employers places them in excellent positions to examine, firsthand, the interest and need for preemployment or extension training for potential employees or those presently employed. Such an intimate contact may include opportunities to make pertinent suggestions of needs for training which the employer may not have recognized.

In addition to the personal contacts with employers which are incidental to daily visitation of CE training agencies, the teacher–coordinator may have opportunity to speak to civic organizations which include employers in their membership. Presentations to such groups could be designed to suggest the values of courses for employees which would eventually accrue to employers. Such suggestions may concern the returns that could be expected by the employer in terms of increased knowledge or skill which would enhance the quality and quantity of production.

In the final analysis, the success of courses of study designed for employed adults is dependent upon the monetary image they reflect to employers as well as to employees. The teacher–coordinator should find ways and means of diplomatically projecting this image in promotional activities. There is no other motivating factor to which employers and employees can be expected to respond in sufficient intensity. Although the "$" sign may have connotations that seem to be inconsistent with educational philosophy, it does represent a realistic approach to continuing education. It is the type of incentive which can be depended upon to inspire the necessary motivation because it will be clearly understood and is applicable to all concerned.

Other factors helpful in determining or anticipating needs for educational opportunity for employed adults are listed below, together with pertinent commentary.

Surveying Needs Caused by Technological Development

The inevitable growth and development of technology in modern business and industry represents a key to the need for continued educational opportunity for employed adults. The business or industrial enterprise unaffected by technological advancement is the exception. The chance of survival is limited by virtue of inevitable inability to compete with others that utilize available and applicable technology.

Alertness on the part of teacher–coordinators relative to technological developments which present needs for new skills and knowledge should keep them headed in the right direction in the development of appropriate continuing educational programs. This awareness, coupled with tendency to be an opportunist, should produce invaluable services to the community.

Examining Needs Caused by Industrial Expansion

The teacher–coordinator should be aligned with special interest groups in the community primarily concerned with the development of local business and industry. Such an affiliation provides opportunity to make known in appropriate circles at appropriate times the services the school is prepared to provide. It also provides advance information concerning new industry or the expansion of existing firms. In either event the teacher–coordinator is destined to be at the right place at the right time to offer the services of the school in providing the preemployment or supplementary training needed to man the new or expanded enterprise under consideration.

Considering Community Occupational Survey Data

Wisdom that results from perennial study of the occupational nature and structure of the community is an essential background upon which to establish and build local programs of vocational education. Vocational education for employed adults is no exception to this general principle. Keeping the local community occupational survey up to date and maintaining familiarity with the information it provides is a potent tool in the hands of a resourceful teacher–coordinator. Adult classes developed in accordance with points of departure established by the study should be apropos and successful, if properly planned and promoted.

Working Through the Advisory Committee

A representative advisory committee should be extremely helpful in establishing bona-fide need for continuing education classes. Intimate familiarity with the occupational structure and nature of the community on the part of the teacher–coordinator, coupled with the wisdom, good judgment, and active cooperation of the advisory committee, should provide the school with accurate leadership in the determination of the occupational areas in which continuing educational opportunity should be provided. It is not suggested that the advisory committee be subjected to the day-to-day problems inherent in this program. It is strongly recommended, however, that continuing education be included in the advisory committee's program of work to the end that its wisdom and good judgment may be brought to bear in the overall planning. This planning should include consideration of the areas of greatest need, the type of educational opportunity to be provided, and the recommendation of craft or occupational committees to work with the teacher–coordinator in course details.

Financing Continuing Education

As a general rule, the state department of vocational education will reimburse a percentage of the salary paid to teachers of approved part-time or evening classes for employed adults. Additional costs are normally paid by the local school.

In view of the fiscal responsibility of the school, it becomes obvious that first consideration must be given to ways and means of financing classes for which definite need has been established. The following suggestions should be helpful in this respect.

Budget Local Funds

When and if local school officials, including the superintendent and the school board, accept responsibility for the provision of educational opportunity for locally employed adults, they should be willing to make local school funds available for the purpose.

The application of local school funds need not be extensive to be effective. A small item in the budget for adult classes will pay big dividends. Suppose, for example, that a state department of vocational education were to agree to reimburse two-thirds of teacher salaries for approved classes, in a given community. An item of $1,000 of local funds in the annual school budget for continuing education matched with $2,000 of state or federal funds, would make a total of $3,000 available for the salaries of teachers of approved adult classes. Three thousand dollars should be sufficient to pay teacher salaries for 25 to 30 twenty-hour classes, depending on the local salary scale, enrolling 300 to 600 people, with the possibility of as many as 1,000. The value of serving educational needs of 1,000 taxpayers and voters, to the economic welfare of the community, would be difficult to overestimate.

The time element and the amount of money were arbitrarily selected for purposes of illustration. It is not intended to imply that more or less hours of instruction may not be necessary in given circumstances, that the local funding should be limited to $1,000, or that the percentage of reimbursement by the state agency will be limited to $66\frac{2}{3}$ percent.

A program of part-time and evening classes properly conceived, organized, and conducted will be a great asset to the community in attracting new industry and the expansion of established firms. In addition, it is difficult to conceive a more rewarding way for the school to extend its program in the direction of more completely meeting the total educational needs of the community.

If the fiscal ability of the local school is not enough to completely finance the adult classes need, with the help of state and federal funds, other sources of funds should become available to the resourceful teacher–coordinator. There follow a few suggestions which may be helpful.

Secure Grants for Continuing Education

Grants-in-aid for adult classes can properly be made to the school by private enterprise. Accordingly, business and industry which stand to benefit from the educational opportunity to be provided by the school may contribute funds to help bear the school's part of the cost. The resourceful teacher–coordinator should find the willingness of local business and industry to contribute to be directly in proportion to their understanding and acceptance of the purposes and values of the service to be rendered. Here again, the monetary values to employers should be brought into focus and exploited to the necessary degree.

Employee organizations are often fiscally able and willing to under-write a portion of the cost of classes that are open to their members.

Other sources of funds may be found in civic clubs and professional organizations sensitive to the economic welfare of the community and its work force.

Establish a Registration Fee

It may be advisable, subject to local policy, to establish and charge a nominal registration fee for all continuing education classes. Funds derived from this source may be used in defraying costs such as the purchase of instructional materials, utilities, and janitorial services, but may not be used to match state and federal funds in the teacher's salary. The fact that state and federal funds normally become involved in educational programs for adult workers places a limitation on the use of registration fees as a major means of financing. Under no circum-stances should such fees be large enough to cause those who attend the classes to feel that they are paying double for the service, once through their tax dollars and again through the registration fee. The use of state or federal funds automatically requires that the educational oppor-tunity be available, without tuition, to all qualified individuals. It is pointed out again that the registration fee can be used only for costs incidental to providing the educational opportunity.

Establishing Classes

The following steps should culminate in the successful establish-ment and conduct of classes for employed adults.

Work with a Craft or Occupational Committee

It is assumed at this point that the general advisory committee, upon the request of the teacher–coordinator, has recommended qualified individuals for membership on craft or occupational committees to deal with the details of courses under consideration. The teacher–coordinator should work formally and informally with these committees in the following areas of concern:

1. Determination of the Course Content
   This function may consist of adjusting the content of an existing course of study to meet local needs. If such a course of study is not available, the teacher–coordinator may resort to the knowledge and experience of the craft or occupational committee in determining course content.
2. Determination of Time Requirements
   After the content of the course in question has been determined, time requirements should be established, including the total hours of instruction and the number and length of class meetings.
3. Determination of the Equipment and Material Needed
   The committee should be helpful in identifying the materials and equipment essential to the successful conduct of the class. It may also be helpful in acquiring special equipment or materials.
4. Securing a Qualified Teacher
   The craft or occupational committee may be the best source of information relative to a qualified teacher for a given course. Its function, therefore, may include the recommendation or the approval of the teacher.

Select the Teacher

Instructors of adult classes should be thoroughly qualified in the field in which they are to teach. In addition to this, they should have gained sufficient stature to command the respect of those who are expected to enroll. It is the responsibility of the school to find such individuals as they are needed. It should be recognized that although these people may be technically qualified and fully respected in their fields, they may have little knowledge of how to teach. It may be necessary, therefore, for the school to provide appropriate instruction in methods, organization of course materials, classroom management, and lesson planning.

Itinerant instructors in specialized fields are sometimes made available by state departments of vocational education. These instructors may be available to local schools upon request without cost. Itinerant instructors will be specialists in their fields and experienced teachers. In addition, they can be expected to have all equipment, teaching aids, and instructional materials needed in the course.

All schools should take advantage of the itinerant instructors available and applicable to the needs in their service areas. It must be understood, however, that it is not possible to provide enough itinerant instructors to meet the total need for continuing education in any community. Most of this need will have to be satisfied through the use of instructors who may be found in the local community.

Teacher–coordinators should come to know. of such individuals who are basically qualified to teach adult classes. They should also know about itinerant instructors available through the state department of vocational education. Local individuals found to be qualified and available may be employed on a "stand-by" or "call" basis to be paid only for the actual time that they teach. An arrangement of this kind lends itself well to the preliminary teacher education which may be necessary under the direction of the teacher–coordinator.

Apply for Prior Approval of Classes

If reimbursement of a portion of the cost of an adult class is expected, prior approval should be requested through appropriate channels. If, for example, a state division of vocational education is expected to reimburse a portion of the cost of a given class, formal approval should be granted and in the hands of local school officials before the opening date of the class. There will be an official form upon which application for approval should be made.

Promote the Class

An important key to success in continuing education is ability to attract those for whom given courses are designed. It was stated earlier that the potential enrollee must want the instruction with sufficient intensity to overcome the desire to pursue desirable leisure-time activities. Promotion, therefore, involves any activity in which the teacher–coordinator may engage that is designed to cause individuals, for whom the course is intended, to want the instruction as a result of their belief that personal needs will be satisfied.

Appropriate personal innovations in the application of conventional promotional methods such as the following should help attract favorable attention. Good judgment in the selection and timing of the promotional methods to be used will enhance the probability of success. The quality which characterizes all promotional activities is also very important. A poorly written letter, for example, is likely to have a negative effect rather than to accomplish the purpose for which it was written.

Prepare News Releases

News releases in the form of articles concerning the course to be offered should be carefully prepared to convey appropriate information to potential class participants and to inspire interest and intensity of desire to attend. Such articles should carry specific information, such as the purpose for which the courses are being offered, beginning dates, the number and length of class meetings, the places of meeting, and the cost of attendance, if any. Here again it is suggested that monetary values be tactfully presented and explained.

Follow-up articles should be carried by the local newspaper to herald the beginning dates of classes and to supplement information contained in previous articles.

Articles such as those suggested above should be written by school officials, preferably the teacher–coordinator, in order to preserve proper inflections in the writing. If, for some reason, this plan does not prove to be a feasible arrangement, it may be necessary to resort to interviews with newspaper reporters to serve as bases of articles to be written by them for publication. The hazard of this technique is the possibility of failure to communicate effectively with the reporter with the inevitable result being a distorted news article. On the other hand, the news reporter who grasps the significance of the article probably will get better results than the nonprofessional news writer.

The editor of the local newspaper and his professional staff are an important public for CE. Time and effort may have been previously applied in developing an understanding and an appreciation of the total scope of the program, including its affiliation with continuing education. If such efforts have been successful, the editor and his staff should be appreciative of the values of courses of study proposed to meet the needs of employed adults in the community.

Consider Paid Advertisements

A paid advertisement may or may not be an appropriate or practical method of alerting given publics to information relevant to their needs. Such advertisements, however, provide broad opportunity for the exercise of originality in design, for the purpose of attracting the attention of those for whom the course in question is intended. Here again, the teacher–coordinator may find it advisable to call on professional personnel of the newspaper for help in designing the ad.

The teacher–coordinator should value the local newspaper as a medium through which to announce and promote classes to be offered. It is often the most effective of all available media.

Make Appropriate Use of Radio and Television

Spot announcements on radio or television are effective in keeping the public aware of a given course of instruction to be offered for employed adults. As a general rule, public service time can be made available for the reading of announcements several times a day, without cost. Local stations may be willing to schedule the announcement to be read as an adjunct to daily newscasts.

The preparation of material for use on radio and TV should also be the responsibility of school officials, if appropriate expertise is available. If such ability is not available, essential data should be submitted to professional staff members of the medium in question, for use in preparation of the script.

In this event school officials should request the opportunity to examine the completed script for accuracy and inflection before it is used, especially when the presentation is to be made by a media staff member rather than a school official.

Mail Letters to Potential Enrollees

It may be appropriate to prepare letters for mailing to individuals assumed to be interested in a given continuing education course. Mailing lists may be obtained from employee organizations primarily concerned with the occupational welfare of their members as well as from business and industry. All other feasible sources of information should be explored.

The content of letters should be much the same as the news articles described earlier (see p. 350) except that the letter should be personalized to the greatest possible extent. The letter should suggest special recognition of the recipient as an individual and imply that he has the privilege of participating in the instructional program being offered. In addition, the letter should include accurate information, such as the time and place of the first meeting and some information about the teacher. The teacher who is well known and has achieved a degree of fame in the area in which he will teach will probably be the most attractive feature of the course. Such a teacher should be featured in all promotional efforts.

Secure Sponsoring Organizations

It is frequently helpful and desirable to interest a local professional or service organization which has vested interest in local employee groups or in other phases of the local economy to sponsor adult classes germane to this interest. Such a sponsoring agency often lends prestige to the educational opportunity being made available and can frequently effectively supplement the promotional efforts of the school. This effort may include the following:

1. Contact with potential enrollees through organizational membership.
2. The use of official organs such as newsletters to publicize the program.
3. An organized telephone contact with potential enrollees.
4. Reference to the program and its potential values in public addresses by members of the sponsoring organizations.
5. The offering of incentives such as some form of recognition for successful completion of the course.

Make Personal Contacts

In the course of regular vistation of students the teacher–coordinator will come into contact with many of those for whom given continuing education courses are to be offered. Mention of a class as a part of a friendly conversation and a special invitation to attend is often an effective promotional procedure. This conversation may give the teacher–coordinator an opportunity to answer pertinent questions about the course which the potential enrollee may not otherwise have an opportunity to ask.

Keeping employers informed of planned courses for employed adults as an adjunct to CE student visitation is also an important phase of the promotional process. Awareness on the part of employers could result in incentives designed to create desire on the part of their employees to attend the class in question.

Less potent but still valuable personal contacts should result from attending association meetings which include potential enrollees in their memberships. This kind of contact would give the teacher–coordinator the opportunity to explain the purposes and values of the course in question and to answer questions which may otherwise go unanswered.

Prepare Posters and Brochures

Attractive posters placed in appropriate locations are helpful in keeping pertinent information concerning scheduled adult classes available for continuous reference by a given segment of the community. Posters should be moved every day or so to prevent them from becoming unnoticed fixtures. Simply moving them a few feet or perhaps changing the position may preserve the ability to continue to attract the necessary attention.

Brochures for mailing or distribution by other means could be effective in promoting continuing education classes. The attractiveness of the design and the quality of their messages are determining factors in their effectiveness. Here again the ingenuity of the teacher–coordinator may become an important factor in the success of this instrument of promotion. If it should become necessary to choose between the use of a poor-quality brochure and the elimination of a segment of the promotional program, better judgment should dictate that the brochure not be distributed.

The teacher–coordinator may find it advisable in some instances to apply all of the methods suggested above in promoting continuing education classes. At other times an announcement of the time and place of meeting of a class may be all that is necessary. The extent and nature of the promotional effort necessary in any given circumstance, therefore, will depend upon the conscious concern of those for whom the classes are to be offered. It is conceivable, for example, that the demand for certain classes could become so great that the school would be forced into a defensive position.

The teacher–coordinator is cautioned not to limit the promotional methods he or she employs to the conventional methods suggested above. In some instances personal ingenuity may produce novel and effective approaches to promotion which would achieve superior results.

Open the Class

The reader is reminded that those who attend the first meeting of an adult class have done so because they have personal needs for information or skills which they have been led to believe the course will satisfy. Keeping this in mind should help those who participate in the first meeting to cultivate this idea rather than to destroy it. If nothing in the first meeting bolsters the above expectation, the return to subsequent meetings will be highly improbable.

Accordingly, the program for the first meeting should be planned very carefully, including exercised awareness of this principle. It would be possible, for example, for the superintendent of schools, in the course of making a welcoming statement, to spook the entire class by means of ill-fated remarks concerning school requirements in areas such as attendance, testing, and grades. Statements in these and other sensitive areas should be avoided because they tend to imply the possibility of circumstances which all adults are prone to avoid at all costs.

Tests or examinations, for example, suggest conditions under which the individual may feel that he will not be able to measure up, with accompanying embarrassment. Grades suggest the possibility of unavoidable comparisons with other members of the class. It is probably enough to say at this point that adults must be treated as adults rather than as youths of school age. They can be expected to remove themselves from circumstances which tend to impose conventional classroom requirements upon them. It stands to reason, therefore, that care must be exercised, in the beginning, to avoid reference to course requirements such as those mentioned above.

Regular and full attendance should be encouraged. The most common practice in this respect probably is the awarding of a billfold-size certificate for an announced percentage of attendance of class meetings. Such a certificate should not carry a grade or any other basis of comparison. It should simply certify satisfactory participation in the course. A sample of the certificate should be shown at the first meeting, together with a full explanation of how it might be earned.

The group should be assured that there will be no examination at the end of the course and that no attempt will be made to determine a grade in any other fashion. Any tests that are given will be turned in without identification and will be used only to help the teacher to determine the effectiveness of the teaching. The teacher–coordinator should be informed concerning the basic principles of adult education in order to avoid inexcusable errors in working with adults.

The following sample agenda should be helpful to inexperienced teacher–coordinators in planning the first meeting of an adult class:

1. Assemble	Teacher–coordinator presiding
2. Welcome and remarks	School official (preferably the superintendent of schools)
3. Introductions and remarks	Teacher–coordinator
4. Orientation and course information	Teacher–coordinator

5. Determination of the most satisfactory time and place for class meetings
6. Exhibiting certificate and explaining how it can be earned
7. Inviting questions and answering them
8. Introducing the teacher
9. Establishing class roll
10. Teacher making initial statement and proceeding to present the first lesson
11. Adjourning

Supervise the Class

Supervisory activities of the teacher–coordinator should be positive and prompt in nature but should always be performed in the guise of being helpful to the teacher, as well as to those who attend the class, rather than to give the impression of trying to find something wrong. The class should be visited periodically but never in accord with an established routine. Visits should be made frequently enough to keep in touch with what is going on and to detect and attack problems in their origin rather than at their height or after they have run their course.

The teacher may be qualified primarily by virtue of successful work experience in his field, but short on classroom expertise. It is necessary, therefore, that classroom performance be observed closely enough to maintain awareness of any difficulties being experienced. Positive identification of problems should prompt intervention at the earliest feasible time by the teacher–coordinator. Helpful suggestions early enough may solve the problem and preserve the instructional program. In addition, the teacher–coordinator should be concerned with a continuous informal evaluation of the teacher. Suitable criteria for such an evaluation procedure could include such items as:

1. Promptness in getting the class under way.
2. Consistency of preparation to teach.

3. Ability to communicate with the class and hold its interest.
4. The use of teaching aids.
5. Efficiency in the use of the entire class period.
6. Class participation.
7. Ability to receive and answer questions.
8. The consistency of class attendance.
9. Holding power.
10. Overall ability to handle the total classroom situation.

Serious classroom problems such as those which often develop in the regular school are not likely to occur in the continuing education classroom. Adult students do not tend to openly take exception to unpleasant circumstances and conditions to which they are subjected. They simply remove themselves from the intolerable environment rather than to become involved in controversial situations. It should be kept in mind that classes composed of adults are not captive audiences as are regular school students. It goes without saying that the holding power of the teacher of adults depends to a great extent upon the ability to sense their needs and to launch positive and aggressive efforts to meet these needs. Failure in these respects may be the basis of problems which originate in the classroom and could account for the high mortality rates which frequently plague continuing education.

Prepare and Submit Reports

Reimbursable classes for employed adults must be reported to the reimbursing agency. State divisions of vocational education normally require an initial report which will include a listing of those initially enrolled together with pertinent information about each of them, and a final report which will list those who have continued their enrollment until the end of the course together with their attendance record. Interim reports such as monthly or other suitable periods of time may be included in the reporting plan. It is usually a supervisory responsibility of the teacher–coordinator to execute these reports and to see that they are promptly submitted to proper authorities. This supervisory responsibility normally includes the initiation and maintenance of a complete system of records involving all continuing education classes.

Publicize the Class

The teacher–coordinator's responsibility for publicizing adult classes does not end with the promotional activities. Specifically, the first meeting of an adult class may be featured by a front-page story in the local newspaper. This publicity may be prepared by the teacher–coordinator or other school officials. An alternative plan might be to invite the editor of the local newspaper, or a member of the reporting staff, to the preliminaries of the first meeting of the class. Listening to a welcoming statement by a school official (preferably the superintendent) and the orientation by the teacher–coordinator and perhaps the opening statement of the teacher of the class should provide ample material for a good news story.

The individual who is to write the story should be encouraged to champion the teacher and those who are to attend the course. It would be advisable to include the names of these people if it can be feasibly done. The story should also emphasize the purpose of the course and suggest the economic values that should accrue to successful participants. The importance of the contribution the school is making to the economy of the community by providing an opportunity for the work force to keep abreast of technological development should be mentioned.

Interim stories would be in order if the class activities and accomplishments are dynamic enough to provide subjects of sufficient interest to the community. Here again, the names of those in attendance should be included in the story. Their employers and friends should appreciate their effort to improve themselves. The value of giving class participants an opportunity of seeing their names in the local newspaper should not be underestimated.

Feature Closing Exercises

The last meeting of the class should be planned as a special occasion. It could be in the form of a banquet to which those completing the course could invite members of their families and friends. The superintendent of schools should be invited to address the group and to present certificates of completion. An occasion of this kind could well take on similarity to a regular high school graduation exercise. The press should be invited and given ample material for a good news story.

Perhaps one of the greatest values that may result from such an occasion is the awakening of school officials to recognition of the service that the school is rendering to the community. They should recognize the potential value of continuing education to the school in serving the total educational needs of the community, which includes the needs of patrons, taxpayers, and voters. Being an opportunist, the superintendent will see in the occasion an opportunity to mention bond elections which are in the offing or other current circumstances which will ultimately culminate in some form of an election. Statements of this nature would, no doubt, be followed by a diplomatic reminder that the school appreciates the opportunity to serve the educational needs of citizens of the community and would appreciate their help in the solution of school and community problems.

If the program planned for the last meeting is of sufficient magnitude and caliber to justify inviting other city officials, such as the mayor, they should also recognize the values of the educational opportunity being provided by the school as it relates to the economy of the community. This occasion should cultivate their willingness to cooperate with school officials in the development of the total educational program.

The suggestion that well-planned closing exercises of a continuing education class can be made to reflect valuable concepts to those who control the destiny of education in all of its aspects should not be allowed to deflect the spotlight from those who have successfully completed the course. As a matter of fact, they are the prima facie evidence of the values that should be recognizable by all concerned individuals.

The following sample agenda may be helpful in planning the closing exercises of a successful adult class:

1. Assemble   Teacher–coordinator
2. Welcome and remarks
3. Introduction of distinguished guests
4. Serving the banquet
5. Introduction of the superintendent
   of schools
6. Address (short)   Superintendent of schools
7. Awarding of certificates   Superintendent of schools
8. Closing remarks   Teacher–coordinator
9. Adjournment

Initiate and Maintain Follow-Up Records

Ways and means must be devised to establish and maintain records of all who complete adult courses. This requirement is based on the probability that many of those who successfully participate will refer to the experience in future job-changing efforts. The school should be in position to respond to inquiries from potential employers.

Teachers would do well, during the course of instruction, to insist that the effectiveness of principles being taught be tested to determine their effectiveness in the solution of job-oriented problems and circumstances. They should explain that the school needs to be informed about the effectiveness of the instruction in order that a continuous process of improvement can be sustained. Information which cannot stand this test has no place in an instructional program for employed adults.

Typical Problems in Continuing Education

Problem 1   Administrative resistance to continuing education as a part of the educational program

School administrators may be reluctant to accept continuing education as a responsibility of the school. Such reluctance may be based on the proposition that the school is responsible only for the "less than college grade" educational opportunity for the educable age group in its service area—more specifically, those individuals living in the community ranging in age from six through 21.

The school administrator with this point of view would probably reason that school funds could not be legally applied to the cost of educational opportunity for employed adults over 21 years of age. By the same token, it may be administratively determined that teacher–coordinators should not apply any part of their time to continuing education. Although the school administrator may be absolutely sincere in such opinions, they are often based on invalid assumption rather than fact.

Teacher–coordinators who find efforts to provide continuing educational opportunities for employed adults opposed by administrative superiors for the above reasons have no alternative but to abide by their mandates. They should not, however, simply capitulate to such administrative attitudes without exerting every possible effort to preserve

359

the opportunity employed adults must have to keep abreast of technological development in the occupational areas in which they are employed.

The enthusiasm, or lack of it, displayed by the teacher–coordinator probably will be a determining factor in the cumulative attitude of the school administration. The suggestion is that the teacher–coordinator who would rather not be encumbered with the responsibility for continuing education may experience little difficulty in cultivating negative attitudes on the part of administrative officials. On the other hand, sincere enthusiasm can be expected to induce the desired administrative response with attending wholehearted cooperation. The modern school administrator will quickly grasp the public relations value of properly conceived and wisely provided educational opportunity for citizens and taxpayers of the community.

Problem 2 Basing continuing education on identifiable needs of which proposed recipients are or can be made aware

The teacher–coordinator who becomes interested in providing continuing educational opportunity will find it fascinating and rewarding. Efforts in this respect may, at times, be rewarded with success or failure without a clear-cut reason for the cause of either, but a reasonable balance between the agonies of failure and the exhiliration of success can be expected. Unfortunately, the reaction of employed adults to classes designed for them is unpredictable. It is safe to assume, however, that the final attitude will be positive rather than negative or indifferent when individuals accept the idea that the class in question will satisfy personal needs of which they are aware and which they want to satisfy. When this state of mind is achieved on the part of enough individuals, satisfactory enrollment can be expected.

Expertise in the identification of the true educational needs of employed adults and the design of courses to meet these needs is a prime key to success in continuing education. This expertise coupled with aptness in the introduction of incentives which will motivate desire to attend should assure success. The combination of needs, wants, incentives, and motives may produce many unpredictable personal reactions, with the result that sincere and intelligent effort may fail to produce the expected results. The teacher–coordinator is cautioned, however, not to generalize from one failure that success is unattainable, but rather to accept failure as a challenge to achieve success on subsequent attempts. As a general rule, failure can be traced to faulty procedure of one form or another. A new attack altered in accordance with identifiable mistakes may produce the success previous attempts failed to achieve.

Problem 3 *Effecting an appropriate blend of effort applied to continuing education with coordinating activities*

It was previously stated that much of the legwork involved in education for employed adults can be accomplished by the teacher–coordinator incidentally with regular visitation of CE students. In other words, teacher–coordinators find themselves in daily contact with employed adults and employers without the necessity of special visits. This association, coupled with frequent opportuniites to work with employee and employer organizations, constitutes the type of community contacts essential to the identification of needs and the promotion of courses designed to meet them.

The teacher–coordinator is cautioned, however, that other phases of continuing education will require the application of time and effort separate and apart from CE. It is this phase of continuing education that should not be allowed to reach proportions which will seriously detract from the teacher–coordinator's regular activities. The problem, therefore, is to effect an appropriate blend of effort which will result in the satisfaction of the most pressing needs for continuing education without causing CE to suffer. That part of the teacher–coordinator's effort applied to continuing education should be considered an investment in program development. If this effort is wisely applied, it should establish a basis upon which continuing educational activities can develop to full potential.

At the right point in this development an assistant should be employed to work primarily with the adult program. The alert teacher–coordinator will see in this expansion the most obvious avenue of growth for vocational education. The results of successful continuing education will be so dynamic that little difficulty should be experienced in convincing wise school administrators of the advisability of expanding the program to the greatest possible extent.

Problem 4 *Finding qualified teachers and preparing them to teach continuing education courses*

School officials, including the teacher–coordinator, are frequently prone to assume that fame and success in a given occupation qualifies an individual to teach without further preparation. Succumbing to such an assumption is frequently the basis of failure. The excellence of business or industrial experience is of little value in teaching without the ability to plan, organize, and present the subject matter to be taught. Continuing education teachers of excellent experience background may be prone to cover their entire course at the first class meeting because they were unaware of the necessity of planning and organization to assure proper emphasis on all areas of the course of study.

The teacher problem is divided into two parts, with the first concern being to find individuals who are qualified by virtue of appropriate and successful work experience and desire to teach.

The craft or occupational committee is probably the best source of teacher recommendations because all of its members will be qualified workers in the field and will know of others of sufficient stature to qualify for the position.

The teacher should be employed with the understanding that a suitable period of time will be applied to orientation and preparation to teach, under the direction of the teacher–coordinator. The preparation period should continue until the teacher is ready to teach and has done the necessary preliminary planning and preparation. Provision to pay the potential teacher for a given period of orientation should be made if at all possible. Failure to make such a provision may cause reluctance to ask the potential teacher to devote the time without pay and thus eliminate the orientation period. This omission would increase the hazard of failure because success seldom results from simply putting a teacher, qualified by work experience alone, in a classroom with adult students who may not be fully convinced that they want to attend the class.

Problem 5   *The effective utilization of general advisory committees*

The effective utilization of advisory committees is often cumbersome and may, at times, slow down urgent processes. As a general rule, however, the additional time required will pay dividends in the form of success factors which cannot be brought to bear in any other way. Effective utilization of such committees is a reflection of good planning and efficient organization.

The program of work suggested and discussed earlier is evidence of such efficiency and will enable the teacher–coordinator to circumvent time-consuming problems inherent in the unplanned program. Accordingly, the teacher–coordinator should present information, relative to the need for classes for employed adults, at an early meeting of the general advisory committee. The committee should be asked to recommend or approve occupational committees for those courses they recommend to be offered during the school year. This process should give the teacher–coordinator an opportunity to plan and organize the continuing education program to include the complete function of craft or occupational committees.

Failure to follow a plan such as that suggested above will tend to negate effective utilization of the general advisory committee and specific occupational committees, thus decreasing the probability of success.

Suggested Activities

1. After reviewing appropriate sources of information, write a complete description of reimbursable part-time and evening classes. Emphasize their most obvious characteristics, applications, and values.
2. Prepare a statement for submission to school administration, recommending the establishment of a continuing education program for employed adults in the community. Be sure to include full explanation of the purposes and values of such a program to the school and community.
3. Write an open letter to all retail establishments in a given community, announcing the availability of continuing educational opportunity for employees. Emphasize the purposes and values of such a program to employers, employees, and the community in general.
4. Design a plan incorporating the use of all appropriate media in a promotional program for continuing education classes. Include all methods deemed appropriate in promotional efforts of this kind.
5. Using the criteria listed on pages 355–356, develop an evaluation instrument for use in appraising the performance of teachers of continuing education classes.

chapter sixteen

Miscellaneous Administrative and Supervisory Responsibilities

The fact that teacher–coordinators must function in multiple areas of responsibility under diversified circumstances renders specific classification of their activities impractical and unnecessary. In other words, they need not be consciously concerned about the distribution of time and effort among teaching, coordination, relationship development, or administration, which are the major divisions of the total responsibility. On the contrary, they should budget and manage available time so as to apply it equitably according to current need without regard for official classification of the activity. It is quite possible, for example, that activities classified as "administrative" may be separated by irregular time intervals depending upon the season of the year and current local circumstances.

The embryonic teacher–coordinator should consider the administrative responsibilities described in this chapter to be typical illustrations rather than an all-inclusive listing.

Community Occupational Surveys

Community occupational surveys are usually conducted when school officials come to recognize the need for dependable occupational information upon which to base local vocational educational plans. Such school officials will have determined that information of this nature is essential to intelligent planning and that it is available through no other source. This decision is a reflection of growing concern, on the part of school officials, for their accountability for the results of the educational program over which they preside. Vocational programs which are not founded on needs that are identifiable in terms of employment opportunity for program graduates, or the needs of employed adults to keep abreast of technological developments in the occupational areas in which they are employed or wish to be employed, are without justifiable purpose.

Sincere and concerned public school officials will recognize the futility of efforts to establish vocational programs to satisfy unknown or obscure needs. Such recognition can be expected to motivate a search for definite and accurate information to relieve the resulting dilemma.

The properly conceived and well-planned community occupational survey is the best-known method of securing the type and quality of information needed by the school to serve as bases for local vocational education programs. Such studies should be perpetual because a relatively small amount of effort each year will keep them up to date.

It will serve the best interest of the teacher–coordinator to head the local occupational study in order to be in position to benefit to the greatest possible extent from the intimate community contact involved. Heading a full-fledged community survey would constitute an unexcelled avenue to school and community familiarity of great value to CE.

The teacher–coordinator may be able to satisfy initial needs of CE through preliminary surveys, which consist simply of canvassing potential training agencies relative to placement possibility for students. The fact that limited surveys of this kind may serve initial needs for community occupational information by no means eliminates the need for a total occupational study upon which to base program growth and development. The teacher–coordinator who does not have the benefit of a total community occupational study cannot be certain that vocational education, including CE, is serving the most urgent needs of the community. As a matter of fact, there may be areas of need about which school officials are completely unaware.

Although the community occupational survey holds many specific values for CE, it also has great significance for vocational education in its total aspects in any school system. Consequently, in accepting leadership responsibility, the teacher–coordinator is cast in an important role for vocational education as a whole.

Intimate knowledge of and extreme sensitivity to community needs should render any recommendation the teacher–coordinator is moved to make, concerning any area of vocational education, acceptable and worthy of consideration on the part of school officials. A schoolwide position of leadership of this caliber should be of great value to CE and greatly enhance respect for the program on the part of all elements of the school and the community.

Student Follow-Up Study

In the final analysis, the success of CE depends upon the success of its graduates in their post–high school adjustment in the world of work. This is normally examined through a formally conducted follow-up study of program gradutes by school officials. Having follow-up information often provides the most authentic clues for the improvement of CE and guidance services. Causes which can be identified as bases of success or failure of former students often serve as dependable barometers of program strengths and weaknesses.

Student follow-up studies should be planned and executed so as to involve actual contact with former students, to the greatest possible extent, for the purpose of determining firsthand how well their educational experiences prepared them for post–high school adjustment. The successful student follow-up study should essentially yield the following types of information:

1. How well students were occupationally oriented and how successful they were in finding the type of work for which they were prepared.
2. An appraisal of the educational experiences the students had in high school in the light of post–high school adjustment problems.
3. Suggestions as to how the high school program might be adjusted so as to be more beneficial to its graduates.

4. Information suitable for recording in permanent records relative to successes and failures with attending anecdotes.

The well-planned and efficiently conducted follow-up of program graduates will succeed or fail in accordance with the degree to which they were conditioned, as students, to respond to subsequent contacts that would be made with them. The impression that students take with them upon leaving the school relative to the sincerity of the concern for their welfare will have a great deal to do with the tendency to respond. If, for example, students were not impressed with the sincerity of the teacher–coordinator's interest in them as individuals, they can be expected to resist response to inquiries concerning success or failure in the world of work or in institutions of higher learning. A general attitude of this nature among program graduates would condemn a follow-up study to failure.

On the other hand, a general feeling that there is genuine concern for the best interest of students on the part of the teacher–coordinator and other school officials should result in sincere desire to keep them informed of their successes. Such attitudes would almost surely result in good response to follow-up inquiries. It should be kept in mind, however, that students cannot be expected to develop the desired attitudes if they are not given plausible information upon which to base their thinking.

The suggestion is that an appropriate amount of teaching time should be devoted to an explanation of the need for follow-up information, how it will be sought, and how it will be used to improve the instructional program. It should be fully explained why the federal government requires that follow-up information be maintained on each student who attends a program reimbursed with federal funds for any part of the cost of instruction. Students should be impressed with the importance of keeping the school supplied with accurate and current mailing addresses so that contact can be made when information is needed or there is information of interest to be mailed to them. Under no circumstances should the student be left with the impression that follow-up surveys are made solely because they are required by the federal government.

The fact that many of the graduates will leave the community in the course of time after graduation relegates the collection of much of the data to the use of mailed questionnaires. The right kind of general attitude on the part of graduates, a good questionnaire, and an accurate mailing list should produce valid follow-up information in sufficient quantity and quality to meet the need of the school for follow-up information on its graduates.

Respondents who have not returned questionnaires within a given time limit should be sent follow-up letters with additional questionnaires enclosed. The second letter should reiterate the importance of the information sought by the school and urge that the recipient take time to provide it.

If no reply to the second letter is received within a specified time, a third letter should be mailed enclosing a third questionnaire, on the assumption that the first two were misplaced or lost. The mailing of additional letters to delinquents is a matter of teacher–coordinator judgment. A letter of appreciation to those who respond should create goodwill and pave the way for future requests for information.

The fact that student follow-up surveys may be dispersed over greater periods of time than is usually the case in more intensive surveys lends less pressure to various phases of the study, such as tabulation, interpretation, drawing conclusions, and making the necessary recommendations. The chances are that the student follow-up survey can be handled by the regular office staff with liberal applications of the teacher–coordinator's time, if the effort is persistent and is initiated early enough.

School officials may elect to contact program graduates who remain in the community in more intimate fashions than through use of the mailed questionnaire. As a matter of fact, contact with many of them may be included in the routine process of coordination because CE graduates often become employers in their home community.

Legal Responsibilities

Teacher–coordinators are not responsible for the administering of federal laws pertaining to vocational education. This fact does not relieve them of the responsibility of being well informed relative to the federal legislative assistance which has inspired the development of vocational education since its inception. Although such knowledge may not be of interest to CE students or any other public, familiarity with federal legislation and its role in the development of vocational education is a distinguishing mark of the professional vocational educator.

For this reason the acquisition of appropriate knowledge and the development of appreciation in this area become important parts of the teacher–coordinator's educational preparation. Special attention should be given to the essence of the following federal laws. Each of these acts was cast in a major role in the development of vocational education:

Smith–Hughes Act (1917)	National Defense Education Act (1958)
George Deen Act (1937)	Vocational Education Act (1963)
George Barden Act (1946)	Vocational Education Amendments of (1968)

The above list is not intended to discount other federal legislation, but rather to emphasize the importance of these particular acts, and the impact they have made, and continue to make, on public education. An intensive study of these and other federal acts should be encountered by the embryonic teacher–coordinator, in the teacher-education program, in the form of courses such as "History and Development of Vocational Education." This area of study may be a part of an undergraduate or graduate program, depending upon when teacher–coordinator preparation begins.

The study of the history and development of vocational education should be accompanied or followed by a study of all phases of vocational education in order that CE may be kept in proper perspective relative to the total program. In other words, it should be understood, appreciated, and accepted that all vocational education may be broadly defined as preparation for satisfactory entrance into the world of work and progress in chosen occupational areas. All areas of vocational education are designed to accomplish these purposes, differing primarily in the occupational areas with which they are concerned. For example, distributive education is concerned with the preparation of individuals for entrance and progress in the field of distribution. Business and office education has the same concern for those individuals choosing to enter office occupations.

Both of these fields of vocational education are attempting to accomplish the same thing in different occupational areas with variations of the same basic class types. CE is an educational "technique" or "method" applicable to both areas as well as to all other divisions of vocational education. It may be employed on a specific occupational basis, such as office occupations, or it may involve all qualified occupations in its "multiple occupational form."

The Federal Wage and Hour Law

The federal Wage and Hour Law establishes fair labor standards and governs their enforcement. It is so comprehensive that the teacher–coordinator could hardly be expected to develop extreme familiarity with it beyond those parts which directly affect CE. Here again, it is not the responsibility of the teacher–coordinator to administer the provisions of the Wage and Hour Law.

As a matter of fact, neither the school or its agents are liable for infractions of this act beyond the rare possibility that personal negligence might be proved against them. The fact remains, however, that the teacher–coordinator, as an agent of the school, bears a strong moral responsibility to the employers of students. Accordingly, the teacher–

coordinator is duty-bound to keep employers informed and to guard against circumstances which could penalize them for their effort to perform a public service through CE.

The fact that the school and its agents are not liable for infractions of the Wage and Hour Law, as it relates to CE, does not eliminate the disastrous effects on the program resulting from employer violations in areas such as wages, hours, and other minimum employment requirements.

The federal Wage and Hour Law covers such a broad area of the economy that it would not be feasible to employ enough inspectors and auditors to monitor all employers in all occupational areas in the United States. The administrators of the act, therefore, resort to unannounced, random spot-checking as one basis for the enforcement of the law. This procedure implies that given employers may violate the law for indefinite periods without penalty. The possibility of being included in random audits without warning, however, is designed to inspire voluntary compliance.

In the early history of the Wage and Hour Law, many employers were unaware of its requirements and the penalties of violation. Small employers often held that they were not covered by the law because they were not specifically advised of their responsibility. Under circumstances of this kind the teacher–coordinator should not permit the employer to enter into any agreement relative to the employment of students which he believes to be in violation of the Wage and Hour Law. The possible result of failure to discharge this responsibility on the part of the teacher–coordinator, coupled with employer unawareness or indifference, is illustrated in the following incident in the early history of CE and the federal Wage and Hour Law.

CE was established in a small city of approximately 20,000 population and operated for a number of years without special concern on the part of the school or its cooperating employers for compliance with the Wage and Hour Law. On a given day, Wage and Hour auditors appeared, unannounced, for the purpose of auditing all the "auto parts" businesses in the city. Two employers were found to have been in violation of the law through the employment of cooperative students at less than the prevailing minimum wage without learners' certificates. The penalty for the employers was a rather heavy fine and the payment of the amount of the underpayment of wages, with interest, to the students involved.

Although the penalty was not in fatal proportions and affected only two "auto parts" employers, devastating effects were suffered by cooperative education. Employers in other occupational areas became alarmed to the point of reconsidering the advisability of continued cooperation with the school as employers of students. Some employers immediately dismissed their students, while others advised the school of their decision to discontinue cooperation at the end of the current school year. The net result of this mutual neglect was that not enough students could be placed the following year to justify the continued operation of the program. Consequently, CE was discontinued for an indefinite period.

The moral of this incident seems to be that although most employers are covered by the Wage and Hour Law, while the school and its agents are not, both are destined to suffer disastrous results from employer violations of the act. Incidents of this nature can be prevented, in the beginning, by the teacher–coordinator in exercising concern for the best interest of employers as well as the school and its students. In this case the teacher–coordinator should have insisted that learners' certificates be secured for the students during the period that they were to be employed at less than the minimum wage. The Wage and Hour Law provides a simple procedure to follow in securing learners' certificates for qualified students.

In the light of this incident, teacher–coordinators are advised to familiarize themselves to the greatest possible extent with the federal Wage and Hour Law of 1938. The exercise of this knowledge in the operation of CE should prevent any possibility of incidents such as that described above.

Workmen's Compensation Law

Workmen's compensation laws have several implications for CE, chief among them being the fixing of on-the-job liability for students as an employer's responsibility to the same extent as that for regular employees. Such laws usually mandate that students count as regular employees even though they may be less than 18 years of age. Insurance carriers may take exception to the employment of students less than 18 on the ground that this age group is more accident-prone than regular employees. Employers tend to escape such problems by refusing to employ CE students.

The probability that workmen's compensation laws will vary among states prompts the suggestion that teacher–coordinators become familiar with these and other pertinent laws of the state in which they are employed. The federal Wage and Hour Law, in concert with workmen's compensation acts, constitutes a network of legal implications for CE which frequently tend to cause problems. Although such problems may create operational difficulties, they should by no means defeat the program. A program properly conceived and soundly operated will not be fatally affected by legal requirements.

The State Plan

Section 8 of the Smith–Hughes Act requires that state boards for vocational education prepare plans showing how federal funds allocated by the law are to be expended. All subsequently enacted federal assistance acts have continued the "state plan" requirement, properly adjusted to satisfy current circumstances.

The state plan, after proper ratification, actually becomes a contract which binds the federal government to provide specified amounts of money and the states to expend it in the fashion described in their state plans. In effect, the federal government agrees to buy X dollars' worth of vocational education, with built-in safeguards to guarantee that it is received. The state plan always reflects the requirements of current federal legislation in that it is required to be rewritten at given intervals to guarantee its timeliness.

The Local Plan

Local plans are designed to satisfy purposes on the local level similar to those of the state plan on the state level. They set forth local intentions to operate certain programs of vocational education to meet needs identified or anticipated on local levels. CE should be a part of the local plan together with its basic operational standards. Such standards should reveal local policy relative to enrollment, related instruction requirements, job-experience requirements, physical facilities specifications, and advisory committee functions.

After the locally prepared "local plan" for vocational education is approved by appropriate state authorities, it in turn becomes an agreement between the local school and the state binding the state to reimburse local schools a percentage of the cost of approved programs, and the local school to operate the programs in accordance with the approved local plan.

Records and Reports

Although the relative importance of the administrative and supervisory responsibilities discussed in Part V would be difficult to establish, there is little doubt that records and reports should be given high priority in teacher–coordinator responsibilities. Accurate and complete records and prompt reporting procedures are vital features of CE. This routine responsibility should not be neglected or delayed.

The integrity of local records and reports is of paramount importance. Any misrepresentation of facts included in the permanent records of students or in the total program record, whether it be intentional or by mistake, will constitute permanent misrepresentation to those who may examine the records in the future. By the same token, misrepresentation of program facts in reports to sponsoring state agencies will, in all probability, be included in annual reports to federal agencies, which will, in turn, be passed along to the Congress and other national bodies concerned with vocational–technical education.

Information submitted in reports to state agencies is normally accepted without question. The integrity of state and federal reports, therefore, rests upon the integrity of the reports received from local programs. This acceptance emphasizes the importance of the veracity of the local report and the care that should be exercised in preparing it. The teacher–coordinator is cautioned to painstakingly "tell it like it is" in all reports, even though the desired image of the local program may not be reflected.

Reports to Sponsoring State Agencies

The vocational–technical division of the state department of education is usually the state agency responsible for the approval and supervision of reimbursable local vocational–technical programs and is the agency to which local program reports are to be submitted. The type of information required by this division of the State Department of Education may vary between states but will properly include:

1. A local plan for vocational–technical education.
2. Annual budget request.
3. Request for approval in advance for the operation of part-time or evening classes.
4. Initial reports for all classes upon which reimbursement is to be requested.

5. Memorandum of training plans.
6. Final reports of all reimbursable classes.

Although additional types of information may be required, the above listing is illustrative of the responsibility of the local school to its state division of vocational–technical education. All reports are due at given times during the year and should be submitted promptly. Neglect on the part of teacher–coordinators in preparing and submitting the reports for which they are responsible is inexcusable and will jeopardize CE. Although it has been suggested that state departments are prone to accept the veracity of information submitted from local levels, the possibility of a local audit should not be completely discounted.

As a matter of fact, a local report may provide guidelines for a supervisory visit from the state office. Such a visit could be promoted by evidence of flagrant misrepresentation which could not be overlooked. State divisions of vocational–technical education normally tend to confine their supervision to positive efforts to be of help to local programs rather than to excursions designed to discover discrepancies. Best results should accrue when state supervisory personnel exhibit confidence in the integrity of local programs, including reports, while local representatives accept the concept that state supervision is dedicated to constructive effort to help improve vocational–technical education on local levels.

Local Reports

Local report requirements may vary from none to as many as are deemed necessary by local school officials. Attention is directed to an earlier statement, the essence of which was that an important factor in teacher–coordinator administrator relationships is attention to "keeping them informed." Accordingly, voluntary reports should be prepared and submitted in sufficient scope to keep school officials properly informed concerning the progress, the problems, and the accomplishments of CE. The sample form on pages 282–283 is an example of the type of voluntary information which should be provided for local school officials.

The teacher–coordinator may also find it advisable to prepare appropriate reports for other important publics, with special reference to the faculty, employee organizations, and the general public. As a matter of fact, a report of program accomplishments could well be the basis of public relations activities during the latter part of the school year.

Local Records

Most schools maintain a cumulative record for each student from the first through the twelfth grade. This record is usually concisely complete, even to the inclusion of significant anecdotes. Although this record satisfies the permanent record requirements of regular high school parents, it fails to meet the total needs of cooperative students. Their permanent records should include additional information such as the following:

1. Occupation in which work experience was gained.
2. Training agency, employer, and on-the-job instructor.
3. Work-experience summary in terms of clock hours devoted to each division of the schedule of work experiences.
4. Summary of the employer's evaluations of work experience.
5. Grade summary for related instruction.
6. Progress record of work experience and directly related assignments.
7. Training-agency changes and reasons for them.

Typical Problems in Administration and Supervision

Problem 1 *Maintenance of a mailing list of program graduates of sufficient accuracy to sustain contact*

The need for follow-up information on program graduates seems remote while they are still in school. As a matter of fact, it is quite difficult to anticipate the need with sufficient intensity to inspire the necessary current action.

Making the acquisition of follow-up information on graduates a club project may be helpful. Firsthand experience with the difficulty of making contact and inspiring response from those who have left the school should be impressive to currently enrolled students.

In addition to such an indirect effort to crystallize the desired student attitudes, specific effort should be devoted to explanation of the importance of follow-up information with specific reference to efforts the school will make to keep in touch with its CE graduates. It should be explained that, in the absence of an address, information, including follow-up questionnaires, will be sent to home addresses with a request for forwarding.

Problem 2 *Applying student follow-up study findings to program improvement*

The most important justification for student follow-up is the need to secure authentic information to be used in the improvement of instruction. The absence of this purpose as an important part of the motivation to make such a study would lend extreme doubt to its advisability. Without intent to use follow-up study information for this purpose relegates the motivation to superficial purposes of insufficient importance to merit the time and effort required. Making follow-up studies solely for the purpose of satisfying federal requirements, for example, cannot be expected to inspire the necessary response.

Problem 3 *Compensating for legal requirements which create problems for CE*

The minimum-wage requirement of the federal Wage and Hour Law tends to focus the attention of the student as well as the employer on the amount of money involved. Students are prone to give inordinate attention to what they earn, while the employer tends to become primarily concerned about the value received for the wages paid. These concerns detract from the educational values of the program and emphasize the less important fiscal values.

Allowing the fiscal aspects of CE to become the most important concern of all publics, with special reference to students, employers, and parents, will tend to defeat other program objectives and relegate major emphasis to monetary returns without concern for career values. Other requirements of state and federal laws may have equally devastating effects on CE when applied by individuals who are without concern for its educational values.

It is the responsibility of school officials, especially the teacher–coordinator, to see that all legal requirements are met with the least possible negative effect on the program. There is no escape, for example, from the fact that students working for employers covered by the Wage and Hour Law must be paid the prevailing minimum wage, or, when learner certificates are secured, three-fourths thereof. Consequently, great effort may be required to develop motivation on the part of students, employers, and parents, based on educational values, as opposed to allowing the money involved to become the most important concern.

Problem 4   *Gaining administrative interest in community occupational study*

School administrators are, for the most part, professionally dedicated, hard-working individuals with sincere concern for the educational needs of those for whom they are responsible. The extent of this concern is normally determined by their own definition of their responsibility and accountability. This will range from concern for the total educational needs of the community to a narrow concept confined to the needs of the educable age group (six to 21) in the community. The narrow concept may range from concern for the total educational needs of the educable age group to primary concern for college-bound students.

The spontaneous attitude of school administrators will depend upon the pattern of professional concern from which they respond. Accordingly, the basic philosophy of school administrators should be examined prior to the submission of a proposal for the community occupational survey designed to serve as a basis for future development of the local educational program. The proposal should be held in abeyance until an appropriate and receptive administrative climate can be developed.

In the final analysis, the professional administrator can be expected to respond favorably to any educational phenomenon which can be satisfactorily substantiated within the realm of currently acceptable educational philosophy. The key to the development of favorable administrative attitudes, therefore, may be the reduction of some elements of educational philosophy to basic definitions such as "The purpose of education is to serve the best interests of all students." Philosophical conflict may develop in the definition of "best interest."

The administrator will be hard pressed, however, to maintain that the best interest of all students is to be "prepared to enter college" in the face of irrefutable proof that a very small percentage of the jobs available for beginners for the foreseeable future will require college degrees. It necessarily follows that major portions of current school populations will accept jobs in occupational areas requiring skill and knowledge unobtainable through college-degree programs. The school must provide opportunity for its students to acquire this skill and knowledge if their "best interests are to be served." In order to gain the knowledge upon which to base such educational opportunity, the school must enter into intensive occupational study of the community.

Problem 5 *Development of interest in community occupational study on the part of community leaders*

The first difficulty in the development of effective public interest may be in the identification of the "power structure" of the community. Community leadership, through whom community action is inspired, may not be clearly definable from normal vantage points. It becomes necessary, therefore, for one who seeks acquaintance with the individuals who make up this elite group to find points of vantage through which the desired contacts can be made.

If key individuals can be interested in community occupational study, subsequent desirable community actions can be expected to follow. Although having the approval of community leadership will not guarantee total acquiescence to community occupational study, the absence of such approval will guarantee failure to achieve desired community action. Approval of community leadership, in effect, opens the right doors to the survey staff and inspires cooperation from all elements of the community. It lends prestige to the study and assures opportunity for its successful consummation, together with subsequent desirable community response.

Suggested Activities

1. List and describe briefly the areas of information that should be sought through community occupational surveys.
2. Design a questionnaire suitable for use in a follow-up study of CE students. Build the instrument around the four basic areas of information listed on page 366.
3. Using the seven items listed on page 375 as topical headings, list the various forms of information which should be recorded in local records. Describe the instruments to be used in the recording process in each case.
4. After a review of current federal and state laws, write a summary of their requirements which create problems for CE.
5. Write a sample local plan for CE designed to satisfy current state plan requirements. (A copy of the state plan should be available from the state division of vocational education in the capital city.)

chapter seventeen

Program Evaluation

Evaluate is formally defined as the "determination or fixing the value of" or "to examine and judge." For the purpose of this writing, however, *evaluation* shall be understood to mean a general appraisal of CE, to determine the strength and the quality of its major functional areas.

The ultimate design of an evaluation program will inevitably reflect the philosophy of the designers in terms of the combinations of program elements selected to be judged and the publics chosen to aid in their appraisal. Accordingly, an evaluation program conceived and designed by school officials or faculty, for example, could be expected to seek confirmation of the program purposes and values which they hold to be of paramount importance.

Evaluative programs designed within the ranks of other publics, such as employers, parents, or students, may seek entirely different types of information from different sources. By the same token, evaluative procedures conceived and designed by teacher–coordinators will be a reflection of what they believe to be the most important aspects of CE, and the most reliable source of information.

It stands to reason, therefore, that evaluative studies should be relieved of the bias of those with vested interests in the program in order that professionally significant results might be rendered. If this is to be achieved, such evaluative programs should be designed by impartial, professionally qualified personnel under sponsorship of appropriate professional organizations.

Evaluating Related Instruction

Activities in the CE related-subjects classroom depart drastically from those carried on in conventional classrooms. For this reason the instruction must be judged by criteria and standards fashioned in terms of its own purposes and characteristics rather than those which set the pattern in conventional classrooms.

The sample evaluation plan of Figure 26 is designed for use in determining the effectiveness of CE classroom instruction in its total setting. It should be applied by unbiased individuals representing agencies outside the local school, such as the state division of vocational education. Following a plan of this nature should relieve the study of the subjectivity which may stem from personal prejudices or philosophical idiosyncrasy.

This plan may also be used by the teacher–coordinator as an instrument of self-evaluation. Regardless of how the instrument is executed, it should finally produce an evaluation of the related instructional program according to the following standards:

> 90 to 100% of the questions answered "yes"   Superior
> 80 to 90% of the questions answered "yes"   Good
> 70 to 80% of the questions answered "yes"   Fair
> Below 70% of the questions answered "yes"   Poor

If, as a self-evaluation instrument, it is administered at regular intervals, the results should serve as a "quality" barometer of related instruction and a firm foundation upon which to base instructional improvement efforts.

Figure 26 Sample Evaluation Plan

Directly Related Instruction—Evaluative Criteria

Physical Facilities   *Yes*   *No*

1. Is the classroom equipped with tables and chairs which provide a minimum of 6 square feet of table-top per student?   ____   ____

2. Does the classroom provide a minimum of 16 square feet per student?   ____   ____

3. Is the classroom amply equipped with storage facilities for reference materials?   ____   ____

380

Yes   No

4. Is the teacher–coordinator's office suitably located for student counseling during supervised and directed study periods?   ____   ____

5. Is the general quality of the classroom on a par with other high school classrooms?   ____   ____

Supervised and Directed Study

1. Does each student have an individual assignment each day?   ____   ____

2. Do all student have study guides, or reasonable facsimilies thereof?   ____   ____

3. Is the daily work experience of the students formally reported and recorded?   ____   ____

4. Is there a properly posted, directly-related-study and job-experience progress record?   ____   ____

5. Is the classroom time of the teacher–coordinator organized so as to include oral testing and student counseling?   ____   ____

Correlation

1. Are classroom assignments and work experience properly correlated?   ____   ____

2. Are incidents of application of technical information to the solution of job-related problems reported?   ____   ____

3. Are employers encouraged to provide opportunity for application of technical information?   ____   ____

4. Is the employer given the opportunity to suggest areas of technical study?   ____   ____

5. Is there a requirement regulating the number of assignments that a student may leave unfinished to initiate a new assignment?   ____   ____

Checking and Evaluating Written Work

1. Do all students turn in written work resulting from daily assignments?   ____   ____

2. Is this work evaluated by the teacher–coordinator and returned to the students?   ____   ____

3. Is attention given to the improvement of writing ability in the evaluative process?   ____   ____

4. Is the checking process applicable without regard for the teacher–coordinator's occupational adeptness?   ____   ____

Yes   *No*

5. Is there a provision which can be invoked which will cause the student to prove the authenticity of information included in the written work? ____ ____

Testing Techniques
1. Does each assignment culminate with a test on the material covered? ____ ____
2. Is the test designed in a form which may be issued to the student upon request? ____ ____
3. Is there an answer book including answers to all test questions? ____ ____
4. Are students required to restudy areas of weakness indicated by the test? ____ ____
5. Are oral tests administered to each student at least twice each term? ____ ____

Classroom Activities
1. Does the teacher–coordinator devote an equitable amount of class time to circulating the classroom for the purpose of helping students with assignments?
2. Do students follow an established routine during the related-subjects class period? ____ ____
3. Is there a schedule for student counseling? ____ ____
4. Is the first few minutes of the period devoted to the posting of the daily job-experience report? ____ ____
5. Do students share equally in housekeeping responsibilities? ____ ____

Student Conduct in the Related-Subjects Classroom
1. Do students enter the classroom in a businesslike manner and begin their work without loss of time? ____ ____
2. In the exercise of classroom freedoms do students accept attending responsibilities? ____ ____
3. Do students devote the entire class period to directly related study as opposed to study for other classes or other unrelated activities? ____ ____
4. Do students refrain from engaging in activities which produce disturbing noise or other forms of distraction? ____ ____
5. Does the related-subjects classroom as a whole reflect an atmosphere which resembles that of library quietness? ____ ____

382

Provisions for Individual Differences   *Yes*   *No*

1. Are there definite provisions for individual differences relative to the amount of production required?   ____ ____

2. Are high achievers given supplementary assignments?   ____ ____

3. Do students understand that their best interest is
   served by concentrated effort on individual assignments as opposed to emphasis on the number of
   assignments completed?   ____ ____

4. Are both slow and rapid learners challenged to their
   best effort?   ____ ____

5. Do the evaluative methods and techniques encourage the improvement of reading and writing
   ability of all students?   ____ ____

Reference Materials and Supplies

1. Is there ample budgetary provision for reference
   materials?   ____ ____

2. Are there at least three reference books for each
   occupation in which students are placed?   ____ ____

3. Are reference materials screened to determine that
   they are written at appropriate reading levels for
   students?   ____ ____

4. Do storage methods and facilities assure the proper
   replacement of each reference book at the end of
   the class period?   ____ ____

5. Is there a definite provision for the storage of notebooks and study guides?   ____ ____

Generally Related Instruction—Evaluative Criteria

Program of Work   *Yes*   *No*

1. Is there a program of work which fixes the time
   elements of generally related units of instruction?   ____ ____

2. Does the program of work fix the dates for the use
   of films and other special visual aids?   ____ ____

3. Are the dates for visiting speakers and student reports indicated?   ____ ____

4. Is the program of work completed prior to the
   opening of school and attuned to the school calendar?   ____ ____

5. Does the program of work include a definite allotment of time for orientation? ____ ____

Teaching Methods

1. Is the instruction organized so as to inspire student participation through the discussion of assigned questions in buzz groups or other small-group techniques? ____ ____

2. Is the conference method used periodically as a problem-solving procedure? ____ ____

3. Are students given individual assignments for special reports? ____ ____

4. Are students tested during or at the time of completion of units of instruction? ____ ____

5. Are first- and second-year students scheduled in separate periods? ____ ____

Generally Related Classroom Activities (Students)

1. Do students enter the classroom in a businesslike manner and proceed with the class routine without loss of time? ____ ____

2. Are students attentive and responsive? ____ ____

3. Are students conditioned to consider the information presented to them in terms of its relevance to on-the-job circumstances? ____ ____

4. Do students take special assignments seriously? ____ ____

5. Do students take notes during classroom instruction? ____ ____

Instructional Aids

1. Are films and other audiovisual aids properly scheduled and used to help the teacher teach, as opposed to dependence upon them as self-contained mediums of instruction? ____ ____

2. Are films and other audiovisual aids scheduled at times when their presentation is germane to the topical areas of instruction being presented? ____ ____

3. Are special speakers from business and industry scheduled at times when their presentations will contribute to current classroom instruction? ____ ____

4. Is the chalkboard used effectively as an aid to instruction and the solution of problems? ____ ____

5. Are special instructional techniques, such as panel discussions, symposiums, conferences, and role playing, used effectively as aids to instruction? ____ ____

Teaching Plan   *Yes*   *No*
1. Is the first portion of the lesson plan devoted to motivation?   ____ ____
2. Does the teacher–coordinator teach from an outline?   ____ ____
3. Are students encouraged to ask questions during the presentation?   ____ ____
4. Is the student given an opportunity to apply the information being presented to his own work experience?   ____ ____
5. Is the test used as an integral part of the teaching process?   ____ ____

Instructional Content
1. Does a 10-day orientation period precede the teaching of other areas of generally related instruction?   ____ ____
2. Is the orientation unit of instruction scheduled to occur before the student goes to work?   ____ ____
3. Are all generally related units of instruction designed to contribute to areas of general interest of all students?   ____ ____
4. Is there a unit of instruction on personal improvement designed to culminate in a personal improvement program on the part of each student?   ____ ____
5. Are the units of generally related instruction presented to second-year students different from those presented to first-year students?   ____ ____

Evaluating Coordination

Coordination has been defined as the process of bringing into harmonious relationship those parts of the school and the community which are essential elements of CE. The degree to which this is accomplished will have a vital bearing on the total program quality that can be achieved.

The sample evaluative instrument in Figure 27 suggests one approach to the evaluation of coordination. Here again, the instrument can be applied by the teacher–coordinator as a means of self-evaluation.

Figure 27   Coordination—Evaluative Criteria

Occupations Included in the Program   Yes   No

1. Do all occupations in which students are placed require a minimum learning period of 2,000 hours to reach proficiency levels?

2. Do all occupations included in the program offer acceptable post-training employment opportunity?

3. Do all occupations offer feasible and justifiable educational potential as a part of the school program?

4. Does the Advisory Committee consider and recommend approval of all occupations for student placement?

5. Is an official listing of approved occupations prepared?

Training-Station Selection

1. Do employers understand and accept the educational purposes and values of CE?

2. Do training stations provide a satisfactory quality and scope of experience?

3. Are qualified on-the-job instructors available in all approved training agencies?

4. Are all training stations satisfactorily located?

5. Does school administration recognize on-the-job instructors as members of the faculty?

Student Selection

1. Is the selection plan designed to ensure enrollment of qualified students?

2. Does school policy return students to the regular program if they are not placed by the deadline date?

3. May students be recalled after this date, if suitable placement opportunity develops?

4. Is vocational intent validated through accepted guidance procedures?

5. Are parents fully advised concerning the responsibilities and values of CE?

Student Placement

1. Is the memorandum of training plan executed as a part of the placement process?

386

	Yes	*No*

2. Is the essence of placement considered to be "getting the right student on the right job"? ____ ____

3. Is the compatibility of student aptitudes, vocational interests, and personal qualities with the success requirements of the job an important consideration in job placement? ____ ____

4. Is a definite effort made to make CE opportunities known to the entire student body? ____ ____

5. Is there a definite plan for the preparation of students for initial job responsibilities, including the job interview? ____ ____

Visitation and Counseling

1. Are training-station visits premised on valid purposes as opposed to visitation without purpose? ____ ____

2. Does the high school principal periodically visit training agencies with the teacher–coordinator? ____ ____

3. Is a visitation record maintained? ____ ____

4. Does training-station visitation serve as an important basis for student counseling? ____ ____

5. Is visitation time equitably distributed among training stations? ____ ____

Advisory Committees

1. Is there a functioning representative advisory committee? ____ ____

2. Are craft and occupational committees properly utilized? ____ ____

3. Are the functions of the advisory committee programmed? ____ ____

4. Is the advisory committee fully accepted and supported by the school administration? ____ ____

5. Does the teacher–coordinator accept and effectively discharge his or her responsibilities in the selection and utilization of the general advisory committee? ____ ____

On the other hand, its application by unbiased representatives of a state department of education, or perhaps a professional association, should produce more objective results. In either event the fully executed instrument can be judged in terms of the standards recorded on page 380.

Evaluating Relationships

In the interest of conservation of space, an evaluative instrument has not been developed for use in evaluating the "relationships" with publics which make important contributions to the environment in which CE is required to function. The need for such an instrument would become evident if related instruction and coordination should score poorly according to the standards recorded on page 380. If these two major elements are strong, it can be assumed that relationships are in good order.

If it becomes necessary to examine the status of relationships with any or all publics, an instrument similar to those suggested for use in evaluating related instruction and coordination should be developed. Questions should be designed so that affirmative answers will be the desired response. Such questions should be confined to the following major areas, as recorded under "Relationship Development" on Figure 1 (p. 9).

Out-of-School Publics

1. Employers
2. Parents
3. Employee organizations
4. News media
5. Civic organizations
6. General public

In-School Publics

1. Administration
2. Faculty
3. Student body
4. Cooperative students
5. Nonprofessional employees

Evaluating Administrative and Supervisory Responsiblities

The possibility that it may become advisable to investigate the administrative and supervisory responsibilities of the teacher–coordinator prompts the suggestion that an evaluative instrument be developed in the same general form as those previously shown in this chapter for use in evaluating "Related Instruction" and "Coordination." All questions should be designed so that the desired condition will inspire an affirmative response. Such questions should be directed at the following areas of teacher–coordinator administrative and supervisory responsibility:

1. Continuing educational opportunity
2. Community occupational data
3. Student follow-up data
4. Legal responsibilities
5. Records and reports

Typical Problems in Program Evaluation

Problem 1 *Maintaining objectivity in self-evaluation*

Several human tendencies come into play as teacher–coordinators consider the necessity of comparing the basic elements of their programs with quality standards and criteria. Perhaps the greatest temptation is to simply find reasons against an evaluative study.

The earlier suggestion that self-evaluation could be an important avenue to self-improvement could be questioned because of the tendency of individuals not to judge themselves sternly and objectively. Their reactions to questions may be in terms of what they know the condition should be or as they have learned to live with it in compensating for adverse local circumstances. Objective reasoning, therefore, should dictate that unbiased individuals be invited to lend objectivity to the study. Representatives of state departments of education or professional organizations may be available for such purposes.

Problem 2 *Follow-through on the findings of evaluative studies*

The fate of evaluative studies, their findings, and resulting recommendations far too often is a permanent resting place in an inactive file. This neglect may result from the teacher–coordinator's reluctance to change aspects of the program which are locally accepted. Such an attitude may persist in the face of concrete evidence of malfunction.

This complacency may apply to any element of the program, but especially to related instruction and coordination.

Suppose, for example, that the program is penalized, through the evaluative process, for unacceptable classroom practices, such as students' use of directly related instructional time for study for other courses. The teacher–coordinator may be reluctant to change such classroom practices which have come to be accepted by cooperative students and other in-school publics. Reluctance may also stem from a lack of courage to face the wrath of students, who can be depended upon to resist any change in this practice. Teacher–coordinators could be excused for failing to correct such malfunctions until the beginning of a new school year, but to categorically ignore obvious program faults is inexcusable.

Evaluation studies without intent to follow through are examples of professional irresponsibility and are misleading to the publics upon which CE depends for environmental sustenance.

Problem 3 *Achieving objectivity in evaluating studies conducted by outside agencies*

Periodic evaluative study of local programs of CE may be initiated by state divisions of vocational–technical education or professional accrediting agencies. The teacher–coordinator should welcome the opportunity of having outside help in detecting areas of program deficiency. In the absence of outside pressures, however, the coordinator should take the initiative in arranging for professional representation of appropriate agencies to participate in evaluative study of the local program. This participation should include supervision of data compilation, interpretation of the findings, and the making of recommendations for program improvement.

The objectivity achieved through such a procedure could reveal program faults which might otherwise remain unnoticed by local school officials. The courage to take such calculated risks, coupled with determination to correct the deficiencies and malfunctions revealed, is a distinguishing characteristic of professionalism.

Problem 4 *Avoiding the tendency to make evaluative studies verify previously assumed conclusions*

Research is often plagued by the tendency to selectively collect information and to draw conclusions therefrom that will substantiate desirable existing circumstances. Such conclusions may fail to identify malfunctions and to indicate where improvements should be made. It is suggested, therefore, that every effort be made to safeguard the integrity of the study, to the end that the findings will serve as dependable guidelines to program improvement.

Problem 5   *Achieving administrative approval of evaluative studies*

Although evaluative studies are not usually expensive procedures, some financial ability is essential. It becomes necessary, therefore, that administrative officials approve the study and make the necessary funds available. Perhaps the most expensive phase of the undertaking would be the cost of travel and local entertainment for out-of-town professionals who may be invited to participate in the study.

Teacher–coordinators can make self-evaluation studies in their own offices with the primary cost being the expenditure of a minimum amount of time. The forms included in this chapter should serve satisfactorily in making such a study.

Evaluative studies involving financial support should be thoroughly planned with accurate cost estimates before being presented to administrative officials. Approval can be expected if funds are available and the presentation is convincing.

Suggested Activities

1. Develop a plan for the application of the instruments for evaluative study of related instruction in CE on pages 381–385. Be specific in dealing with ways and means of applying the criteria. Indicate how the results of the study should be used in program improvement.
2. Develop a plan for use in applying the evaluative instrument for coordination, beginning on page 386. Here again, be specific in dealing with the evaluative criteria. Indicate how the results of the study should benefit the program.
3. Assuming that a given CE program scores poorly in related instruction and coordination, develop an instrument similar to those shown on pages 381–387 for use in evaluating relationships with out-of-school publics as listed on page 388.
4. Based on the assumption above, develop a similar instrument for use in evaluating relationships with in-school publics as listed on page 388.
5. Prepare a statement to be submitted for administrative approval of a formal evaluation of the CE program. Include a tentative budget providing funds for essential expenses.

Index